TEXAS —
A Year with the Boys

Other Books By William Hoffman

BEYOND REACH: THE SEARCH FOR THE TITANIC

DAVID: REPORT ON A ROCKEFELLER

DOCTORS ON THE NEW FRONTIER

PAUL MELLON: PORTRAIT OF AN OIL BARON

QUEEN JULIANA: THE STORY OF THE RICHEST
  WOMAN IN THE WORLD

SIDNEY (a biography of Sidney Poitier)

THE STOCKHOLDER

THE MONEY PLAYER

THE BRIDGE BUM

BLACK CHAMPIONS CHALLENGE AMERICAN
  SPORTS

TEXAS

A YEAR WITH

THE BOYS

William Hoffman

TAYLOR PUBLISHING COMPANY
Dallas, Texas

Copyright © 1983 by William Hoffman

Published by Taylor Publishing Company
1550 West Mockingbird Lane, Dallas, Texas 75235

All rights reserved.
No part of this publication may be
reproduced in any form, or by any
means, without permission in writing
from the publisher.

Library of Congress Catalog Card Number: 83-51251

ISBN: 0-87833-337-1

Printed in the United States of America

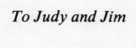
To Judy and Jim

One

I was sitting with Jim Seligmann, my old friend and literary agent, reminiscing about the day thirteen years before when we first met. It was a torturous first meeting, but out of it came twenty-one books and a long-standing friendship. We were just shooting the breeze without ever thinking a hurricane was about to enter our lives.

The phone rang.

"I'm in a lot of trouble, boy," were the first words Seligmann ever heard from Jack Grimm. Of course these were the first words. I would hear them a thousand times.

"Who is this?"

"Jack Grimm, boy."

"I've never heard of you."

"That's your fault. But let's cut through the preliminaries. I'm going to find the *Titanic* and I need a writer to be there. You got a writer?"

"I still don't know who you are."

"Want me to mail a bank statement? I need a writer."

Seligmann, sixty-two — the guy calling him "boy" was fifty-six — cupped his hand over the receiver: "You want to look for the *Titanic?*"

"I thought it was found."

"No."

I picked up the telephone and said hello.

"You a writer?"

"Yes."

"Get your ass to Woods Hole tomorrow morning. I'll make you rich."

"Where's Woods Hole?"

"Be there at seven, boy."

If I had had any sense I would have rejected Grimm's demand out of hand; but as a writer I was naturally curious, and also strangely attracted by the arrogant and self-assured manner of the invitation. If I had hesitated, I might even have decided it was something shady, but so were half the deals being struck on Wall Street. Nothing new for a New Yorker. So I went.

I caught the Eastern shuttle to Boston and a bus to Woods Hole. It was midnight when I arrived. Seven hours early.

Woods Hole is a remarkable old New England town, quaint colonial houses, sea air, taverns still strong at midnight, snap of salt in the warm June wind. The great oceanographic institution is in Woods Hole. Music pours out of the bars, saturates the deserted street, this has to be where Melville walked.

Finding myself lost, I hitchhike.

"Where you going?" The man is fat, sports a "Lone Star Beer" tee shirt, has a beard.

"Trying to find the ship *Gyre.*"

His hair is wild and he has the look of a fanatic. "I'll take you to the *Gyre.*"

He nearly runs his car into the bay. It screeches to a jerking, back-and-forth stop next to a ship that has to be the *Gyre* and he lurches outside and scales a gangplank. I follow, more uncertainly, and ask the first face I see who that man is.

"The Captain of the *Gyre.* Don Armand. Captain Don Armand."

My God. Jack Grimm. Don Armand. These two Texans are going to find the *Titanic?*

Jack Grimm had arranged for a monkey, named Titan, to accompany the search. The monkey had been trained to point to a spot on the map where the *Titanic* was believed to rest, a monumental accomplishment, the millionaire believed, and one that would lend class to the movie he would make about the search. Dr. Fred Spiess, chief scientist, director of the prestigious Scripps Institution of

Oceanography, known throughout the world as the "Father of Underwater Research," heard about the monkey and didn't approve of the scheme at all.

Spiess thought bringing the monkey along would only hold up to ridicule what he considered a very serious search. He talked it over with the other noted scientists who were scheduled to accompany the expedition and issued an ultimatum: "Jack," he said, "this is not a circus. Either the monkey goes or we go, but not both."

"Well, boy," said Grimm, "the monkey's going. Fire the scientists." Whereupon the expedition almost never took place at all. Saner heads ultimately prevailed, however, and Grimm agreed to leave the monkey behind. But the voyage almost ended before it began.

Life aboard the *Gyre,* which is 174 feet long but registered as a motorboat in Texas, had assumed a predictable routine after six days at sea. The scientists were busy sixteen hours a day testing the equipment we would use to try to find *Titanic.* Grimm was busy what seemed an equal amount of time conducting a poker game in the ship's galley.

Regulars in the game were John Burris, a deckhand from Galveston, and Bobby Blanco, a Cuban from Florida who was an investor in the expedition. The results were monotonous in their similarity: an astounding amount of time Grimm was raking in the pot. He wore a Texas A&M cap, a Lyndon Johnson cat-that-swallowed-the-mouse smile, and tennis shoes, and would break from the game only to exchange *Titanic* or "Aggie" jokes with Captain Armand.

> "A priest, a rabbi, and a black man met St. Peter at the Pearly Gates. 'What's the most famous ship that ever sank?' St. Peter asked the priest. 'The *Titanic,'* was the answer. 'Good,' said St. Peter, 'you can enter Heaven. Now,' he said to the rabbi, 'how many people died aboard *Titanic?'* 'Fifteen hundred.' 'Close enough,' said St. Peter. 'You can also enter. Name them,' he said to the black."

"Know why Aggies drink their cocktails without ice?" Grimm asked Armand.

"Why?"

"The guy with the recipe graduated."

The jokes drove Bobby Blanco wild. It was bad enough that he felt he would lose his investment, that we would never find *Titanic,* but the daily poker losses to Grimm coupled with the millionaire's down-home humor were too much to bear. At least if the investment foundered the Cuban was in good company: Nelson Bunker Hunt, he of trying to corner the silver market and lamenting that inflation had eroded the value of his billion dollars, also owned a piece of the action.

Getting mad had not helped. Bobby would slam his fist on the table, and leap from his seat cursing, breathing fire, whenever a hand went against him, which was often, but Grimm retained his composure. He talked about how fickle chance was, how imponderable was Lady Luck's will.

Bobby even tried praying aloud during the game, and when that failed he resorted to voodoo. During each crucial hand he would rise from his chair and intone a Haitian curse — "Wombie! Wombie! Wombie!" — over Grimm's head. But the results never varied. Someone sitting opposite the oilman at the table might have thought his opponent was a mountain of chips, so high had his stack grown that he was virtually invisible behind it.

Once Bobby, his face contorted in pain and anger, stormed away from the table, trailing Spanish expletives behind him, fervently vowing never to play again with "that crazy moneybags." "He'll be back," Grimm predicted confidently. "He can't stay away. He's like an old fire horse."

Grimm was different from card sharps one read about in books or watched in movies. Kibitzers speculated that he was either the luckiest man on earth or cheating, but he never coaxed players into staying in the game by giving them hope and intentionally losing a hand or two. Each session started with him winning, progressed with him winning, and ended with him winning. He was merciless and relentless, in a good-old-boy way. The winning became wearisome to everyone but him, and constantly he contributed to Bobby's deepening despair with droll shafts of crackerbarrel insight: "I believe in the Golden Rule, that is, he who has the gold, rules"; but then, more thoughtfully, "The fattest pig is always butchered first"; and finally, at peace with himself, "A full house is better than a sharp stick in the eye."

Grimm's luck was undeniable. He was by light years the richest person on the *Gyre,* so of course it was he who continually found lost money on the deck of the ship. He had the sea legs that could be expected of a Texas oilman, and to his credit never exhibited bravado when the North Sea blew angry, but he could be as sure-footed as Jacques Cousteau when he spotted a quarter to be picked up from the storm-lashed fantail.

James Drury, television's "The Virginian," was aboard the *Gyre* to narrate the movie Grimm was making about the search. Drury had been born in New York City, raised primarily on a ranch in Oregon, appeared in plays even as a boy, eventually went to Hollywood and got his big break when he beat out more than seventy other hopefuls for the title role that made him famous.

"The Virginian" was a quality ninety-minute weekly Western that would have been Number One in the genre had it not been for "Gunsmoke." As it was, the show spent its entire nine years in the top-twenty-ranked programs, largely, it appears, because of Drury and his insistence that high standards be maintained despite the cost.

"The pattern is dismally the same," said the former Virginian as he kibitzed the card game. "A good series is produced. The public loves it and wants more. The producers think the public is composed of Barnum's suckers and try to cut corners. Downhill goes the series and soon it's off the air."

Drury, still movie-star handsome and wearing a beret cut from a bath towel, had no intention of letting that happen, and his methods of preventing it included refusing to work. This was hardly a tactic designed to endear himself to the show's bosses, and they thought long and hard about replacing him. But it was impossible: he was The Virginian in the minds of the American people, just as James Arness was Matt Dillon, and a replacement would have meant disaster. Drury kept his job, but he also made enemies.

"The Virginian" *netted* more than $1,000,000 for each of its almost three hundred episodes, but that didn't matter to the moguls. When it finally went off the air, Drury couldn't find work in Hollywood. No one needed an uppity actor who stopped production with sit-down strikes.

Drury now lived in Houston in a big house that had to be entered through what seemed to be a dense jungle, but actually was a huge atrium. He was a favorite of Grimm, not leastwise because he was a spokesman for the National Rifle Association, which in the tycoon's eyes made Drury a patriot.

And Drury did believe in the right of the American citizen to own a gun, having several of his own in his Houston home. Once he heard a rustling at his window, stuffed a pistol into his pajamas, and went to investigate. He heard the noise again, and almost in a single motion whipped out the gun and turned on a light. He had drawn down on a philodendron the wind had been brushing against the window.

But Drury was too smart to get into Grimm's card game. "I don't know how to play," he said, when the millionaire asked him to join.

"I saw you playing," said John Burris, the deckhand, "on an episode of 'The Virginian'."

"That was a stand-in."

"I think I can help you," said Grimm. "It's probably a mistake, because I hate to play beginners — they always win first time out. But it's all in fun, so I'll overcome my misgivings."

"Really, no."

"Well, boy," said Grimm, turning to me, "that leaves you. We can count on you, right?"

"A friendly game?"

"Absolutely. We're all friends. And we really need another player. Myself, and brothers Burris and Blanco, it's just not enough for a good game."

"I suppose I could sit in."

"Good. You won't regret it. I have to admit, my luck has been uncanny lately, but it can't last. You're getting in at a good time."

"How's that?"

"The laws of probability, boy. They're unchanging. Immutable. Absolutely inflexible. They're why insurance companies can't lose money. They're why smart gamblers would bet on you tonight."

"You really think so?"

"Figure it out for yourself. You keep betting heads long enough, you have to lose. That's what I've been doing. And tails are long overdue to turn up."

Up on the bow after dinner a beautiful afternoon had changed into an even more lovely early evening. The shining green water and pale blue/orange sky competed peacefully for a Most Serene in the Universe award. The *Gyre* moved almost imperceptibly, and the sun was warm and comforting, perfect for sleeping under. There was just enough of a hint of breeze for the fresh salt sea to clear the sinuses.

"You really don't know how to play poker?" I asked Drury.

"Not against Grimm, I don't."

"He's that good?"

"What do you think?"

"He said . . ."

"Forget what he said. He finished second in the World Series of Poker in Las Vegas against some of the most ruthless man-eaters on the planet. Won a bundle of money in the tournament. It was on national television. Rumor has it the only person who can beat him is his wife."

"Why would he pretend . . ."

"He's rich. He likes to win."

"So you think I'm pretty sure to lose?"

"Don't you?"

"Well . . ."

"I've been waiting to meet someone like you for a long time. Look, I've got this bridge in Brooklyn, and . . ."

Drury was depressing so I ambled around to the fantail where Bobby Blanco was baiting a shark hook with sirloin steak. He said he was glad to see me, that we needed to discuss strategy.

"I don't know," I said. "I see all those IOUs Grimm has collected from you and Burris. Maybe I shouldn't play."

"That's just the reason we need to talk," said Bobby. "You don't want to sign anything over to him. It's different with Burris. What can Grimm do about him, anyway?"

"Have some Texas thugs break his legs?"

"Not Grimm's style. He knows he can't collect from Burris. Not so with us. We make money once in a while. He could collect from us."

"He's not getting anything from me. I'm not going to play. He's too lucky, or something."

"You're not seeing the big picture. Do you know how much money Grimm has?"

"He has more than me."

"He's rich. R-I-C-H rich. What an opportunity. We've got him all to ourselves on a long cruise. It's a golden opportunity few people ever get offered."

"I hear he's ranked second in the world. I know I'm not ranked first."

"In *poker*. He's second in the world in poker. We're going to get him to play blackjack."

"There's that big a difference?"

"Night and day."

"I heard him suggest we switch to blackjack. That doesn't sound encouraging."

"It's what makes it perfect. It was *his* idea. He can't complain we conned him. He's walked into a trap."

"I don't see any trap. I don't think I want anything to do with this, Bobby."

"You'll always be small potatoes with that attitude. Is that what you want?"

"Well . . ."

"Follow my plan and we'll leave this ship with a tidy nest egg."

"How tidy?"

"Grimm's no piker. We could win a lot."

"I'm not going to cheat, Bobby."

"Who's talking about cheating? Besides, Grimm is the suspicious sort, and would sniff out a cheat right away."

"Then how do we do it?"

"We outsmart him."

Outsmart him? It seemed obvious Einstein was brighter than, say, former heavyweight champion Jack Dempsey, but in a fist fight the intelligent money would probably be on Dempsey. I asked Bobby what he meant by outsmarting him.

"Does Grimm seem like a scholar to you?" he asked.

"In geology, maybe. He's found a lot of oil wells."

"Forget geology. Forget oil wells. I'm talking about brains."

"Geology is brains. I think."

"*Book* learning."

"All right, I agree, I don't think he stays awake late at night reading Proust."

"Exactly. You've got it."

Bobby was baiting another hook. It appeared he was attaching an entire prime rib. His eyes were a bit wild, they seemed occasionally to spin like pinballs, but if he had a way of transferring some of Grimm's money to us, he was worth hearing out. Bobby spit on the meat before lowering it into the water, absolutely normal and recognizable to anyone who grew up next to the Mississippi and observed people going after the big catfish. Spitting on bait, said established wisdom, added a final touch that fish found irresistible.

"Grimm is instinctive," Bobby analyzed. "Elemental Man. He possesses a certain bash-them-over-the-head Texas intelligence, a cunning a cut above that of a wolf, but he can't cope with modern minds."

"Go ahead."

"Cro-Magnon man wiped out Neanderthal, right?"

"Right."

"Because Cro-Magnon was smarter. And capitalists beat feudalists, right?"

"Right."

"On the same theory, we wipe out Grimm, right?"

"I don't know, Bobby. It seems . . ."

"We apply good old modern-day know-how against him. I've read every book there is on blackjack, memorized them, burned the principles into my head, and in just a few hours I can teach you all the fundamentals. We play scientifically and we'll own this caveman."

"I doubt if we'll really own him."

"Maybe we'll show some mercy. I sort of like his wife Jackie."

"What's she like?"

"A character. Has to be to be married to Grimm."

"Maybe we should kidnap Jack and demand a ransom."

"Jackie wouldn't pay it. Listen, let's get serious about this blackjack business. It's the opportunity of a lifetime. We'll go back to the cabin and I'll teach you everything I know."

Bobby baited a final hook, tossed it overboard, mused for a moment about how delicious shark filets are, and then we headed for the cabin.

Jack Cosgrove, a photographer, was reading a Western novel, and Nik Petrik, another photographer, was asleep. Bobby began by explaining when to stay or hit on twelve, then talked about the right time to double down when holding ten or eleven.

"You still scheming?" said Cosgrove.

"A righteous transfer of funds," said Bobby. "Cosgrove, you could join us."

The veteran Cosgrove had covered several wars, been all around the world, interviewed and filmed dictators, revolutionaries, vain movie stars, kings of finance, South American peasants, Mafia dons, and so on. He started once again to read his Zane Grey novel. "I don't gamble," he said. "I don't think Grimm does either."

Unmoved, Bobby dissected the intricacies of when to split pairs, the percentage that favored the dealer, the correct time to take "insurance" against blackjack, and how (this was by necessity a crash course) to count cards.

"We don't deviate," he concluded. "We go strictly by the book. And we insist that the limit on bets be raised."

"Grimm will agree to that," mumbled Cosgrove.

"Look," said Bobby, "you're not part of this. Go back to reading about sunsets."

We arrived in the galley promptly at nine, just as the movie up in the lounge was letting out. There was no roughing it on this expedition: food was often steak or lobster or both. Grimm had financed the search the year before, 1980, but had not accompanied the voyage, and members of the expedition said the meals were terrible.

Eddie Vos, who had spent thirty years at sea, was seated at the table where the game would be played. Above him, on a shelf beneath the porthole, were round racks filled with chips and a dozen new decks of cards. The galley itself was smoky but well-lighted; the table was bolted to the floor as a precaution against rough seas.

Eddie Vos smiled and shook his head as Bobby told him of our plans. The old seaman had been watching the nightly slaughter for almost a week.

"Don't be so morose, Eddie," Bobby said.

"You boys don't stand a chance."

"I should quit while I'm behind?"

"Offer him double what you owe now. If you're lucky, he'll accept, and you won't have to play him any more."

"Don't listen to this negative guy," Bobby said. "Grimm is late. He probably knows something is up and is sweating it out."

If Grimm was "sweating," it was not evident. He came into the galley telling Captain Armand a joke:

A Jewish man named Goldberg was sitting in a bar next to a Chinese. Suddenly he turned and punched the Chinese in the nose. "Why did you do that?" the Chinese asked. "That's for Pearl Harbor. I hate Japanese." "But I'm Chinese," said the Chinese. "Chinese, Japanese, it's all the same." The Chinese thought about this for a moment and then punched Goldberg on the nose. "Why did you do that?" he was asked. "For the *Titanic*." "But I had nothing to do with the *Titanic."* "Iceberg, Goldberg," said the Chinese. "It's all the same."

"Here I am, boys," said the millionaire, pulling up a chair. "Should we start?"

"Why," I asked, "do you always say 'Here I am?' It's obvious you're wherever you are."

"A good question," said Grimm. "The reason . . ."

"Let's get down to business," Bobby interrupted, and proceeded to lay down the new conditions for the game: blackjack instead of poker, and higher bets. Grimm, congratulating Bobby for realizing that his "luck was bound to change," agreed to both provisos. "Deep down," he said, "I'm just a sucker for games of chance."

With a big crowd packed into the galley (the scientists were amused by the nightly card game), the deck was cut to see who would deal and Grimm won. The only way to take the deal away from him was to catch a blackjack, an ace along with a face card or ten.

But right from the start the only person getting blackjack was Grimm. That was not what hurt. *Twelve times in a row,* over a period of ninety minutes, with a six (the worst possible card) showing, the tycoon dealt himself "21."

"I'm in big trouble, boys," he would say, each time the six appeared. "Don't show mercy. Double down and make me suffer."

It seemed just not to be possible, but there was a solution available. "I've got to go to the lab," I said.

"Don't be gone long," said the millionaire. "I feel in my bones that the flow of cards is shifting."

"Carl," was the way Dr. Lowenstein was approached. Lowenstein, of the Scripps Institution of Oceanography, was in charge of the *Gyre's* super-sophisticated computer. He was a computer expert who taught other computer experts. Undoubtedly a genius, he lived in a mental world inhabited by few others, was a hard man to get an answer from. Once I asked him the time. "What time do you mean?" he answered. "The real time, or the time everyone mistakenly thinks it is?" Lowenstein pointed out that there are 31,556,925.975 seconds in a year, and no calendar devised is accurate enough for that kind of measurement. "We lose a day every 3,200 years," he said. "The year 2100 won't be a Leap Year."

"Carl," I said, having rushed in from the galley, "how about putting that computer to a practical use?"

"That's how it's being used now."

"For HEBBLE? Be serious." HEBBLE was what we were doing before looking for the *Titanic*. It was a search for a spot on the ocean bottom that was free of practically everything; ideal for the scientists to study underwater currents. HEBBLE drove Grimm crazy. He wanted to be about the job of finding *Titanic*. "What HEBBLE is," Grimm groused, "is a search for nothing." That is precisely what it was.

"Look, Carl," I said, "what I want has an important application."

John Farre's ears had pricked up. He was a husky, no-nonsense scientist from Columbia University. His authoritarian manner had prompted the movie crew to nickname him "Kaiser," and even Grimm was afraid of him. "Leave Dr. Lowenstein alone," ordered Farre.

"Farre, you're a reasonable man. I only want Lowenstein to compute what the odds are for hitting '21' twelve times in a row with a six showing."

"This is a scientific expedition," said Farre. "It's not a gambling cruise."

"Could you do it?" I asked Lowenstein.

"Yes."

"Would you?"

"No."

"We could use someone on the winch-watch," said Farre. "It might cool you off."

"Give me a break, Farre. All I want is to know if Grimm is cheating."

"We're not going to become involved in this."

Back in the galley, Grimm was advising, "Increase your bets, boys. When your luck changes, and it's due to happen any time, you'll want to take full advantage."

Bobby cursed in Spanish, but this argument impressed the young deckhand, John Burris. "There's another thing we've got going for us," he said. "Grimm is older than we are. He's bound to tire. All we have to do is keep him playing long enough."

"Good thinking," said the tycoon.

"He'll never be *chief* deckhand with that kind of reasoning," observed Eddie Vos.

But Grimm, never losing his sincere face, insisted Burris had a sound point, and launched into a long story about a game he had witnessed as a boy in Oklahoma. It involved a struggling young farm couple trying to hang onto their homestead, a greedy banker wanting to evict them, and a concerned oil man (what else?) who plays blackjack with the banker to try to stop the foreclosure. Grimm was five minutes into the narrative when Bobby told him he didn't want to hear any more.

As though drawn by a powerful magnet, the chips continued to move steadily to Grimm's side of the table. Other players, of course, occasionally won hands, but never on any sort of consistent basis. About midnight Bobby Blanco announced, "That's it. I'm quitting. I've got a little money left in the bank in Tampa, but I'll be damned if I'm giving it to Diamond Jim Brady here."

"I'll take another IOU," said Grimm.

"You will?"

"You're a man of your word, Bobby."

"You can't quit," said Burris. "It will give him an excuse to break up the game while he's ahead. Fatigue will set in soon."

"This boy needs shore leave," said Eddie Vos.

"It's monotonous," said photographer Jack Cosgrove. "I think I'll go finish my book."

"Why don't you sit in for a few hands," Grimm suggested to the cameraman. The streetwise Cosgrove feigned a stroke, then ambled off shaking his head.

To acquire more chips, Bobby signed an IOU on a scrap of paper and Grimm added it to some twenty other scraps of paper he carried in his shirt pocket.

"Those are all IOUs?" I asked.

"There's not so many of them."

"Must be twenty."

"I don't keep track."

"Of course he doesn't," said Eddie Vos, raising his eyebrows and pretending to play a violin.

"Most of them are signed by widows and orphans," said Bobby. "Just deal the cards."

Grimm seemed hurt, particularly by the snickering of bystanders over the pocket full of IOUs. Later, in Abilene, one of his secretaries remarked about his facility for laying his hands on the IOUs. "He's uncanny, all right. But he's all thumbs when looking for a UOME."

Fresh with new chips acquired from the IOU, Bobby dedicated himself to coming back. His eyes shown with a new alertness. His entire body seemed to quiver with concentration. Often, before a crucial card was dealt, he rose from his seat, and exhorted the gods with "Wombie! Wombie! Wombie!"

"What does 'wombie' mean?" I asked him.

"Dooms Grimm and his descendants."

But nothing changed. Bobby and Burris signed updated IOUs, and I signed my first. Burris's theory that the millionaire would tire was evaporating to smoke. Grimm looked cool and refreshed. His opponents were drained, as much from the constant, unchanging routine of losing as from the long session.

"Why not stop punishing yourselves?" suggested Eddie Vos.

Grimm is a card-counter, and about 2 A.M. there occurred a hand that was typical of all past, present, and future sessions. The millionaire had already dealt halfway through the deck, and most of the cards that had appeared were low ones, fours, fives, sixes, and the like. "I'm in a lot of trouble, boys," said Grimm.

"Stop talking and deal the cards," said Bobby.

"I'm just trying to be helpful," said Grimm.

Eddie Vos had to choke back a coughing seizure.

"It's true," said Grimm, still able to portray a man deeply aggrieved when his motives were doubted. "I'm telling you, the deck is rich in face cards."

"Mostly small ones have been played," said Bobby.

"That's right. And it means the odds have shifted from the dealer to the players."

"For once," said Bobby, "I agree with Diamond Jim."

"Well, boys, double your bets. I'm ripe to be plucked."

"Could I play more than one hand?" Bobby asked.

"You can play eight hands if you want, Bobby."

And that's what he did. He played eight hands at once, his bets stacked across the table in front of him like a phalanx.

"A smart move," said Grimm. "A blackjack is bound to show up somewhere, what with all those high cards still in the deck."

Grimm was right: a blackjack did show up, but not in one of the *eight* hands Bobby was playing. It appeared in the *one* hand the millionaire played.

"Madre de Dios!" said Bobby softly. "Maybe suicide is the answer."

It was clear the concept of scientific blackjack had long since been abandoned, but it was not until 3:30 A.M. that Grimm dealt the hand that broke up the game. The millionaire had a six showing, Bobby had doubled his bet and was on his knees screaming "Wombie!" Grimm turned over a jack, which meant he had sixteen, and the Cuban was holding a pair of kings. "Wombie! Wombie! Wombie! Wombie! Wombie!"

"I'm in trouble, boys."

It was as if super-sensitive radar zeroed in on the cards Grimm held in his hand. Even Eddie Vos, who never doubted the tycoon would win, was curious about what seemed an almost supernatural run of luck. If Grimm were going to deal a second, or from the bottom of the deck, or out of his sleeve, or whatever, he would have to do it in front of some very suspicious eyes.

Grimm turned over a five. If hanky-panky had been involved, he was Houdini's reincarnation. The room stood still waiting for Bobby's reaction, and this time he didn't disappoint. Grimm said, "Well, boys, Lady Luck is sure to smile on you soon," and then came the explosion. From his kneeling stance Bobby made a three-foot vertical leap, resembling Julius Erving going up for a dunk, and when he landed he was in full stride, racing out of the galley and down a corridor, back through the corridor and out to the deck, to the galley once again and then up stairs that led to the radio room, shouting in Spanish every step of the way.

"It's healthy," the rich man judged, "that he's not repressed."

Everyone on the ship at one time or another stopped to watch what became a nightly contest as one-sided as Crazy Horse versus Custer. Co-chief scientist Bill Ryan of Columbia University could barely contain his distaste: what particularly appalled him was the large debt being run up by the deckhand, Burris. He figured Bobby and I deserved whatever we got. The other co-chief scientist, Scripps Institute's stern Fred Spiess, surprisingly thought it was a great good show, and his eyes twinkled (did he know something?) each time Grimm pulled in another pot. Scripps scientist Mary Linzer was sympathetic, saying the pain being endured seemed worse than any enjoyment deriving from the game.

Soon no one in the nightly session, except Grimm, had cash any more, so a good deal of time was spent updating IOUs, a bookkeeping job the oilman performed with proper solemnity. His filing system had appeared crude at first, cluttered as it was with slips of paper from Abilene debtors, but he could unerringly zero in on the proper document whenever someone needed more chips. He of course had early on assumed the role of banker.

It was clearly fruitless (why then each morning would hope rear its ugly head?), but thoughts of all Grimm's money — even some of it — in our more worthy pockets kept us coming back throughout the 30-day expedition.

Jim Drury made a brief appearance in the game: he won the first hand dealt to him, said something about being the only man on earth ahead of Grimm, and quit.

It was during one of the card games that Grimm suggested I might want to move to Texas to write the book about the *Titanic* search. "You'll like Abilene, boy," he said. "Beautiful country, and it's nice and quiet. You can get a lot of work done there."

"I don't know. I've never been to Texas."

"People keep their word in Texas. A Texan makes you a promise, you can count on his keeping it."

"I kind of like New York."

"Look, boy, you come to Abilene when this expedition is over. See what you think. There'll be a big charity affair going on — we hold it every year for crippled kids — and you'll meet lots of stars. Besides, I've got all the information in Abilene that you'll ever need to write about *Titanic*. Been collecting it a long time."

"It wouldn't hurt to take a look."

"Right, boy. Maybe we'll even make a Texan out of you."

"I doubt it."

"Whatever. I know you'll enjoy meeting the boys."

The night before we docked in Boston, I asked Bobby Blanco who the boys are.

"God knows," he said.

Two

The West Texas Rehabilitation Center each year helps hundreds of disabled and crippled children, and relies not a whit on taxpayer money. Abilenians are justifiably proud of the center, generously support it with cash donations, and once each year have a big fundraiser featuring top-name stars. Bob Hope usually hosted the show, but this year it was Glen Campbell.

I was ensconced at Kiva Inn, having been driven there by Grimm from the small Abilene airport. The millionaire had been on "Good Morning, America" the day before, which was the day after we docked in Boston, and was eager to see the underwater pictures the scientists were developing. He was convinced we had photographed part of *Titanic*, and was not unaware that this could earn him a small place in history books.

Grimm was not opposed to publicity, and as time went by, and I met other rich Texans, I developed a theory about why they tended toward the spectacular and outrageous (just one example for now: Stanley Marsh 3 of Amarillo, who owns what he describes as a pool table that is the size of a football field). The Texans, I believe, having accumulated fortunes as large as any in the East, resent that their accomplishments are not so well documented, and find that the mere possession of money is not sufficient to satisfy their need

17

for recognition. You can read practically every day about a Rockefeller or DuPont, but not about the obscure men with big egos who have dug fortunes out of the Texas desert.

Lee Cullum, editor of *D Magazine* in Dallas and a member of the wealthy Tom Thumb supermarket family, disagrees with this analysis. "The Texas rich," she says, "have accumulated their money recently, and they're not ashamed of it as some of those in the East are. Many Texans made it themselves. A lot of those in the East inherited."

No one could accuse Jack Grimm of being ashamed. Besides *Titanic,* he had financed well-publicized searches for the Loch Ness monster, Noah's Árk, Bigfoot, Big Bird (this probably a figment of a moonshiner's imagination), and the Tibetan snow leopard, and had commissioned a sculpture to be carved on a mountain he owned outside Abilene that would be four times the size of the one on Mount Rushmore. He said when he finished with *Titanic* he would probably look for Atlantis.

As expected Grimm drove his Cadillac very fast coming in from the airport, and I couldn't tell if he was pulling my leg with his talk about how beautiful Abilene is. I remembered one national magazine describing it as a place where nothing happens, and with the terrific heat of this August day bouncing off desolate sand, and millions of large dead insects on the roadside, and a profusion of new fast-food emporiums already old and dusty . . . no, it did not look beautiful, but I didn't say so to Grimm.

"Look over there, boy!" he said, skidding to a stop in the center of the road. He was pointing at what seemed to be a large, round, grey rock. "That's an armadillo, boy."

"What do they do?"

"We hold armadillo races."

"I don't believe you."

"Betting on horses is illegal in Texas, so we bet on armadillos. They're fast little devils, once you get them going."

"People raise armadillos?"

"They train 'em, but mostly it's a waste of time. They run when they want to. Makes it pretty hard to handicap a race."

"I'd like to see an armadillo race."

"You will. And you'll want to see the Armadillo Alympics, too. And the rattlesnake hunt."

"Armadillo Olympics?"

"*A* lympics. We wouldn't want it confused with the real thing."

Grimm made one more stop before dropping me at Kiva Inn. He screeched into the Petroleum Club, saying he would be just a minute: "I want to see if one of the boys has an extra plane." He didn't explain why he needed an airplane, but apparently it was as routine as borrowing a neighbor's cup of sugar.

There were two types of vehicles in the Petroleum Club parking lot: Cadillacs and pickup trucks. Many of the pickups had gun racks in the back. On the *Titanic* expedition, Grimm had said, "The Russians will have a helluva time taking Abilene."

At the Kiva Inn I was put in the hands of B. J. Billing, a husky Vietnam veteran I assumed was Grimm's go-fer. When I was settled in the room I started to tell him about the *Titanic* search, but soon learned he had just been on a more interesting adventure. At least it had been more dangerous.

"Grimm asked me a couple months ago," B.J. said, "if I'd like to be on top of the world. Foolishly, I said yes. I thought by top-of-the-world he meant rich. I ended up in Tibet lucky to be alive."

Somehow Grimm had obtained eight visas to China, which he used chiefly to give to some fundamentalist religious people. One of these was the president of The Praise the Lord Construction Company in Toronto, Canada. B.J. was sent along, ostensibly to make a movie about China and Tibet, but mostly he helped the religious zealots. They had smuggled thousands of Chinese-language Bibles into the Communist stronghold, and proceeded to play hide-and-seek with Red security agents as they passed out the illegal material to anyone who would accept it.

B.J. met singer John Denver in China — he wrote the popular "Shanghai Breezes" while the two were together — and Denver was convinced all of them would be killed. What evidently saved them, at least from arrest, was that the Chinese believed B.J. was Grimm's financial agent and able to make deals involving oil exploration or building a hotel in Peking.

"Grimm wouldn't do business with the Chinese," I said.

"There are a billion of them," said B.J.

"He's very anti-communist."

"He's also a businessman. Can you imagine his eyes lighting up when he thinks of a billion customers?"

The more B.J. talked about his trip to China and Tibet, the more I thought he should consider writing a book about the adventure. In

Tibet he had lived with Tenzing Norgay, the Sherpa guide responsible for Sir Edmund Hillary's 1953 conquest of Mount Everest, 29,028 feet high. When the exhausted Hillary seemed unable to continue his historic climb, it was Tenzing Norgay who kept him going. Norgay is known to very few people in the United States, but in actual fact he was the one who first scaled the great mountain.

And B.J. visited areas of China, and met Chinese people, no living Westerner had ever encountered. One high Chinese official connected with the trip was a born-again Christian, an understandably nervous man in constant fear that the Bible-distributors would be arrested.

Also, B.J. had a scheduled appointment with the Dalai Lama, the exiled spiritual leader of Tibet now living in northern India. Plans were afoot for the Dalai Lama and tens of thousands of his followers to set up a retreat in Colorado. I said I thought this newsworthy information certainly should be a part of the book.

"Grimm owns the rights," B.J. said.

"How's that?"

"He paid for the trip. I work for him."

"Well, the book is a good idea."

"I think we should talk to him about it."

B.J.'s job had many facets. He made films for the eccentric millionaire; he eliminated chaos from schemes like the search for the *Titanic,* or a hang-gliding competition Grimm sponsored to be held on his mountain, or a climb by paraplegics in wheelchairs up the highest mountain in Texas; plus in his spare time he beat the backwoods to obtain oil lease renewals. B.J. told me about the farmer whose house could only be reached by driving over six miles of pasture.

"I'm with the Grimm Oil Company," B.J. told the farmer. "It's that time again. Time to renew the lease."

"Well, I think I'll do that," the farmer said. "But first I want to go to town, talk with the Gandy boys, see what Exxon is paying these days."

About this time Grimm called the farmhouse to see if the papers were signed. "Not yet," he was told. "Mr. Threewitt wants to go into town to find out what Exxon is paying."

"Don't let him do that, boy," warned the tycoon.

I learned that Grimm as a young graduate of the University of Oklahoma hit oil on the first well he drilled, had perhaps the best ratio in all of Texas of wells drilled to oil found, and now also was involved in gold and silver mines, retail marketing, and real estate. He and his wife spent their honeymoon panning for gold in Nevada. He seemed to be as lucky making money as he had been on the ship playing cards and finding loose change.

There seemed to be a reason why for years Bob Hope, and this year Glen Campbell, might come to out-of-the-way Abilene for a charity benefit. Granted probably their hearts were in the right place, but many areas of the nation had worthy causes to be helped, and why choose this particular one? The reason suggested was that Abilene had a high percentage of millionaires among its population, Jack Grimm being only the most visible, and if money were ever needed for personal reasons or for financing a movie or other venture, they were a likely source to tap.

B.J. told me that a number of rich Texans had invested in the movie business, usually with unhappy results. The production would get off to a good enough start, a worthwhile idea, promising script, talented actors, plenty of up-front money, but then the process would deteriorate. The oil mogul and the "creative" people could not have less in common, and after a few weeks the rich man would try to take over the running of the operation. Usually this meant cutting down on expenses — "Dammit, why can't the star do his own stunts?" or "Why the hell don't we take a picture of a picture of the Empire State Building instead of going all the way to New York to film it?" or "If we put a commercial for Trailways in the film they'll loan us a bus for free."

"If they'd just put up the money," B.J. judged, "and leave the movie-makers alone, they might turn a nice profit. But they start to think they're Cecil B. DeMille and the film ends up terrible."

Of course, any actor who drank, chased women, or took drugs, was not wanted for a movie, and this eliminated most top-name stars. The Texans also tended to believe most Hollywood people were "AC-DC, you know, not like us," and this contributed to friction. Charles Bronson was runaway Best Actor winner in a poll of oilmen, followed by Lee Van Cleef and Clint Eastwood.

Similar unusual tastes were found in education. "Tell me the truth now," one prosperous wildcatter asked, "what's the better school, Harvard or Hardin-Simmons?"

"Hardin-Simmons has more Bible courses," I said.

"I thought you'd see it my way."

Grimm had only been gone an hour when he entered the Kiva Inn room without knocking, Jim Drury in tow, and said we didn't have much time. Much time for what?

"The banquet tonight. And the big Glen Campbell show afterward. Get up, boy. Show some life. We've got places to go, people to see, things to do."

"The banquet's not till seven. It's only four."

"You're not going like that?" I was wearing slacks and a sweater, and had on a pair of new shoes.

"I thought I'd put on a jacket."

"Don't you want me to be proud of you, boy? Come on. We'll rent you a tuxedo."

"I don't wear tuxedos."

"A nice white one. He'd look good in a white tuxedo, wouldn't he, Drury?"

"Like a famous author," said Drury.

"Well," I said, "that's right. I'm an author, not a fashion model. Authors don't wear tuxedos."

"Dammit, boy, be somebody. Look sharp."

"You wearing a tuxedo?" I asked Drury.

"A black one. I brought it from Houston."

"I'd rather wear a black one."

"Wear a white one," said Grimm. "You'll stand out."

"I don't want to stand out."

"When you move here, you'll want people to know you."

Grimm found a quarter on the sidewalk when we stepped out of the motel room. I told Drury this sort of consistent good fortune, like the cards he dealt himself on the *Gyre,* made me suspicious.

"He's just lucky," Drury said.

"All the time?"

"I think so. He's a fire-eater, you know. He's never taken lessons, but doesn't burn himself."

The tuxedo place was closed, but Grimm beat on the door and the owner opened up. He seemed honored that the rich man would come to his store, wouldn't take cash for the tuxedo ("I'll send a bill to the oil company"), and peppered Grimm with questions about the oil business, a subject on the minds of many Abilenians. At the recent 100th anniversary celebration of Abilene's founding, a group of oilmen, for educational purposes, set up a skeleton rig on the fairgrounds. The purpose was to show children how a well was drilled: what happened was that oil was discovered. Of course, there presently was a legal fight over ownership of the oil between politicians and the men who drilled the well.

With Grimm driving very fast, he, his wife Jackie, Drury and I drove to the Civic Center for the cocktail party, dinner, and show that preceded the main show, the Glen Campbell concert. Drury and I were the only two in tuxedos, and there were some five hundred people present. Most of the people Grimm introduced me to had initials for first names — T.B., O.R., W.N., H.C. — and were wildcatters, oil well suppliers, ranchers, and bankers. I asked Grimm if Abilene had the highest millionaire-to-general-population ratio in the country.

"Don't think so," he said. "But we've got plenty of them around here, don't we?"

Later I looked it up. Palm Springs, California, had the highest percentage of millionaires in America, with Odessa/Midland, Texas, next.

There was an abundance of food at the cocktail party, tables stacked high with barbecued ribs and fresh gulf shrimp. Women wore big glittering diamonds on their fingers and around their necks, while the men tended toward gold. A grizzled oilman, wearing a wide Texas hat, was talking about upcoming tax cuts. He kept referring to the president as "Brother Reagan."

When we were seated for the banquet, but before the prime rib was served, "celebrities" were introduced to the gathering by the people who paid for the tables where they sat. Drury received loud applause. In Abilene he was still The Virginian, a straight-thinking, straight-shooting straight guy.

Grimm introduced me as "the author of twenty-two bestsellers." "Jack," I whispered, "that's twenty-two *books*. No one has written twenty-two bestsellers."

"A slip-of-the-tongue, boy," Grimm said. "But who knows the difference?"

Entertainment after dinner featured Rex Allen, a country and western singer, dancer Donald O'Connor, and the beautiful Mexican singer, Anaconti, who appeared regularly on the Lawrence Welk Show. When Anaconti completed her number, the master of ceremonies declared, "We're getting a better class of wetback this year."

The Glen Campbell concert was held before 2,000 people in the main auditorium of the Civic Center, and Drury and I sat in the front row. Rumor was that Campbell had lost a sizable sum of cash that afternoon to Abilene golfing versions of Grimm at a card table, good old boys on a run of luck. But Campbell put on a fine show for the crowd, and they loved it, bringing him back numerous times with applause and calls for just one more song.

Drury and the singer are friends, and after the show we went to Campbell's dressing room to say hello. Campbell was seated at one end of the large room, his girl friend, pop music star Tanya Tucker, at the other. The two evidently had been having a spectacular fight, and Drury wisely decided not to stay long.

On the way to his home, with Grimm driving even faster than before, his wife Jackie was criticizing his "thoughtlessness." His grandson's birthday was approaching, and the millionaire had not yet bought a present. As Jackie went on, Grimm grew more tense. He gripped the steering wheel tighter, applied more pressure to the gas pedal, his shrewd little eyes darted back and forth as though looking for an escape. "Well," he finally spluttered, "I'll get him something in the morning. I'll buy him a pair of guns."

The boy's next birthday was his twelfth, and Jackie snorted at this idea. She was going to be a lot of fun.

Jackie Grimm was a still-very-attractive blonde who married Grimm while the two were enrolled at the University of Oklahoma. She did not in the least resemble the stereotype of the Rich Texas Wife drawling sweet honey-soaked nothings. She panned for gold with Grimm on their honeymoon, refused to be discouraged when it appeared he might not strike it rich in the oilfields, encouraged him on his fantasy searches for such legends as Loch Ness Monster and *Titanic,* and could beat him playing cards. Recently the two had gone to Las Vegas agreeing each would have a stake of $10,000. Grimm lost it all, but Jackie built hers to $40,000. She turned him down when he asked for a loan.

A bit of the flavor of Abilene could be captured by reading bumper stickers as Grimm sped toward his home. The city was proud of its nickname — "Buckle of the Bible Belt" — and many of the bumper stickers bore religious slogans. But there were others: "We Don't Care How Y'All Do It Up North" and another, advertising a new organization, "DAMM — Drunks Against Mad Mothers."

Grimm's big house featured antiques, Picasso prints, a 16th Century desk, one of the first slot machines ever made, and a nickelodeon. There was a painting in the bedroom that at a distance appeared to be a woman's luscious derriere, but up-close was a drawing of Abraham Lincoln. The Grimms kept two dogs: Beauregard, a bright poodle, the "inside dog" who never went outside, and Bee Bee, who had a bad heart, the "outside dog" who never was allowed inside. The house featured the biggest bathtub I had ever seen, and in the backyard were a swimming pool and pecan trees. Grimm exhibited a piece of wood he was certain had come from Noah's Ark, and part of the carpet that had been aboard the *Titanic* (removed by a worker before the ship sailed, found its way into the tycoon's hands by way of a historical society impressed with his efforts to locate the lost behemoth). Grimm donated one small thread from that carpet to a March of Dimes fundraiser, and it brought $2,000 at auction.

Just about anything recovered from the *Titanic* would have enormous value, so Grimm stood to gain far more than fame if he found the great ship. And reportedly there was cargo of immense actual worth that was lost with *Titanic:* a fortune in gold bullion, jewels, a diamond-encrusted copy of Omar Khayyam's *Rubaiyat*. "This book," said a speaker in front of a university women's group, "all by itself, would be worth the millions Grimm and his friends put up." The precious manuscript, so all research indicated, was in a waterproof safe.

But Grimm had other motives besides making money. The managing editor of his hometown newspaper described him as "a man with hounds at his heels," a reference to his continuing, restless quest for involvment in unusual projects. Grimm was an adventurer, the everyday tedium of normal life bored him, and he had the money to alleviate his malaise. Jim Drury called him a "grown man living in a little kid's world."

Another concern, once the expedition began, perhaps Grimm's strongest concern, was the welfare of his investors, or more accurately, perhaps, the image the investors have of him. These were his peers, and he had persuaded them to invest in a very risky endeavor. He seldom failed them on oil deals. He did not want to fail them with the *Titanic* search. I suspected he had dressed me in the tuxedo to demonstrate that a first-rate writer was doing the book about the expedition.

Jackie Grimm was emphatic when she talked about treasures

that could be salvaged from the *Titanic,* and specifically the copy of the *Rubaiyat.* "Jack's not like some of those rich eastern 'philanthropists,' " she said. "He wouldn't hide the book away in our house so only we could appreciate it. He'd give it to a museum or a library."

Grimm's return search for the *Titanic* in the summer of 1983 reportedly turned up new evidence of the lost liner, but not *Titanic* herself. Armed with renewed confidence, the possibility of aid from the world's largest privately owned submersible, the *Aluminaut,* and an offer from astronaut Alan Shepard to pilot the craft if Grimm decided to go for it, the expedition was mounted with all the glory of the earlier ventures. The *Aluminaut's* nine-foot exterior arms would have been able to reach into the liner to recover artifacts, but that "new frontier" was to remain only a dream for Shepard and a compelling lure for the determined oilman.

But that night in his living room in Abilene, Grimm was sure of success. In fact, when *Titanic* was behind him, he told us, he would probably go search for the Lost Continent of Atlantis. The idea did not seem as strange as it would have had I not been aboard the *Gyre* and listened to the *Titanic* expedition's co-chief scientist, Dr. William Ryan of Columbia University. Ryan, who had been chairman of the New York Academy of Sciences, said he knew where the legendary Atlantis is, and, what's more, the reason why it sank.

Atlantis, Ryan said, was in the middle of the Aegean Sea. It was demolished in 1450 B.C. by a huge eruption that could have been as much as a thousand times more powerful than Mount St. Helens. The disaster occurred during the Minoan civilization, and could explain why that civilization was destroyed. What is left of Atlantis is now known as the Santorini Islands.

The center of Santorini, the main island, simply collapsed and sunk to the bottom of the ocean. "There might never have been a Western civilization," Ryan said, "if the wind had been blowing in a different direction that day." Huge clouds of volcanic ash were carried over to Crete and wiped out all agriculture. King Midas' palace was ruined by the ash, and the people of Crete fled to Greece.

But what if the wind had been blowing differently?

"Probably everyone would have migrated to Lebanon or Africa," said Ryan. "Probably no Western civilization."

The destruction of Atlantis, said Ryan, could also explain the

Biblical story of the parting of the Red Sea for Moses. The eruption took place — worked out by the dating of sediments and archaeology — at a time when the Israeli nation was in captivity in Egypt. Huge tidal waves would have resulted, which probably would have caused the Red Sea to recede. "Not a parting of the waters," Ryan said, "but it might have seemed that way to the people there."

"That would be something," Grimm said. "To find *Titanic* and Atlantis."

But he had *Titanic* on his mind this evening, having so recently returned from looking for her, and his eyes sparkled when he talked about the ship. "She wasn't unique," he was saying. "She had a twin sister, the *Olympic,* and when *Titanic* gave her CQD the *Olympic* was five hundred miles away going in the opposite direction. The *Olympic* came charging to the rescue but was too late."

Grimm described the progress of his search as having "a heifer corralled in a box canyon," but he knew more about the ship than almost anyone on earth. He ticked off the names of the famous people who died: Benjamin Guggenheim, copper magnate, head of a family with reputed wealth of $95 million; George B. Widener, $5 million, Philadelphia socialite and financier; John Jacob Astor, richest person aboard *Titanic,* $150 million, the 47-year-old real estate king who was on a honeymoon with his nineteen-year-old bride; and Isidor Straus, $50 million, a former U.S. Congressman and partner in R.H. Macy & Company.

Many oil men of Grimm's generation struck riches fairly early, but never became as enduringly successful in the business. With several million dollars in hand, they preferred to move to the more cosmopolitan atmospheres of Houston or Dallas, and allow their fledgling, albeit startlingly profitable, operations to be run by others. Grimm stayed put, overseeing his growing empire (ownership in some 400 producing wells), bumping over dusty, almost nonexistent roads personally to make certain everything hummed along smoothly.

This night Grimm was bored. He kept jumping up from his chair to walk outside, which was interesting to watch because he actually walked sideways, a sort of sidle one might use to slip around a corner. "Why do you walk sideways?" I asked.

"Old war wound, boy."

I knew he had been wounded on Okinawa, but I doubted that it caused the walk.

Several other guests had arrived, a psychiatrist, and banker types who seemed eager to loan Grimm money. We began to fantasize about who we would like to be if reincarnation were real and we could choose our identities in a later life. One person wanted to come back as another Einstein. A second understated that he thought Dante Alighieri had been "rather interesting." A third leaned to "someone like Queen Victoria."

"How about you, Jack? Who would you like to be?"

"Yes, Jack, what character will you come back as?"

It was a tough question, and the tycoon's eyes darted, as they always did when he thought hard and fast. "Well," he finally announced, and everyone knew he would tell the truth, "I'd like to come back as me."

Grimm drove me to the airport the next morning. "Tell me, boy," he said, "what do you think of Abilene?"

"Is it always this hot?"

"No. It gets a lot hotter."

"Well, the people are friendly." I considered this answer to be noncommittal. I had never been any place where the people had been *un*friendly.

"Damn right. You'll like it, if you decide to live here."

"It would certainly be different. You're different."

"I don't think so. There are plenty down here like me."

"You're kidding."

"Look it up, boy. We're not the same as those in the East. We have more fun, for one thing. But you're a writer. Look it up."

Three

I sat in the big third-floor reading room of the New York Public Library, 42nd Street and Fifth Avenue, and read first about Texas. I had forgotten my old school lessons about how big it is. You travel a shorter distance getting from El Paso to Los Angeles, California, than from El Paso to Texarkana. Similarly, Texarkana is farther from El Paso than it is from Chicago, Illinois. In short, residents of the largest cities in California and Illinois are closer geographically to population centers in Texas than the Texas cities are to each other.

The state I considered moving to could be compared to most countries, except it is richer and larger. Texas is bigger in size than every nation in Western Europe. It has 26 times the area of Belgium, 9 times that of Austria, 5½ that of Czechoslovakia and Greece, and is three times larger than West Germany. Texas is bigger than England, France, or Italy. The South Asian country of Bangladesh — population 93,100,000 — is 500% smaller than Texas, yet has 6½ times the population.

Texas, it was easy to see, is also rich, Rich, RICH. That's R-I-C-H, as in oil. In 1981 only fifteen countries in the world produced more oil than Texas. Nations such as India (population 700,000,000), Brazil (124,700,000), and Pakistan (89,000,000), not to mention industrial giants like Japan and West Germany, would consider themselves fortunate to possess just a fraction of Texas's energy reserves. Texas, only one state among fifty, also outproduces the vast majority of nations in such lucrative and critical crops as grain, vegetables, fruit, peanuts, and cotton, and in the area of livestock, cattle, hogs, and sheep. Nonnatives would scarcely be aware of the fact — people do not normally think of beaches when Texas comes to mind — but the Port of Houston is the nation's number one shipper of goods. There are 29 universities in the Houston area alone, and 33 institutions of higher learning within thirty miles of Dallas. By the year 2000 Texas is expected to be America's most populous state.

But what fascinated me was Grimm's claim that he was in the mainstream, just an average guy compared to his class peers. Forget that he spent a fortune looking for the *Titanic,* the Loch Ness Monster, and Noah's Ark, and intended to go ahead with that sculpture four times the size of Mount Rushmore's. There were others, he said, just as unusual, and it was these, this sun-shadowed early afternoon, that I began to read about.

"Some people," read the newspaper story, "say that Cullen Davis has finally become convinced that his millions can solve any problem, that money has made him invincible."

Thus was I introduced to the saga of Fort Worth's Cullen Davis, a saga I did not believe could take place in the East. In the East there are the Old Rich, Established Money, cautious, careful, colorless men like David Rockefeller (former chairman of Chase Manhattan Bank) and Paul Mellon (billionaire bland-as-milk major stockholder in Gulf Oil) who hire public relations experts to keep them *out* of the news, who cringe at even the whisper that they might be controversial, flamboyant or, God forbid, different. But in Texas what I researched, and in the case of Grimm had met, was a unique, almost bizarre collection of wealthy eccentrics who made the antics of television's J. R. Ewing seem mild in comparison.

There was nothing in Cullen Davis's childhood to indicate he would be different. A quiet youngster, mild, unassuming, no one seemed even aware the boy was heir to one of Texas's greatest fortunes. Certainly young Cullen never mentioned it.

"To tell you the truth," said a guidance counsellor at Arlington Heights High School, from where Cullen graduated, "I didn't even remember he had gone here. It was like Lee Harvey Oswald (another Arlington Heights student). I had to get out my annual and look him up when all this publicity started."

"All this publicity" was the indictment of Cullen Davis for murder in a case that was sensational even by Texas standards. Texans, who have lived through the Kennedy assassination, Charles Whitman's Texas Tower murder spree, and a seemingly endless chain of other killings (later, in a single autumn week in 1982, there were *five mass murders*), have become somewhat inured to violence. In fact, according to the FBI's Uniform Crime Reports, the Lone Star State possesses nine of the nation's thirty cities where you are most likely to be murdered. To compete for attention in this crowded field, the case has to be unusual, and Cullen Davis's was. It had sex, drugs, and piles of money. Cullen Davis, whose personal wealth was estimated to be between $50 million and $300 million, was the richest murder defendant in U.S. history.

Cullen's father, founder of the family's oil-based fortune, was a strict disciplinarian — his nickname "Stinky" aptly described what numerous people thought of him — and it was not until his death that unusual personality characteristics became discernible in Cullen. His second marriage, on August 29, 1968, to Priscilla Wilburn (it was her third), surprised many of his friends. The fun-loving Priscilla did not fit in with Forth Worth's staid upper-crust society, and it was rumored Cullen himself was hardly the model monogamous male.

On August 3, 1976, two years after Priscilla filed for divorce, police were called to the $6 million Davis mansion where they found Davis's stepdaughter, Andrea Wilburn, and Stan Farr, a former Texas Christian University basketball player and Priscilla's lover, shot to death. Priscilla and a friend, Gus Gavril, were wounded. Police said the killer was "a mysterious man in black," but shortly thereafter arrested Cullen Davis and charged him with capital murder.

I couldn't put down the stories on Cullen Davis, and wondered if Grimm, who seemed to know most rich people in Texas, knew him.

Many sociologists, and some criminologists, believe in this country there is a double standard of justice, one for the rich and one for the rest of society. It has even been suggested that trying a very wealthy person is a waste of taxpayer money, because the chance of conviction is virtually nil. Fort Worth prosecutors were eager to disprove this cheerless, negative perception of justice, and in Cullen

Davis, at least where money was concerned, they had the ideal defendant: he was undeniably rich.

From their father, Cullen and his two brothers had inherited Kendavis Industries, a widely diversified conglomerate with eighty corporations worldwide, including the world's largest independent oil field supply company. Much of the rubber tooling for Apollo moon shots was made by a Kendavis subsidiary, and another subsidiary is the largest U.S. distributor of Ford industrial engines. In 1977, the year Cullen Davis went to trial, the company of which he was one-third owner had sales of $1.29 billion.

Texas is a state legendary for extravagant spending (Neiman-Marcus department stores, perhaps the planet's most expensive, does a land-office business catering to the rich), and perhaps unintentionally Cullen Davis's willingness to spend money to save himself proved a point defense attorneys have long tried to establish: that in a criminal prosecution the state has a big advantage, because it is operating on almost unlimited funds, provided by taxpayers, funds which defendants cannot hope to match. What defendant has an entire police department at his beck and call to investigate? What defendant can afford to use sophisticated computers and laboratory techniques routinely available to the prosecutor? Cullen Davis turned the tables upside-down: despite the state's obvious eagerness to prove to a skeptical public that equal justice applies to all, *Cullen outspent the prosecution.* His tab ran into the millions.

The trial would have generated headlines on its own merits, but adding immeasurable color to the proceedings was Cullen's defense attorney, the very successful and very expensive Richard "Racehorse" Haynes. Haynes is known for dazzling juries, and he was in peak form representing Cullen Davis.

Gus Gavril, paralyzed in the shooting incident, identified the black-wigged gunman as Cullen Davis. Countering Gavril's testimony was Davis's then-girlfriend, Karen Master, who testified the millionaire was in bed with her at the time. The jury chose to believe Karen Master, and on November 17, 1977, returned a verdict of not guilty. That day Cullen celebrated his good fortune by having cocktails with the judge.

In another state a millionaire accused of murder might be expected to low-key it, keep himself out of newspapers, but as I was slowly learning, the rich in Texas are different. Ten months later Cullen Davis was arrested and charged with attempting to hire Charles David McCrory, a friend-turned-police-informant, to kill Judge Joe H. Eidson. Eidson was the judge presiding over the Cullen/Priscilla divorce case. The arrest came after FBI agents tape recorded a meeting between Davis and McCrory where Davis allegedly paid $25,000 for the killing. But, of course, since this was Texas, there was more: McCrory testified that Cullen Davis wanted *fifteen people killed*. This time the best Racehorse Haynes could win for his client was a jury deadlock, 8-4 for conviction.

During the attempted murder-for-hire trial, a prominent Fort Worth businessman talked about Cullen Davis: "During the first trial," he said, "I would say that most businessmen were behind him to a man. But now, I would have to say that most of them think he's guilty."

The divorce proceedings, put on hold during Cullen's two trials, were as steamy as the media anticipated. It developed that Cullen Davis, a top pool player, often journeyed to the Playboy Mansion in Chicago for high-stakes games. Cullen and Priscilla each charged the other with marital infidelity. District Judge Clyde Ashworth, who replaced Judge Eidson, awarded Priscilla $3.4 million. She had asked for more that $50 million. Cullen married Karen Master the day the divorce was official.

In 1980 Cullen Davis said he underwent a born-again religious experience and found God. His ex-wife, Priscilla, probably would not have been impressed. Previously she had said, "He is a liar. I realize that he's been acquitted of the crimes, but that doesn't mean he isn't guilty."

I expected that the last had probably not been heard from Cullen Davis, and was proved right more than a year after my visit to the New York Public Library. Cullen Davis had credited his conversion to television evangelist James Robison, and in October, 1982, donated more than $1 million worth of jade, ivory, and gold art objects to be sold at auction, the proceeds of the sale to benefit Robison's ministry. But Robison soon had a change of heart. "The Lord didn't want me to receive them," he said of the art objects, which related to Eastern religions. "It was not biblical, and as far as I was concerned it represented a false religion."

With hammers in hand, Robison and Cullen Davis smashed the

art objects to pieces in the driveway of Cullen's mansion. "I do not want to do anything that does not please the Lord," said Cullen Davis.

Demolishing precious art objects — one of them was a four-foot jade pagoda valued at more than $500,000 — might appear to many observers as an act unlikely to please the Almighty, but few would dispute Cullen's analysis of his two trials: "If I had been poor . . . I would have ended up in the penitentiary in no time flat."

There were no reference listings such as "Whackos, Texas," but it was not difficult to determine that the Texas rich were a breed unto themselves. For example, Stanley Marsh 3 (he insists the "3" be written this way), who would be undisputed King of the Eccentrics if he lived anywhere else, yet a stick-out even in Texas where the competition clearly is extra-stiff.

At Marsh 3's home, just outside of Amarillo, he keeps a very unpleasant and ugly Bactrian camel who enjoys spitting on people and chasing them. Marsh 3's residence is called Toad Hall and actually is a large ranch in the central panhandle area. The ranch is also home for llamas, alpacas, vicunas, and South American ostriches.

Stanley Marsh 3 likes animals. He owns a yak bull named Yelverton which he is breeding to Hereford cows to produce "cattle-yaks," and to buffalo cows to obtain "buffa-yaks." A reporter once said that writing or talking about Stanley Marsh 3 is extremely hard because people don't believe he could exist. Before his premature demise from an overdose of chocolate, a tattooed pig called Minnesota Fats was Marsh 3's favorite drinking buddy. Minnesota Fats was stuffed and hung in Stanley Marsh 3's office.

Like Cullen Davis, Stanley Marsh 3's background would not have seemed conducive to producing an eccentric. The tall, broad-shouldered, middle-aged multimillionaire has a master's degree from the University of Pennsylvania's highly-regarded Wharton School of Business, a staid, establishment institution not likely to teach the pros and cons of some of the investments Marsh 3 has considered. One of his favorite schemes was the construction of the Potter County Sphinx (a lion with a human face), which he intended would rival the colossal stone figure near the pyramids of Gizeh in Egypt. Another plan was to encircle Goat Mountain, the area's tallest, with a shiny, sky-colored, dog collar-like fence to give the appearance of a floating mountain top.

This Amarillo mogul — he has sizable holdings in cattle, banking, natural gas, and owns TV stations — seemed to me to be a person to meet, should I decide to move to Texas, if only to learn why he was so fascinated by Egypt. On a field he owns he had implanted used Cadillacs at the exact angles which the Great Pyramids rise from the ground. He also possessed an outside "pool table" the size of several football fields.

A recent visitor to Toad Hall was guided by one of the multimillionaire's aides. "You know," said the aide, puzzled, "people think he's strange, weird, and crazy."

"Well?"

There was no answer.

For some reason, numerous individuals who meet Stanley Marsh 3 ask him what art is. Marsh 3 enjoys taking them to a field where he has posted the large block letters "A," "R," and "T." "That's art," says the rich man. Another large sign, posted on his own property to discourage a proposed nearby housing development, reads: "Future Home of the World's Largest Poisonous Snake Farm."

Marsh 3, of course, enjoys practical jokes. At a party he gave for a Japanese trade delegation, the only guests he invited were Texans who had to be at least six feet four inches tall. He journeyed to the bribery trial of former Texas Governor John Connally wearing boots dipped in cow manure. At his sister-in-law's wedding he dressed a dwarf in an Aunt Jemima dress. At another wedding he hid a skunk in the bride's dressing room. For reasons he says elude him, Stanley Marsh 3 made Richard Nixon's "Enemies List."

Marsh 3 was another who promised periodically to keep popping up in the news. Indeed, he recently wore red tie, tails, and sneakers to referee a professional wrestling match. He was the bout's major attraction, and unlike wealthy Eastern counterparts who shudder at the prospect of contact with *hoi polloi,* enjoyed exchanging insults with the spectators.

It was getting along toward 6 P.M. dinner time, but I'd located material on another rich, worthy Texan, Baron Enrico di Portanova, who seemed cut from a different but no less interesting cloth. I decided to see what he was up to.

He was born Roy Paul di Portanova on August 16, 1933, the son of an Italian playboy, Paoli di Portanova, and Lillie Cranz Cullen, an American heiress; the "Enrico" and the "Baron" did not come until later. Whatever his real name, obviously this unusual Texan was as colorful as he was rich. And rich he was: his own lawyer, a typically restrained, conservative member of his profession, said his annual income was $8 million, his net worth $50 million.

Enrico di Portanova, while not interested in armadillo racing or rattlesnake hunting, takes a backseat to no one where throwing money around is concerned. He air-conditioned the *entire backyard* of his mother-in-law's huge Houston home (his wife explained that "We like good weather"). Di Portanova built Arabesque, the largest villa in Acapulco. It has 36 bedrooms, 26 bathrooms, and two indoor waterfalls. Arabesque rises out of the water like the Taj Mahal, and its approaches are guarded by machine-gun-wielding private guards. Di Portanova's apartment in Rome features a roof-top garden copied from the fabulous gardens at Pompeii. He gives away Cadillacs as gifts, and has been known to lose as much as $150,000 during a single night gambling at Monte Carlo.

Enrico di Portanova's money comes from his grandfather, Hugh Roy Cullen, called the King of the Wildcatters, a man the high-living Baron could not less resemble. Hugh Roy Cullen's greatest achievement was finding the Tim O'Connor field, a mile-deep, billion-dollar bonanza of oil near Victoria, Texas, and he was a right-wing, hard-boiled, no-nonsense admirer of Herbert Hoover (he hated Franklin D. Roosevelt) and the puritan work ethic. His grandson Enrico turned out to be a party-loving, jet-setting, live-and-let-live sort who has evinced no inclination to prove his mettle through hard work. He prefers entertaining a variety of social butterflies, including Nancy and Henry Kissinger, at Arabesque, and rubbing shoulders with the likes of Prince Rainier of Monaco.

Nor did Baron Ricky, as he is called, inherit his tastes from his mother, Lillie Cranz Cullen, a 400-pound woman who shunned Texas to reside in the seedy Times Square section of New York City, cut buttons from her coats and replaced them with safety pins, and prowled the streets of Manhattan in tattered, ragged, old-fashioned black clothes carrying shopping bags. The clerk closest to her at the hotel where she lived had to talk with her through a closed door.

Actually, the Baron is probably not really a baron at all, but because of his money few question his right to use the title. As one researcher pointed out, none of the standard reference works on European nobility make any mention of his family. Nor has he chosen to marry nobility, many of whom have come upon hard times and are not averse to exchanging wedding vows with rich Americans.

Enrico di Portanova's first wife was Ljuba Otasevic, a stunningly beautiful raven-haired woman who had been a member of Yugoslavia's national women's basketball team. Together they were a striking couple. Baron Ricky was handsome, urbane, sophisticated, no Nelson Bunker Hunt in tennis shoes he, and Ljuba was gorgeous enough to catch the eyes of executives at Universal International, who signed her to a motion picture contract.

In the mid-1960s all of Baron Ricky's money could not prevent management from evicting him from his posh Houston apartment at Inwood Manor. Neighbors reportedly complained that Ljuba was keeping them awake at night by dribbling basketballs on her living room floor, and a monkey that lived with them took its toll on the furnishings. Next, with a full complement of servants, they moved to a mansion on two pine-covered acres of land.

The marriage, each charging the other with adultery, ended in 1971. Ljuba, with high-powered Percy Foreman as her lawyer, received $1.01 million, plus all of her jewelry, furs, and a Houston townhouse. Baron Ricky also had to pay Percy Foreman's astronomical legal bill, which alone was nearly $300,000.

Enrico di Portanova's second wife was Sandy Hovas from Lamar, Texas, nicknamed "Buckets" in high school. Soon after the marriage Sandy was known as Sandra. Next she was Sondra. Then Alessandra. Now, if you please, you can call her Baroness Alessandra.

In 1980 *The New York Times* reported that Baron Ricky was buying Manhattan's exclusive "21" club for Sandy as a present, but the deal was never consummated.

Baron Ricky's friends could argue that all is not fun and games for him. The smallest republic in the world, San Marino, whose chief industry is postage stamps, named him consul general to the United States.

Baron Ricky made me wonder if even the Texas rich might some day grow fat and soft. It wouldn't happen to Grimm, or those I had met in Abilene who drove the pickups with gun racks in the back, but Baron Ricky was *third generation.* The founding fathers of Eastern dynasties, the original Rockefeller, Mellon, and DuPont, had been rough-hewn, hard-eyed men of action, true believers that the accumulation of money signaled the Almighty's approval of their actions. Yet most of their offspring were infected by no notable compulsion to toil twenty-hour days or roll up their sleeves to prove they could do the job more efficiently than any worker. The inheriting sons and daughters, although not averse to watching the fortune swell, take on a life of its own, preferred chasing foxes and leisurely sipping tea.

In a letter to a friend, former TWA executive Edward Condon, Enrico di Portanova confided his foremost ambition: "to think of nothing other than the best things in life, sun, sex, and spaghetti."

I wanted to read more about the men whose money shaped Texas, but it was 9 P.M. and a library worker was telling me to leave. She said I could come back in the morning, and I said I would.

Outside it was already pitch black, not the fresh star-splattered black of Abilene, but a sickly grey-yellow black that made Manhattan seem old and unhealthy. Through smog that hurt the eyes I saw the blinking neon lights of Broadway, Street of Dreams, and the lights cast eerie shadows.

The night was humid, but the city had no warmth. It was stone and steel and iron, chimneys, smoke, dreariness. Newspapers, garbage, and rags soaked in casual sidewalk water puddles. Horns honked. Steam whooshed out of grates.

The 42nd Street sidewalk from Fifth Avenue to Seventh was virtually deserted, but then it came alive, all at once, a brazen burlesque show featuring a cast of thousands, society's rejects: pushers, pimps, muggers, prostitutes, numbers runners, alcoholics, dope addicts, misfits and maniacs of every description, but, mostly, just plain half-clothed, underfed, disfranchised people so stupefied by years of mistreatment that often they could not summon up the strength even to complain.

There are few places in Manhattan where a single block can be walked without having to walk around or step over a derelict or other unfortunate, more eloquent testimony to a society in decay than any politician's speech extolling New York as the Big Apple or Fun City. The richest town in the world, financial headquarters of the wealthiest nation mankind ever built, does not take care of its own citizens.

But New York is also exciting, and not in the self-satisfied way an Abilene rancher, who recently visited the city and was robbed at gun point in front of a police station, had described. "I must admit," he said, "the adrenalin does flow when you're looking over your shoulder for muggers." This same not-unlikable man had a plan he said would have won the Vietnam War: "Let the Viet Cong march all the way across this country; when they get to Central Park they'll find somebody tougher than they are."

New York City is also theater, ballet, opera, museums, art galleries and, most important to me, the big book publishing houses. I talked to a friend, after my first foray to Abilene, about moving there. "I've been to Texas," he said. "Except for Austin, and maybe Dallas, it's feudalism straight out of the thirteenth century."

"The people seem friendly."

"Scratch Dallas. The Hunts run Dallas."

"Grimm knows Bunker Hunt. Says he's a nice guy."

"Right. Come to think of it, you can forget Austin, too. A bunch of Neanderthal politicians taking orders from the oil barons."

"I didn't see any muggers in Abilene."

"You won't, either. Hitler would admire some of the laws they have there. I know a guy who got ninety-nine years for marijuana possession. Possession, not sale."

"That was in the Sixties."

"Texas. Ugh."

Still, I wondered if I shouldn't give it a try. I suspected it was just that I was growing older, but the muggers, who appeared to be everywhere and increasingly resembled an organized army, had begun to scare me. What I had in common with the Abilene rancher was that I had been robbed two blocks from where he was held up.

"Besides," my friend said, "muggers are just poor people trying to stay alive. You always were for poor people."

There were plenty of them between Seventh and Eighth Avenues as I walked toward the subway that would take me to my apartment. On a wall, as I went down the steps to the "A" train, was a message in graffiti: "Abandon hope all Ye who enter here."

Four

"Your Honor," said G. Brockett Irving, lawyer for Billy Sol Estes, "I think we can show that the ten million dollars went to Lyndon Johnson as business expenses."

I was reading about Billy Sol Estes, who had a home in Abilene, this rainy August morning. It was during a 1979 federal court trial for income tax evasion that Billy Sol's lawyer told U.S. District Judge Robert Hill that the $10 million claimed by IRS was paid to Lyndon Johnson as "business expenses." Hill refused to allow the attorney to continue, although letting him continue might have been a public service, because, he ruled, any payments to Johnson had no bearing on money owed to IRS.

Billy Sol Estes from Pecos, Texas, was a small-town product who made it big. He was friendly and charming, a Scripture-quoting, Bible-thumping con man who was convicted on engineering the largest swindle in U.S. history. The get-rich scam might have generated only passing attention, briefly entertained bored readers as an interesting oddity and then been forgotten, except Billy Sol Estes knew important people: the late mayor of Chicago, Richard Daley; former Texas governor and Nixon cabinet official, John Connally; the late Speaker of the U.S. House of Representatives, Sam Rayburn; the powerful late Louisiana U.S. senator, Earl Long;

40

former Teamsters president, Jimmy Hoffa; and former president Lyndon B. Johnson.

While it lasted, Billy Sol's now-you-see-it, now-you-don't fiscal sleight-of-hand was a thing to behold. He induced West Texas farmers to lease anhydrous ammonia tanks from him and then to make monthly payments on the tanks to large finance companies, which fought with one another to buy the paper at a discount. It was a great deal for everybody. The farmers met their payments with money received from Billy Sol, who sweetened the pot with an additional ten percent. The finance companies were ecstatic because of the lucrative interest they charged. Happiest of all was Billy Sol, who funneled hundreds of thousands of dollars to the farmers so they could meet the payments with funds he received from the U.S. Department of Agriculture.

The problem was, the anhydrous ammonia tanks did not exist. But before the whole, complex house of cards collapsed, Billy Sol had made millions. He lived in a mansion with a huge swimming pool and double tennis courts, and got around in one of his two airplanes. Most interesting, he had acquired some very influential friends. Former President Harry Truman and his wife hastily had to cancel a planned vacation at the mansion when Billy Sol was indicted.

Billy Sol served 6½ years of his fifteen-year sentence for mail fraud and conspiracy, but many students of the case thought others should have gone to jail also. "It took three to tango in that deal," said one of Billy Sol's friends, referring to the finance companies and the farmers. *Thirty thousand* chattel mortgages were secured by fertilizer tanks that did not exist. Surely, the friend insisted, the finance companies had to know what was going on, and so did the farmers, whose payments were being made by Billy Sol.

Billy Sol was released from prison on condition that he not engage in "promotional" activities, but it was too much to ask from this King of the Wheeler-Dealers. He was sent back to jail for making $500,000 from the sale of phantom chemical steam cleaners, machines used on oil well equipment. "Even the guy who sold the Brooklyn Bridge," commented one admiring journalist, "couldn't compare to Billy Sol. At least the Brooklyn Bridge exists."

In 1977, the Internal Revenue Service, claiming Billy Sol owed more than $10 million in taxes from the fertilizer tank scheme, tape recorded a conversation between the swindler and an undercover agent posing as a Chicago financier with mob connections. Billy Sol had a good deal to say about his friend, Lyndon Johnson:

"If you committed yourself to him and paid him enough money, he'd make the deals he would make with you, anything you want done . . . and he would. It's just that simple."

"But, hell, you know you'd think $10,000 (a) good contribution. Hell, he'd call on you for half a million dollars at a time. I mean he'd say, I want half a million dollars delivered just like you know you would bologna. I'd say, 'Hell, it's 9 o'clock, Lyndon.' He'd say, 'Goddammit, I didn't ask you what time it was, goddammit.' He says, 'Get me my goddam money to the airport.' "

Billy Sol had more to say about Lyndon Johnson:

"Lyndon was a ruthless bastard, a ruthless gentleman."

"If you had grain elevators you wanted full . . . hell, when he was living and paid enough and you wanted allocations, you'd just get allocations. It's real simple. He'd do anything, but he expected the same from you."

"Now Sam Rayburn was a man that would take contributions for people running for Congress but would take nothing for himself. But, hell, Lyndon couldn't get enough in his sack."

Billy Sol Estes, rumored in his heyday to have amassed a fortune of $150 million, has considered writing a book. I wondered if it would detail his dealings with Lyndon Johnson, John Connally, and others, if it would shed light on the involvement, if any, of the four people left dead in the scandal's aftermath in bizarre accidents and suicides. Billy Sol never testified at his trials, nor has he ever told his side of the story publicly. *The Dallas Morning News,* way back on May 2, 1971, wrote that "Businessmen and politicians from here to Washington to Wall Street and back have waited nervously" in fear Billy Sol will speak out.

I wasn't sure I was learning much about Texas, but I was convincing myself that the state had a justifiable claim to being number one where housing stranger-than-fiction rich people is concerned. Next I was attracted, because of the nickname, to "Mad Eddie" Chiles. Not "Mad" meaning insane or screwy, but angry, enraged, fed up to the gills. Primarily he is ticked off at the government, which he sees as the chief reason for all of humanity's problems. Since Eddie Chiles grew very rich under this form of government, I had difficulty figuring out why he was mad, but I knew many citizens shared his distaste: they simply do not have the means at their disposal to disseminate their views. Eddie Chiles does.

In 60-second spots, aired on 500 radio stations in 14 states, Eddie delivered his "Mad Ads," called diatribes by some observers, which point out what he believes is wrong with this country. What is wrong, says Eddie, is too much government interference in our lives, and depending on your point of view he is either a dangerous right-wing demagogue or an admirably outspoken champion of individual freedom.

What everyone can agree upon is that Eddie is different. It is impossible to imagine a David Rockefeller biting the bullet and venturing into the political trenches with straight-from-the-shoulder language, and *personally* taking a stand. David pays people to do that for him, and even then the language is often so obscurantist that few understand what is being proposed. A child can understand where Mad Eddie Chiles is coming from.

The government, says Eddie, should do three things, and three things only: "Defend our shores, deliver our mail, and leave us the hell alone."

Mad Eddie, whom I thought it would be fun to meet, is the founder and chief executive officer of the Western Company of North America, an oil well (what else?) servicing operation that does a $400 million business annually. The ads he runs are tax deductible, which enrages activist Fort Worth attorney Don Gladden: "When the IRS allows him to do that, it means all of us are subsidizing his politics."

Helping the needy is not one of the three functions of government envisioned by Eddie, but somehow I was not surprised that he is willing to accept federal largesse for himself. Critics carp that he has taken federally guaranteed loans to finance more than half of his drilling rigs.

Mad Eddie is the majority stockholder in the major league Texas Rangers baseball team, an outfit whose consistent second-division finishes could not have contributed to banking his fires of anger.

Eddie's political views, expounded in the Mad Ads, seem to be conservative even by Texas standards. His chief political guru is Arthur J. Finkelstein, a poll taker for NCPAC (National Conservative Political Action Committee) and a former strategist for Richard Nixon's Committee to Re-Elect the President (CREEP).

No reason exists, claims Eddie Chiles, not to use his money to hawk his viewpoints. "We've still got the First Amendment," he says. "The Constitution doesn't say a rich man won't have this right. They didn't repeal the golden rule when they wrote the Constitution. That is, the golden rule that says, 'He who owns the gold makes the rules.' "

Buying the Texas Rangers and delivering radio commercials brought charges that Mad Eddie was using his money to enter the Fort Worth hierarchy. Eddie Chiles was genuinely astounded. "Why?" he asked. "I *am* the Fort Worth hierarchy."

In a state where Neiman-Marcus advertised submarines as birthday presents and financier H. Ross Perot proposed to feed *all* American POWs in Vietnam, it was not necessary in a brief crash course on Texas eccentrics to include one who has passed away, but O. L. Nelms seemed so unusual and at the same time typical that he deserved a closer look. Nelms (died in 1972) was a big, husky, hard-drinking real estate operator and builder who enlisted the entire state in his pursuit of a personal goal: becoming rich.

Nelms inherited no money, nor did he benefit from formal education: "I never got past the third grade. School bored me. I thought it was a waste of time. All I wanted to do was make money."

To his early customers O. L. Nelms passed out cigars with a message printed on the wrapper: "Help O. L. Nelms Make a Million Dollars." After he succeeded, for twenty years, *every day,* he took out ads in Texas newspapers: "Thanks to All of You for Helping O. L. Nelms Make a Million." But Nelms wanted more, and later the ads read, "Thanks for Helping O. L. Nelms Make *Another* Million."

The gimmick worked. Million after million poured in. And always O. L. Nelms was grateful. More amazing, so evidently were his customers. Somehow people all over the state could share vicariously in the real estate operator's good fortune, if only they did business with him. If people could not be rich (and how many could?), then they could take pleasure reading about the good life they had bestowed on O. L. Nelms. Besides the newspaper ads, 85 large truck-trailers were painted with the Thanks for Helping message.

O. L. Nelms made his name one of the best known in Texas, but he wanted it to live on after him. He decided to set aside between $5 million and $10 million of his fortune to finance cocktail parties in his honor after his death. He envisioned a thousand people attending each party, and guests could drink as much as they wanted. "Why," he said, "it takes ten drinks to do for me what one drink will do for some other people. But then I have soaked in alcohol for the last forty years."

The plan was for Nelms to be preserved in an open $25,000 silver casket and carted from one party to another, where he could be toasted as the really fine fellow he was. O. L. Nelms anticipated that his heirs might not share his enthusiasm for financing grandiose cocktail parties, and added a provision in his will disinheriting anyone trying to interfere with the merriment, or any heir who wanted to bury him.

Alas, it was too complicated even for the expensive stable of legal talent O. L. Nelms employed to draft the unbreakable will, and he was buried shortly after his death. A few parties in his honor have been held, however, and occasionally an aging truck can still be spotted on a dusty Texas road, bearing the paint-peeled thanks of O. L. Nelms to all of those who helped make him rich.

I briefly considered, and then rejected, becoming better acquainted with a variety of other wealthy Texans. The Hunt brothers, for example, Lamar, Bunker, and W. Herbert, with a combined family fortune estimated between $8 billion and $12 billion, had recently been shown to have paid no federal income taxes in 1976. Frankly, and maybe this was cynicism, I never suspected they had paid taxes, and I figured everyone knew about the Hunts anyway. H. Ross Perot was another who was too well-known, although his rescue of hostages from Iran, something the U.S. Government couldn't pull off, was a feat of Texas-size proportions. Of course, the late Howard Hughes was a Texan, with exploits to compare with anyone's, but like the Hunts plenty was known about him.

David Hannah, Jr., if he succeeded, was someone to keep an eye on. He was saying the Lord wanted him to launch the world's first privately financed space vehicle, a gargantuan and super-ambitious task even for a rich Texan. The Russians might be able to do it, and NASA with its elite scientists and billions of dollars of funding from Washington, but a Houston real estate developer and elder emeritus in the First Presbyterian Church?

Hannah seemed an admirable character. He first became interested in space flight when he read a futuristic article in *Smithsonian* magazine that envisioned a utopia in space, free of poverty, powered by abundant solar energy, rich with minerals from asteroids, an absolutely beautiful and idyllic place where mankind could live in harmony.

What Hannah did was persuade 57 people to invest at least $25,000 apiece in his Space Services, Inc., whose goal was to stake a claim to outer space for private industry. The first investor was Toddie Lee Wynne, multimillionaire founder of American Liberty Oil Company, who told his wife: "Honey, I'm not bettin' on the horse, I'm bettin' on the jockey."

Some of the investors were idealistic; others were not. Maybe, just maybe, a fortune could be made out there: if not for themselves, then for their children or grandchildren. A future David Hannah might even be selling real estate in space, or the boundless reserves of precious ore that are out there waiting to be tapped.

Hannah was not unaware there might be more immediate, practical benefits. A truck leasing company could use the space machine to keep track of its vehicles. A petroleum company could monitor its wells in remote locations. Still, not many investors really had confidence the space machine would even fly, much less be a money-maker. What they had invested was pocket money for them, the chance to be part of an adventure that would be talked about over and over on golf courses and at country clubs. But fly? Even NASA could not, in the last analysis, guarantee that its expensive paraphernalia would fly.

It was not until later that I read how the soft-spoken, God-fearing Hannah met with success. The flight of his *Conestoga I* went off without a hitch. His plans, he said, plans the Lord wanted him to carry out, included a number of more sophisticated flights in 1984 and 1986.

The time was 6 P.M. and I'd be bucking rush hour, but I decided to head back to the apartment. What I'd mainly learned was that Texas was a state packed with rich zanies, any one of whom would stand out in another place; in New Hampshire, for example, a Stanley Marsh 3 would be the state's best known citizen.

Back at the apartment I intended to start typing notes taken on the *Titanic* expedition, then have a late-night corned beef sandwich. As I headed up 42nd Street for the subway, walking past the most diverse collection of characters on earth, I was reminded of some of the rules I'd heard for avoiding muggers. One rule was never to date a woman who admired courage: she would encourage you to resist the mugger, thus dramatically adding to the certainty of losing money the possibility of being seriously injured or killed. Another rule was always to dress as if you'd just come off a 500-mile cross-country hike. Talking to yourself was also recommended; muggers, like other sensible citizens, are afraid of crazy people.

I went down into the Eighth Avenue subway stop under the "Abandon hope" graffiti and went past popcorn and hot dog stands to the second level below ground. For 75¢ you could stand in a crowd six-deep in heat so humid you could soak a newspaper with sweat from your hand. I couldn't see Mad Eddie Chiles or Baron Ricky ever waiting for a subway train.

When the train thundered into the station, there was the eternal standoff between the crowd trying to get off the train and the big mob wanting to get on. Of course, only half the doors of the train opened. The push toward them was terrific. If you let yourself go limp you can be carried along, but you'll probably have to wait for the next train. There always seem to be aggressive sorts, usually husky linebacker types who enjoy the contact, or little old ladies with blue hair, veterans of decades of subway embarking and disembarking, expert with the umbrellas they carry with ends sharpened like a knife point. The danger of fights is always present when the train stops during rush hour, but usually the combatants are packed too close together to raise their hands to throw a punch. When the train is ready to get going, each door is closed on three or four people half in and half out of the car. These always somehow manage to get inside before the train is rolling.

The train I rode was never air-conditioned and often the inside lights didn't work, but I knew it didn't have to be that way. Trains servicing more fashionable areas were always cool and well-lit and usually you could see a policeman. Of course, the cop wasn't needed on these trains. Where he was needed you didn't find him. Street wisdom held that there were certain routes even the police were afraid to travel.

By the time we were out of Manhattan into Brooklyn the subway car had cleared enough so individuals could be distinguished. It was a not untypical collection. A hippie with backpack and bandana carrying a copy of the *Yaqui Book of Knowledge*. A middle-aged OTB bettor looking exhausted but still studying the *Racing Form*, though it was academic now. An Abe Lincoln look-alike in black suit with his fly open, leaning over a high school girl who didn't want to hear what he was saying. A drunk in a topcoat in this boiling heat, bottle of Muscatel in his pocket. I felt a heavy weight on my foot.

"You're ruining my shoes, asshole," he said.

He was medium height and thin, yellow teeth, three-day growth of beard. He wore a brown stained suit and no shirt — no shirt at all. He was standing on *my* foot.

"You're standing on my foot," I said.

"You scuff my shoes and I'll cut you."

I saw the knife in the palm of his hand by his side, and thought *you don't really need this hassle.* The old Jimmy Stewart would have known how to solve the situation. Well, maybe not. Jimmy Stewart might have tried to persuade Abe Lincoln to leave the girl alone, and not been capable of any further action.

I tried to move my foot out from under his, but he pressed down harder. Finally a mighty pull yanked the foot free. He squatted down to look over his shoes. A perfect time to knee him in the face. I remembered my small town Wisconsin childhood and a couple boys who couldn't find enough fights in which to become involved. I thought New York would dampen even their enthusiasm.

"You're lucky, asshole," he said. "My shoes are okay."

He was just crazy, his brain boiled to mush by a super-heated chaotic city both beautiful and bestial. But he was also dangerous, you could see in his eyes he didn't care, and nothing could be done about it in a city constituted like New York. The system was veering out of control. Very little worked, and the politicians and businessmen who ran the show didn't care. Try to get electric service connected in Manhattan. Con Ed, as ruthless a corporation as exists, rightly figures they don't need new customers, that the reverse is true. Con Ed, of course, has the highest electric rates in the nation, and the poorest record of service: witness the several blackouts, just one of which cost more than a billion dollars. Anyway, it is possible to go on about the filthy streets, banks that only loan money to corporations, never to people, the inability even to walk a hundred yards in most areas without having to step over some sleeping unfortunate, and so on, and it was easy to understand that arguing with this fellow about his shoes wasn't going to matter much to the cosmos.

I reached the Brooklyn Heights apartment, put on some coffee, and started to type from the four notebooks I'd filled on the *Titanic* trip. I'd worked about an hour when the phone rang.

"You gonna move to Texas?" It was Jim Drury.

"A guy on the subway was trying to convince me it's a good idea."

"I know what you mean."

"What's up, Drury? I don't get many calls from TV stars."

"I want you to come to Dallas tomorrow. I'll have your ticket and a special invitation ready at the American Airlines counter, and a friend will pick you up at the gate."

"What's going on?"

"It takes time to go into. Just figure you'll meet some interesting people, all expenses paid."

"I don't know, Drury." My mind raced. I'd loved New York when I was younger. Maybe I'd appreciate her more if I got away for a while.

"I think you'll make money," Drury said. "You're not against that, are you?"

"No. But . . . "

"The ticket will be waiting for you. The flight leaves about three."

Drury hung up. I decided to go (why not?), but to travel as lightly as possible — meaning the clothes on my back. I probably wouldn't be in Dallas long.

Five

He had been watching, and making me nervous, since before the American Airlines jet left the ground from Kennedy. We had aisle seats, directly across from each other, and halfway to Dallas I decided to meet the problem head-on.

"I'm Bill Hoffman."

"Fred Satterfield, Bill. I noticed that invitation on your lap."

"Oh." I picked up the invitation and looked it over for what really was the first time. It was actually a four-color brochure advertising an outfit called "Bloods of Quality," owned by somebody named L.G. Mosley, and announcing a barbecue and press conference. Enclosed with the brochure was a business card promoting the J.R. Ewing Silver Piece, a coin featuring Larry Hagman's face, and a letter from Jim Drury saying a good time would be had by all. Besides the good time, Drury promised an announcement of "worldwide importance."

"I didn't get an invitation," said Satterfield. He seemed hurt.

"It doesn't seem to me you'll be missing much. A silver coin with J.R. Ewing's face on it."

"Lots of important people will be there," he said, sadly. He seemed to be genuinely heartbroken. "People with money. Plenty of deals could be made."

"Deals?"

"I make my living making deals. I'll make a deal with anybody."

"You know L.G. Mosley? The one giving the party."

"Everybody knows L.G."

"I don't."

"Well, I just don't understand it. I should be invited to something like this."

"I'm sorry."

"It was probably an oversight. I'll be there, you can bet on that."

Satterfield was perhaps thirty-five, thin, not quite six feet tall, wore a Texas hat over curly brown hair, silk tie, silk shirt, silk jacket, and had, appropriately, *gold* eyes, which matched the hunks of diamond-studded gold jewelry around his neck, wrists, and fingers. The Mosley invitation seemed to make me an important person in his view, and he asked what I did. I told him.

"I guess there's pretty good money in that," he said.

"Only if the books sell a lot."

"What you working on now?"

"A book about the search for the *Titanic.*"

Satterfield whistled. "Jack Grimm," he said. "He's big time."

"You know Jack?"

"I wish I did. He's a heavy hitter. Old Jack Grimm. I've got some deals that would do us both some good."

I couldn't figure Satterfield out. The way he talked about himself, he had plenty of money. And he handed me a card indicating he owned an expensive ranch. Still, he was sitting in the coach section with me. The gold he wore was expensive and bulky, but most rich people I'd met in the East didn't wear jewelry so openly, or so much of it. And they didn't constantly talk to a stranger about "deals."

The plane arrived at 8 P.M., and I went down the ramp with Satterfield right behind me, talking into my ear, assuring me we would see each other at the Mosley party. Drury had told me a friend of his, Jim Gosdin, would meet the flight. I had talked with Gosdin on the phone, and he refused my offered description. He said he would recognize me.

I recognized *him.* He wore a white silk suit and gold belt buckle with "G" — for Gosdin — etched into it, dark Alfa Romeo sunglasses, and boots made from deepwater Atlantic Ocean catfish. I thought he and Satterfield, who wore eelskin boots, had dressed out of the same closet. Gosdin had his hand out and was about to shake Satterfield's when I introduced myself. Satterfield insisted I introduce him, also.

"The surprise is on me," Gosdin said, looking me over. I could tell he thought he had an impossible task. I was wearing an orange tee shirt and blue jeans. "Let's get your luggage and be on the way."

"I didn't bring any luggage."

"Travelling light. A good idea." But everything about Gosdin indicated he didn't think the idea was good. The crease in his pants was so sharp you could shave on it. Hundreds of hard manicurist-hours had gone into his fingernails.

Illegally parked just outside the airport's main entrance was the longest white Cadillac limousine I had ever seen. The driver, Nathan Shay, said it was an "honor" to meet me. "The famous Bob Hoffman," he mused. "Jim Drury tells me you're a terrific writer."

"*Bill* Hoffman."

"Bob, I just know you'll find a good story here."

Nathan was five feet seven and just as wide; he resembled Luca Brazi of "The Godfather."

I sat in the backseat, which was cavernous, and felt like a fool. Someone outside the limousine could not see inside, but the windows were so dark you couldn't see outside either. Nathan talked about book writing. Gosdin made one telephone call after another. The limousine also had a TV and bar.

There really seemed no reason to be here. The clotheshorse Gosdin and Nathan the Gorilla could not have been more mismatched, we were driving to God knew where, and someone — I never did find out the name — had to be picking up a pretty stiff tab for this. Drury had said only that I would find excellent material for a story.

After a long ride we pulled into the parking lot of Ramada Inn on Central Expressway, and while Nathan waited, Gosdin checked me in. I asked Gosdin, who was becoming accustomed to the jeans and orange tee shirt, if Nathan made out okay as a chauffeur.

"He's not a chauffeur. He's sales manager for the company marketing the J.R. Ewing silver piece."

"I'd buy anything he wanted to sell."

"Nathan's all right. Not nearly as tough as he looks."

"What's your connection?"

"I'm a friend of Drury's. He didn't think you were ready for some of the people you're going to meet."

"What does that mean?"

"It can't be described. You'll have to learn firsthand."

"How about Satterfield, the guy on the plane? He kept telling me he was rich. Ranches — four of them. Horses and cattle. Oil wells. Gas. You ever hear of him?"

"No. But he might be rich."

"The ones I know don't tell you."

"Well, he might not be rich. A lot of people here say they are, and aren't. To hear people talk, in bars and restaurants, you'd think each one had an oil field going. Some of them do."

"He said I'd be seeing him again. I don't believe it."

"Don't bet on that. If he is rich, there's no telling what he's got in mind."

After checking in at Ramada, we drove to Gosdin's North Dallas apartment. Drury was already there.

The apartment was spanking clean, and of course Gosdin asked me to wipe my shoes on the mat before going in. He brought a beer — "Moosehead, plenty more where that came from" — and asked me to use a coaster. He had a gold and silver ashtray lined with crystal, a Gucci that cost $140, and winced when I moved toward it with a cigarette; lightning-like, he switched the ashtray for one that was merely gold-trimmed.

I couldn't imagine there was anything to complain about in this pleasure palace apartment, but Drury found something. "This Artesia water I'm drinking," he said. "Don't you have Perrier?"

Gosdin had known Drury a long time. He snorted into his hand, then whispered to me: "Drury smokes three packs of Pall Mall Straights a day. I guarantee you, his taste buds are ruined. No way he can tell the difference between Artesia and Perrier."

It occurred to me this evening, the first night of my second trip to Texas, that almost everyone I had met so far was either pretty well off or very well off. The people Grimm had introduced me to in Abilene were hardly the crowd I ran around with. Satterfield, whom I couldn't decide about, Gosdin, Drury, and the limousine-driving Nathan also seemed to be doing all right. I was sure there were poor people. I just hadn't met them yet.

Gosdin, Nathan, and I drank until 4:30 A.M., and Drury, down-ing mineral water, matched us bottle for bottle. I began to like Gosdin. When I told him I thought Grimm was the ultimate eccen-

tric, he promised I soon would be meeting many others from which
to choose. Also, despite prodigious consumption, Gosdin's efforts
kept the apartment from looking as if anyone lived there. At the end
of the long evening Drury invited me to his Houston home for a few
days during the next week. He said a well-to-do rancher was writing
a book and might want to pay for some professional help.

I felt at 7 A.M. when I answered my Ramada Inn phone that
maybe I was dead. I wanted to swallow a gallon of cold orange
juice.

"Can you meet us in Drury's room in twenty minutes?" Gosdin
asked.

"Who's us?"

"Me and Tom Taylor. He's president of the National Mint.
Wants to know if you could do a story about his company."

"Give me a break, Gosdin. I didn't use my head last night, but it
still hurts."

"Taylor has a lot of money."

"So does everyone else I've met in Texas. I want to sleep."

"Look, dummy, he's willing to give *you* some of that money."

"I'll see you in twenty minutes."

Somehow I knew Gosdin was capable of being shocked again by
my orange tee shirt and blue jeans, and that he himself would look
as if he had just stepped out of a bandbox. He wore heel-less Gucci
driving shoes, a cotton-knit cream-color polo shirt, and Bill Blass
slacks. I still hadn't seen his eyes. This time the dark glasses were
amber, the Porsche Carrera brand.

Drury was propped on his bed talking on the telephone. I couldn't
tell if he'd been to sleep. He had the true actor's habit of never being seen if not at his best.

Tom Taylor was a surprise. Sitting at a table in front of a fresh
pot of coffee, he was dressed like neither a jewelry store mannikin
nor a cowboy: no big diamonds, no gaudy gold pendants, no boots,
no ten-gallon hat, no string tie with spurs jangling from the end.
Taylor's attire was a conservative blue suit, white shirt, and sensible
black shoes. He was small, neat, and spoke quietly.

I couldn't follow what he was saying. The hangover, and wondering why I was in Texas, made it hard to concentrate.

"You don't seem to be concentrating," Taylor said.

"I'm sorry."

"As I was saying . . ."

"He'd concentrate better," said Gosdin, "if you did something to get his attention."

"Right," said Taylor. He reached into his wallet, counted out ten one-hundred-dollar bills, and handed them to me. I let them sit on the table.

But Gosdin was right. My concentration was improved. And Texas seemed a little brighter. I'd arrived less than twelve hours before, and already was a thousand dollars ahead. Unless of course I was expected to kill someone for it.

Tom Taylor's National Mint was going to market a gold piece, "make it available to every American." There had never been a mass-marketed U.S. gold piece. Until recently it had been illegal even to buy gold, and the government, by dictate, kept the price of the metal artificially low. Taylor talked about how gold historically had always had value and always would. It was extremely malleable: gold can be made so thin that 250,000 sheets are needed to produce a layer just one inch thick, and a single ounce of gold could be drawn into a wire fifty miles long. And it was rare. All the gold in the world could be placed onto a single oil tanker, or contained in a cube measuring only eighteen yards on each side. Possession of gold had always been the best hedge against too much paper money, inflation, and an economic crisis, which Taylor believed had a very good chance of occurring. He talked about Germans after World War I having to push wheelbarrows full of marks to the grocery store to purchase a loaf of bread.

This soft-talking, earnest entrepreneur knew the entire history of gold. It could be traced back to almost 9000 B.C. King Croesus of Lydia (now Western Turkey) had his image stamped on gold pieces; thus the state was guaranteeing their value. Spaniards massacred more than 50,000 Indians to steal the gold of Montezuma and Guatemoc. Pizarro, equally lustful for the precious metal, wreaked a similar havoc on Peru. In 1851, the discovery of gold in Australia by Edward Hargraeves, who had come up empty as a "Forty-niner" in the U.S., increased that country's population from 400,000 to 1,200,000.

To finance the Vietnam War, President Lyndon B. Johnson persuaded Congress to repeal a law requiring that paper currency be backed by 25% in gold bullion. Thus the U.S. dollar, at one time resting on a 100% gold foundation, was now strictly a medium of exchange, and good only so long as people accepted it as good.

Taylor had worked out a plan whereby banks nationwide would sell his gold piece — "as accessible as meat at a grocery" — and it was priced inexpensively enough for even most working people to afford. What Taylor wanted me to do was write an article about gold for a national publication, mentioning that his company would soon have a gold piece available for the mass market. No matter how good the idea, the gold pieces wouldn't sell if potential customers didn't know about them.

"You'll be competing with the Krugerrand," I said.

"Yes. And with Canada's Maple Leaf and Mexico's Eagle."

What Taylor didn't understand was that although I wanted the thousand dollars, and could make more than that on the article (I knew just the magazine to go to), I had never written advertising and didn't want to start. The money Taylor had given me was to obtain national exposure for his company. Advertising.

"I don't like the government of South Africa," I said.

"You shouldn't. The government owns the Krugerrands. South Africa, through sales of that coin, takes two billion dollars away from us each year in foreign exchange. That money could stay in the U.S., providing jobs, and cash for investment."

"That doesn't concern me."

"You worried about pressure? I see your point. The South African government is tough. It'll fight dirty if we start to cut into its business."

"Hoffman wrote a book about Rockefeller," Gosdin said. "I don't think he's worried about pressure."

I told Taylor that South Africa is the most racist country in the world. The government's official policy of apartheid denies all legal rights to the black majority. Actor Sidney Poitier, just to get into the country to film *Cry, the Beloved Country,* was forced to declare that he was white producer Zoltan Korda's slave. I knew the South African government used some of the money it received from selling the Krugerrand to buy torture devices the police use on Africans.

"You think that matters to people?"

"It does to some. It's the best reason I know for buying your gold piece instead of South Africa's."

"Well, if that can help promote the gold piece, go ahead."

Gosdin and I left the room together. Drury was still propped on a pillow talking on the phone. Since acting had become more or less part-time to him, he was involved in a dozen businesses, and it seemed if just one of them hit he would be doing just fine. Drury had his hands into oil exploration, a new process for extracting gold, a worm ranch promotion, importing goods from Eastern Europe, and selling insurance. I wished him well — he was a good enough person, had gotten a raw deal from Hollywood on "The Virginian" — but wondered about the wisdom of trying to be a jack-of-all-trades. It was tough enough for me to attempt to do one thing well.

"What now?" I asked Gosdin. It was not yet 9 A.M. this Saturday morning, and it seemed my business in Texas was concluded. It could have been handled on the telephone, I thought.

"Get some rest," Gosdin said. "I'll come by about noon and we'll have lunch."

"Why don't I go back to New York?"

"And miss L.G. Mosley's party?" He seemed shocked. "You've got to attend L.G.'s party."

"Why?"

"You're a writer, that's why. No writer in the world would pass up the chance to see a show like this one."

"The party's not till tomorrow. I could be home by then."

"What's the matter with you? You've got a nice room in a fancy motel. Order room service till your heart's content. I'll take you out later and show you Dallas. It doesn't cost you a dime. Do you get a lot of offers like this?"

"No. And I don't understand this one."

I really didn't.

"Well, just stay loose. Get some rest. I'll see you at noon."

I went straight for the bed, but one step away from it, the telephone rang. I picked it up and said hello.

"Bill. How are you?"

"Who is this?"

"Fred Satterfield, Bill. I was hoping you'd be in."

"Who?"

"Fred Satterfield. I met you on the plane last night."

"Right. Fred. What can I do for you?"

"I'd like to come and see you."

"I'm pretty tired right now."

"I'm down in the lobby."

"Why do you want to see me?"

"We can talk some business."

"I don't know. I'm really tired."

"I've got my banker with me."

"Your banker?"

"We'd appreciate your giving us some time."

Why not? I thought. I didn't know whether to be paranoid, or just to relax and enjoy a uniquely Texas experience. Anyway, I was curious about the outcome. Certainly the all-expenses trip to Dallas for something that could have been handled by mail or telephone was unusual enough. Fred Satterfield, met on an airplane, was a bonus.

He arrived in Western boots, big Texas hat, silk business suit; his gold eyes were shining. His "banker," who really was a banker, it turned out, dressed more causally: the wide ten-gallon Stetson, but khaki pants and plaid shirt. At the time I didn't believe he was a banker.

"Bill," Satterfield said, getting right to business as soon as he sat down in the semi-dark room, "as I told you, my business is making deals, and the best one I've got I've brought over to you. I'm sure you know what a private placement memorandum is. I've got thirty-five units, each on a third for a quarter basis. They're in the Austin chalk, relatively shallow. The A.F.E., considering depth, might seem high to you, but it's not when location is taken into account. All permits from the Railroad Commission . . ."

This was amazing. I hadn't understood a word he said. I guessed it had something to do with trains. He had a black-bound book in his hands which I hoped he wasn't going to show me. I had a hangover and wanted to get back to my interrupted sleep. The banker wasn't saying a word as Satterfield continued in a language that might as well have been Arabic.

". . . and you'll find the geology interesting. We do it different from y'all up north. We had the geology done by a guy here in Dallas. The very best. The operator — man from Midland/Odessa — is first-rate. Everything's contracted for right down to the last sucker rod. The whole shooting match is on ready, just waiting for the package to . . ."

My headache was worse. This whole trip was a mystery to me. Someone had paid what to me was a good sum of money to finance a jaunt to Texas that would culminate in a barbecue, and now a man I'd met only the night before was talking a foreign language to me. And with his banker looking on. I had a bone-deep feeling I'd gotten into something I was better off without. The only time I ever heard from bankers — bank employees, really — was when I missed a car payment. I decided to get to the point.

"I have no idea what you're talking about," I said, interrupting something about pumpjacks.

Satterfield looked surprised. "I'm trying to sell you oil leases," he said. "A right good deal, too."

"Oil leases?" I started to laugh.

The laugh must have been genuine, because the earnest Satterfield recognized immediately he had approached the wrong customer.

"So I can't sell you anything," he said.

"I'm afraid not."

His disappointment was only momentary. "Well," he said, "Since I can't sell you anything, maybe I can buy something from you."

This got my attention. "Maybe you can," I said, getting up from the chair where I had been sitting and walking over to a table where I had placed the manila envelope. It contained the first two hundred pages of a novel I'd been working on. I'd brought it in case anyone wanted to see a sample of my writing.

"You could buy the movie rights to this book," I said.

"Is it a good book?"

"You bet."

"I'll do it. How much do you want?"

"How about $7,500 for a one-year option? You can renew each year for $7,500 more, up to ten years. If a movie's made, I get paid what's left up to $75,000."

This was pretty standard for a motion picture contract before a book's value increased by becoming a public success, or dwindled because nobody read it.

"You've got a deal," said Satterfield.

I had gone through motion picture negotiations before, but never any that took less than thirty seconds. I couldn't believe Satterfield knew anything about movies. He hadn't asked if I had a publisher for the book (I did), or even what the book was about. He was on his feet picking up the manuscript pages and heading for the door.

"Where are you going?" I asked.

"Downstairs to get some copies."

The banker and I were left alone to stare at each other. He

seemed only a shadow sitting in the chair across the room, legs crossed, hands folded. The silence, at least for me, was embarrassing.

"You really a banker?"

"I am."

"Big bank here in Texas?"

"It's not in Texas."

"That's good. I guess."

Several minutes went by. I imagined the Sphinx would have seemed a blabbermouth compared to the man who sat still in that chair.

"Satterfield told me on the plane last night that he liked to make deals," I said.

"Fred's right good in that department."

"How does it work?"

"You saw it. He sells. If he can't sell, he buys. He sells and buys."

The banker wasn't unfriendly. He just was no volunteer of information. He sat very still, face two-thirds obscured by the big hat, and gazed passively straight ahead. Not for a moment did I believe Satterfield was going through with the arrangement, but I couldn't envision how the scenario would end.

He was gone thirty minutes. I answered the knock at the door and he came bustling past with an armful of manuscript pages. He had persuaded a Ramada Inn assistant manager to let him use the Xerox machine. He also had drawn up a rough half-page contract that was unlike anything I'd seen. It was packed with misspellings and contained none of the language customary in such an agreement. I suspected, however, that it was legal, and accomplished the intended purpose of transferring film rights from me to him.

"If that's okay with you," Satterfield said, "just go ahead and sign and I'll give you my check."

Aha! I thought, so here's the catch. *His check*. The check wouldn't be any good. But even a moment's analysis of this conclusion rendered it absurd. If the check were no good, neither was the contract. But why go through that hassle?

"I'd prefer cash," I said.

"I don't carry that much with me," Satterfield said, "But we'll just set up another meeting and I'll turn it over."

"It's Saturday. Banks are closed."

"No problem there."

That's nice, I thought. I knew I could remember a hundred times when *$50 cash* on a weekend had been as unattainable as pure virtue. Getting $7,500 cash seemed as easy as rolling off a log for Satterfield. That is, if this weren't just some sort of scam I was unable to fathom.

"Well, what do we do?" I asked.

"I could have the cash for you at L.G.'s party tomorrow."

"Oh. You got an invitation."

"Of course."

"I suppose the party would be okay."

"That's it then," said Satterfield, up on his feet and ready to go. He shook hands firmly and said he hoped we both came out good on the deal. "I've got other people to see today," he added. "Gotta keep workin', gotta keep after it."

I shook hands with the banker, too. I couldn't see his eyes beneath the broad brim of the Stetson.

Six

"You did what?" Gosdin's voice was filled with disbelief. It was just after noon this Saturday, and Gosdin's knuckles were white and his hands shook as he steered the Cadillac south on the Central Expressway. The Dallas day was brutally hot, a killer like the many the summer before, and I could *see* the heat waves.

"I told you," I said. "I sold a movie rights option on my novel to Satterfield for $7,500."

Gosdin seemed genuinely shaken. "I don't get upset very often," he said, which I could believe. He seemed cool, collected, urbane. Until now. My recount of the Satterfield meeting had agitated him beyond anything I thought was a reasonable response. "But I'm upset now. I hate, just hate, to see anyone be a fool."

"It's not really your concern."

"I've made it my concern. Besides, I told Drury I'd look after you. Besides that, I like you. I think you're talented. I think it's crazy to take a shafting like this."

"My arm wasn't twisted. I told him what I wanted and he said okay."

"You need a keeper."

I wished he would drop the subject. I imagined his motivation, and on this I was right, to be a care for my well-being. But what I

62

had done was not so crazy, or so I thought. But Gosdin wasn't going to let loose of the issue.

"I don't know what you're used to in New York," he said, "but I'm sure it's different from Texas. You're swimming with piranhas here. They'll eat you alive."

Despite its being Saturday, we were in the middle of a traffic jam. I asked about this, but Gosdin wanted to talk about Satterfield and movie rights to an uncompleted novel.

"Look," I said. "You're probably swinging at phantoms. Satterfield's not going to hand me $7,500 cash. I doubt if he knows anything about books, and I suspect less about movies. As a matter of fact, I doubt if you know much about movies."

"I know if you get offered $7,500 in thirty seconds, you could have gotten four, five times more."

"I'm probably not getting anything. We don't know anything about Satterfield."

"Want to bet on that? You'll get the $7,500, unless you run as fast as you can away from this deal."

"You said you didn't know anything about him."

"I don't. But as soon as we get where we're going, I'll make some calls and find out. My guess is he's got money."

Where we were going was Tony Roma's restaurant, a barbecued ribs place Gosdin said was popular with Dallas Cowboys football players. In fact, the restaurant's proprietor was Cowboys owner Clint Murchison, one of the richest men in Texas. I ordered a beer (could I really be doing this after the session last night?), and Gosdin determinedly went off to a pay telephone booth. I waited, watching a Blue Jays-Yankees game on television.

"The news is bad," Gosdin said a few minutes later, pulling back a chair and distastefully eyeing the beer.

"Satterfield's broke."

"He's loaded, you dummy."

"Well, I don't know how he got that way. I'll bet *you* he knows nothing about movies. He's bought something, and can't possibly know what to do with it."

"He knows how to syndicate."

"Come again?"

"*Syndicate.* He knows how to syndicate quarter horse racers. Sells breeding shares to a number of investors. Let me give an example: he might sell breeding shares to a stallion for $7,500 each —

does that figure ring a bell? — to maybe forty different people. Get it. Forty people times $7,500. You don't have to be the Wizard of Wall Street to understand this."

"You don't know that's what he's planning to do," I said.

"I know he's not a benefactor of the arts. He intends to make money on this, quite a lot of it. He's not small change."

Gosdin ordered a beer, "just so you won't have to drink alone," and ran down some of what he had learned about Satterfield's investments. These included cattle and horses, gold mines, real estate, ranches, oil, and loaning money. Satterfield was a native Texan, considered a plus on financial statements since so many outsiders had come to Dallas or Houston and failed. It seems Fred and his older brother started working at an early age for their father, breaking, training, and transporting horses. This was scut work, but along the way he picked up the knack of buying and selling. He learned how to deal. He became a millionaire before age thirty; now, at thirty-five, he was a multimillionaire on a long winning streak.

"What about his family?" I was joking. Gosdin hadn't been gone longer than five minutes.

"Three kids. Wife's a champion horsewoman."

"Sounds like I've made $7,500. More, if he renews the option."

"You're not listening to what I say. Do you have an agent? Someone who keeps you out of trouble?"

"A couple of them. Why?"

"Give them a call. Maybe you trust them more than me. Let them tell you what a bad deal this is."

"Agents don't work weekends. You could argue that they don't work at all."

"Call one at home. If you keep running down this one track, it will be too late on Monday."

So I called New York.

"Bill! How's Texas?" Agents are always enthusiastic.

"I made a movie deal on the novel."

"Wonderful!"

"With a rich Texan."

"Marvelous!"

"I get the money tomorrow."

"Terrific!" Agents also gravitate toward adjectives and one-word sentences.

"$7,500. A one-year option against $75,000."

I thought maybe the line had gone dead. It was as quiet as the moments before a tornado strikes.

"Are you still there?" I asked.

"That's not a lot of money, Bill."

These situations are never easy. I'd never been able to learn how to say what I mean and still be diplomatic.

"It's $7,500 more," I said, "than *you've* been offered for the book."

"We haven't really been trying, Bill. We're waiting for you to finish. You know this business as well as I do. It's better to sell a finished book to the movies."

"When it's finished, will you get more than $7,500 up front?"

"I would certainly think so."

"But at least you're sure we'll get a sale?"

"I would absolutely hope so."

Back at the table I ordered another beer and figured I'd loll the day away. I supposed I had an obligation to attend L.G. Mosley's party, then it would be back to New York. The trip, though financially profitable, hadn't accomplished a thing towards deciding if I would accept Jack Grimm's invitation and move to Abilene to do the *Titanic* book. I wondered what Grimm would think about all of this. I figured he was familiar with the Satterfields of the world. I imagined he also had experience making off-the-cuff deals. Since beginning to write books fifteen years earlier, my experience had been with lawyers, and they usually seemed to make what was a simple arrangement quite complex, when their eternal wrangling didn't kill the contract entirely. If there weren't problems, lawyers appeared to have to create them. How else to justify a sturdy fee?

Gosdin wasn't going to let me waste the day. He had a pathological aversion to bad deals, and was convinced the one with Satterfield was the worst of the worst. I could tell his day was going to be spent persuading me to wriggle out of the verbal agreement.

"What did the agent say?"

"Agrees with you."

"That should settle it. Why else do you have an agent?"

"Agents don't have to pay my bills. They can shoot for the moon as often as they want, but I have to live on what's paid for my work."

"He told you he could get you more, didn't he?"

"He's good with phrases like 'hope so' and 'think so'."

"This world doesn't come with a guarantee."

"Well, dammit, I don't want to talk about it. I'm $8,500 richer and haven't been here twenty-four hours."

Gosdin, a picture of fashion in silk shirt and top-of-the-line Pierre Cardin slacks — I couldn't imagine the Texas heat wilting this style-setter — decided on a different tack. "Are we talking about a pretty good book?" he asked.

"Yes. It's a thriller."

"Did Satterfield impress you as a sensitive artist?"

"No."

"Imagine your book as a musical comedy, because that's what it's likely to be when the movie's made. I can see it now. Soupy Sales in the dramatic lead. Charo can play your tortured heroine."

This approach was likely to be more successful with me than the you're-getting-screwed routine. I knew the deal could turn out bad financially. I knew also that down the road there might be no deal at all. It was a chance you took. At this particular moment I preferred the bird-in-hand. But I certainly didn't want a good story mauled by a deal-making Texas millionaire whose only association with movies was watching them.

"I thought," I said, "that Satterfield would sell parts of it. Make a profit. I don't care if he makes a profit."

"He might make a movie. He might have to if his investors get edgy. They'll want a return on their money, too."

"Sounds like a pyramid scheme."

"Exactly. Everybody makes money until those right at the end."

"We don't know that's what he plans," I said.

"He won't come out a loser, we know that. The man's sharp. He didn't arrive on last night's melon truck. He has to have been sharp to have succeeded in Texas. There are real man-eaters here."

"Well, you've convinced me. I won't sign the deal unless I get some sort of consulting position if and when they make a movie. Soupy Sales, you say? Good Lord!"

"You shouldn't sign the deal at all. You should . . ."

"Jimbo!"

His voice was loud bass, very loud, and he himself was big and broad and wore a ten-gallon Stetson, overalls, and string tie. He had spotted Gosdin from twenty feet, and now was in full locomotion, striding towards us with purpose. He looked like Paul Bunyan.

"Jimbo! You old son of a swine, how long has it been?" He

slammed a hand the size of a pork roast on Gosdin's back, a whack so solid I thought my new friend's hair might be jarred askew, but the blow was survived with a fleeting wince.

"Art," said Gosdin.

"Mind if I join you boys?" He had already sat down, a big Billy Carter grin on his face. He was huge: six-feet-six, I guessed, with a large, hard stomach.

"Art," said Gosdin, "this is Bill Hoffman. He's a writer from New York."

I just knew what was coming, and there was no way to avoid it. I could feel bones crack in my hand as we shook. I'm sure he didn't hold the hand as long as it seemed. His eyes, cold and steady, belonged to a different face from this jolly grinning mask. The eyes, confident to the point of cocky, said he knew me and what made me tick. I didn't think he did.

I shot Gosdin a what-the-hell-is-this look, and he shrugged a make-the-best-of-it, I'm-sorry reply.

"Art's big in the oil and gas business, aren't you, Art?"

"I get by. Thank God for the Arabs, I say."

"Why's that?" I asked.

"They got the prices up so you can pay through the nose. We didn't have the guts to do it. I tell you, I'm on my knees every night thanking God for the Arabs."

"You're joking."

"I don't joke about oil. Been mighty good to me. But I did hear a good joke. What's two niggers in a shoe box?"

"It's the racist hour," I said to Gosdin.

"A pair of loafers," said Art, rubbing his stomach and beginning to laugh. "I know another one," he said.

"That's all right," said Gosdin.

"You're locked in a room and a bomb is going to explode in thirty seconds. Only one person can save you, and you get one guess who it is. If you're wrong, boom! you're dead. Who's the person? Ronald Reagan, Santa Claus, the Easter Bunny, or an ambitious Mexican? Which one?"

"Ronald Reagan," I said.

"Right! Say, you're not as slow a mind as I thought. How did you know it was Reagan?"

"I guessed."

"It's because the other three don't exist." Now Art was really laughing hard. "Get it. The other three don't exist."

"I doubt if Reagan would save me either," said Gosdin.

"Why, sure he would," said Art. "Brother Reagan's all right. My taxes aren't going to be anything like they were."

"Well, Bill," said Gosdin, "we've got places to go. Art," he said, getting up, "it's been real."

"You boys can't leave." He seemed to mean it literally. He had his big hand on Gosdin's shoulder and pulled him down. "Some of my boys are coming in for ribs. Have another beer. Waitress!" his voice roared across the crowded restaurant. "More beer!"

We were at a series of very long tables that stretched the length of the wall, and Art's "boys," fifteen or sixteen of them, arrived in ones and twos. All of them ordered Tony Roma's excellent ribs, and seemed there chiefly to listen to and agree with what their boss said. Art was a director and they were his choir.

He had a vast repertoire of ethnic jokes, all of which he seemed to relate while staring directly into my eyes. He wanted to see my reaction. Later I noticed many Texans would go out of their way to tell these jokes, testing the listener. It was as though they were saying, see, we can get away with this down here. I'm sure they would have found it the height of bad taste if confronted by stories of an opposite bent. Most of them weren't bone-deep racists, though I suspected that my new acquaintance Art fit that category. He kept the jokes coming in a steady, slow narrative style, and as his audience increased around the table, so did the appreciative laughter.

I imagined Art projected precisely the image that Dallas, at least since the Kennedy assassination, was trying to rid itself of. What little I'd seen of the city was favorable, a clean modern metropolis bursting with energy, so different from many of the dying cities of the North, and there were genuine efforts afoot to make Dallas an entertainment and cultural center also. Art, a throwback to another time, hardly fit in even to the new economic scheme, which required international contacts. Many of the new generation of Texas businessmen, though perhaps not Renaissance Men, could surely force the words "black" or "African" out of their mouths if negotiating a lucrative oil deal with a Nigerian. I doubted, as the giant oil man showed no sign of running out of steam, if Art could.

Yet there was a purpose to all of this, as I should have suspected. Art surely had not become rich sitting in a restaurant swilling beer.

When he got to the point, it was swift and blunt.

"I hear y'all write books," he said.

"How did you hear that?"

"Old Art has his ways."

"Well, it's true."

"I might have a deal for you." Pitchers of beer had replaced mugs, and he filled the glasses of everyone within reaching distance.

"You know," he said to Gosdin, "about my movie."

"I heard you were making one."

"It's finished. Has been for six months. Damn good picture, isn't it, boys?"

Mumbles of assent greeted this evaluation.

"I'd like," Art said, now talking to me, "for you to see it. I've got a little spread outside of town. Couple hundred acres. You'd be right comfortable there watching the movie."

"I'm no judge of films."

"You don't have to be to see how good this one is. Cost me three goddamn million dollars, and I can't get it shown anywhere. A few distributors got the market locked up tight as a drum."

"I don't see how I could help."

"Three million," Gosdin said. "Must have had a lot of money you didn't want to pay Uncle Sam."

"The last few years been good ones. But not that good. Damn unions got me by the nuts and wouldn't stop pulling. Have to pay union scale for a guy just to turn on a light. Shit, I said I could turn on the light. They said, do that and you ain't got a movie."

"You didn't film it in Texas," I said.

"Should of. We got the sense to keep unions out of here."

"I don't know what I could do."

"You're a book writer, aren't you? Write me a book. Nothing to it. Base the book on my screenplay, and when the book is a success people will demand to see the movie. Those thievin' distributors won't be able to give me the back of the hand then."

"I've got more work than I can handle now."

"Dammit, just *see* the movie. You'll be begging me to do the book. Tell him, boys, tell him how good it is."

The expected response of "Great" and "Just Great" and "Tell him, Art" chorused like what is heard from pews when the minister has the congregation wound up.

"You see," said Art. "This movie cost me a bundle, three million dollars in case you've forgotten, but I've got something customers'll stand in line to see. Three million dollars. Damn."

"I'm sorry," I said, though I wasn't. "But I'm too busy. You should find somebody else."

"I'm forty years old and you're the first book writer I've met. Sure as hell can't wait another forty years. Damn distributors. What do they know? Damn three million dollars."

"I could give you the name of my agent. You could probably get a writer that way."

"I want you. I heard you're good, and I need a good book. Something so good they'll have to show the movie."

"Where did you hear about me?" First Satterfield, out of nowhere on a plane, and now Art. No, Satterfield hadn't been first. Grimm had been. His phone call to New York had come out of the blue. I was uncomfortable enough, drinking with someone with whom I had nothing in common, but it was worse wondering why I suddenly was meeting so many rich people.

"Never mind that. Come see the movie. Like I said, you'll be begging me to do this."

"I'm just not up to seeing a movie."

"Playing hard to get, eh?"

"No. I really don't want to see a movie. If you want to tell me what it's about, that's okay."

It took him a half hour. His "boys" provided adulatory background noises, and I wondered if he always traveled with an entourage. They reminded me of the yes-men and go-fers I'd seen around Muhammad Ali's training camp when I once interviewed him for an article. They drew pay for agreeing with the boss.

The movie plot unerringly followed the plot line of an excellent award-winning short story I'd read, and I asked if that's where it came from. Art said no; he'd never heard of the short story. I suggested that he read it.

Actually, the story seemed quite good. *If* it hadn't been plagiarized. But even the twist at the end was the same I'd read in that excellent short story.

"How would you like to get your teeth into this?" Art said when he had finished.

"I don't have the time."

Now he was getting angry. He wasn't used to being told no. His already red face colored a deeper shade. "Time?" he said. "What time? You could do this in two weeks."

"Two weeks?" My voice was filled with disbelief.

Art misunderstood. "Two weeks too long? You could do it in a week, right?"

"No, I couldn't."

"Take as much time as you need. You can have three weeks. And here comes the part that'll get you. I'll pay you $10,000. That's a lot of money for something you can do sleepwalking."

The last sentence didn't register. Only later did I muse on how little this oilman knew about books, or what little respect he had for them and how difficult they are. Instead I was adding sums in my head: $1,000 from Tom Taylor, $7,500 from Satterfield, now $10,000 more. I wondered if there were printing presses in Texas.

Art misunderstood again. "Worried if I'll pay you, eh? Old Art always pays. And he'll give you the money right now 'cause he trusts you. Lot of money just for a book, isn't it?"

I looked at Gosdin. I hoped he understood I wanted to get away from here.

"I've got the money right here," Art said. He pulled out a wallet as big as a bank pouch and was about to open it.

"I'm not going to do your book."

His face beet red, he misunderstood still again. "I know about you goddamn Jew writers from New York," he growled. "You think you can play virgin-hard-to-get and still fuck me. Well, smartass Jew, you can't. You're not bleeding me for a cent more."

"Let's go," I said to Gosdin. I was up and past Art and headed for the door. I hoped Gosdin was behind me.

He was. We didn't say a word until we were inside his car and the engine was started. "Welcome to Texas," he said.

"Art's something," I said. "Satterfield didn't fill me with a lot of warmth, but he's Mr. Charm alongside this guy."

"I liked the way you handled it."

"You did? I thought Art was your friend."

"He's someone you meet in my business."

"What is your business? I've asked before."

"It's hard to describe. Listen, where do you want to spend the rest of the afternoon?"

"Why did he think I was Jewish?"

"He thinks everybody from New York is. He thinks Rockefeller

is. It's all a conspiracy. The Jews and the Commies scheming
against good guys like him."

"How about going to where Kennedy was shot? Is it too far?
That was a moment in my life I won't forget."

He drove through the heat, a Willie Nelson tape playing in the
Cadillac, and I knew we were close to the place before we saw it. I
wondered what it was like to have thirty seconds left in your life and
not know it. A silly thought.

Dealey Plaza was much smaller than I imagined. A real shooting
gallery. I'd been led to believe Oswald had a difficult shot, but looking at the School Book Depository, and then to where the car carrying Kennedy had been, killing the President seemed no feat at all.
Not that I would ever believe Oswald acted alone. The Zapruder
film, clearly showing the victim's head moving front to back — a
shot from in front, unless one of Newton's laws had been repealed
— and the mountains of other evidence gathered pointed to a conclusion I believed even the blind could see.

Maybe it was 20/20 hindsight, but what struck me at this
historic spot was that it looked like a killing would take place here.
Tall buildings staring straight down into a fish barrel. Hadn't it
looked like a shooting gallery (it certainly did now) to those Secret
Service agents who traveled the terrible route the day before Kennedy had? It wasn't as if they hadn't been warned of danger. Adlai
Stevenson had been shoved around in Dallas a couple weeks before.
The very morning of the assassination an ad paid for by a rich Texan appeared in the *Dallas Morning News* making it clear Kennedy
wouldn't be missed. The most obvious precaution, making sure no
killer waited in a window or on a building's roof, had not been taken
by men whose *only* job was to protect their boss.

There were maybe forty or fifty people, faces sad, pensive,
wandering in a sort of daze about the area. I thought it was good
Dallas city officials hadn't changed it much. The people, I imagined, were from out of town. They were old enough to remember
clearly that November 22 eighteen years ago. It had been a day
they would remember forever. But people, I suspected, would be
coming here a thousand and eighteen years from now.

I tried to open the door of what had been the School Book
Depository. I figured most visitors did this, only to be sent on their
way by a guard. Maybe I'd have better luck getting up to that sixth
floor and the window the Warren Commission said Oswald fired

from. I would give the guard a story about my wanting to write what would be the thousandth book on the assassination. But the door to the building was locked.

Gosdin and I just wandered around. Over and over I thought of having thirty seconds to live and being rich, handsome, powerful, expecting to live fifty years in a style even Pharaohs couldn't envision. I looked up the street Kennedy had traveled, his limousine about to turn left, people cheering, beautiful wife at his side, the whole world in his pocket. Now the limousine was turning left. How long did he have? Ten seconds? And the last words he ever heard, from Governor John Connally's wife, Nellie: "You can't say the people of Dallas don't love you."

We walked over to the grassy knoll and to the railroad tracks. On the grassy knoll, I believed, was where the real killer waited. Oh, Oswald might have been in that window, and there might have been another man in one of the tall buildings behind, but where we stood was where the assassin whose frontal shot Zapruder's camera had recorded had been.

"The killer was right around here," I said.

"I think so too," Gosdin said.

"The person who did it couldn't be alive." I figured this had to be true. Setting aside all moral judgments, I wondered how anyone could accept such an assignment. Surely a sane person knew by murdering the President he was murdering himself. Those who hired him could never let him live.

Time raced by. We sat on the grass for a while and watched cars and the faces of people. Those of the visitors who had come to this shrine, for that is what it is for many Americans, were solemn. Fathers pointed up to the window of the Depository and tried to explain to little boys what happened. I wondered what was in the minds of drivers when they turned left and drove over *the spot.*

Compared to other cities, Dallas was relatively free of graffiti, but there was plenty of it in Dealey Plaza. Most of the graffiti had to do with the assassination, and it might have seemed irreverent to some, but I didn't see it that way. Often the only way to live with a terrible tragedy is to joke about it. *Titanic* jokes — gallows humor — make it possible to exist with the unbearable.

The most determined of the graffiti artists signed his work "Garret Gerishkin" — could anyone really be named that? — and offered a number of unusual solutions to the assassination: "The gun was hidden in Zapruder's camera;" "E. Howard Hunt was the Umbrella Man;" and "The Killer — with phony Secret Service credentials — stood on the railroad bridge."

Garret Gerishkin evidently had been studying the Kennedy assassination for years, and returning faithfully to the scene to record his conclusions. Some of his observations seemed to have been written many years earlier (they were weathered, barely decipherable), while others were fresh and might have been recorded yesterday.

"Do you think Garret's here today?" I asked Gosdin.

"Probably."

"Which one is he?"

"Listen," Gosdin said. "It's past five. We've been invited to a party tonight. Why don't you buy some clothes? Tonight you'll meet a broader cross section of our town."

"I thought I'd just have a few beers at the Ramada bar and get to bed early."

"Ramada doesn't have a bar. It's a new hotel and the bar's not in yet. You just don't want to buy clothes."

"Why can't I go like I am?"

"You look like a slob."

"Well, who's going to be at this party?"

"You worried about meeting another Art?"

"That's it."

"Be more curious. You're living a lot of stories you'll be able to tell your grandkids."

We went to a place called (what else?) The Gucci Salon, where Gosdin's former wife worked. The first thing I noticed was a table lamp costing $500. "This is the wrong store," I said.

"You're successful. Look it for once in your life."

"You're just worried about how I'll look to your friends."

"They're not my friends. If I wanted to give them a treat I'd let you go like you are. That orange tee shirt. Nouveau Skid Row. It'd give them something to tell *their* grandkids."

"I'm not going to shop here."

"Okay. I'll take you to Target. But I am making sure you get a change of clothes."

I learned more about Gosdin as we drove around North Dallas. He was a native Texan (Lubbock) without a trace of Texanese in his voice, a graduate of Texas Tech, and he was fiercely dedicated to working for himself. He promoted concerts, did advertising work, and was a person people came to when they needed something solved. He knew an astonishing number of people, from the richest to the poorest, in every imaginable type of business. If you invented a widget, chances are Gosdin could find someone who marketed widgets. His outstanding personal quality — I believed him when he said his harassment of me on the Satterfield deal was out of character — was an ability to listen.

The party was held in a condominium complex, and the big, well-lit swimming pool was reserved exclusively for the party's use. It seemed at first to be a singles gathering like you expect to see in California for types in their early thirties, but closer examination revealed some financial heavy hitters also had come: some oil and gas independents, a couple of real estate developers, a well-known East Texas rancher in for Mosley's party, and a Texas representative of Chase Manhattan Bank, David Rockefeller's colossus in New York.

I met the rancher first. "This beef sure will taste good," he said to Gosdin, referring to the meat barbecuing on the big pit near the poolside.

"It smells good," said Gosdin. I didn't think this was the answer the rancher wanted to hear.

He drew us closer, talking in a conspiratorial tone. "I said, it will *taste* good."

Gosdin's expression was blank. "I'm sure it will," he said.

"Beef always tastes better," said the rancher, "when it doesn't cost anything. I rustled that old heifer."

"Rustled it?" I said.

"Went to my neighbor's last night and just wriggled through that old fence and took him. I tell you, with the cost of beef these days, it's hard to enjoy just for thinkin' about it."

"Do you raise cattle?"

"That's how I know the cost. Plumb outrageous, isn't it?"

I met the banker and an oilman. The oilman told a story about a banker. The oilman was into buying bankrupt corporations and through complicated maneuvering turning a healthy profit by selling off assets. One company he bought for the proverbial song turned out to hold valuable properties somehow overlooked by the previous owner. "So there I was," the oilman said, "ready to move all the files out of the old headquarters. All of a sudden this banker shows up. He'd foreclosed on the corporation, sold it to me for what he could get, and now he realized he'd made a mistake. So I'm telling him to get out of my way, and he's saying the deal's off. I've got this heavy file cabinet up on my hand dolly and he lies down in front of the door. Flat out on his back in front of that door. 'What you goin' to do now?' he says. I says, 'I'm comin' right over the top.' But I couldn't really, him bein' kind of heavy. So I kept nudgin' the file cabinet and the dolly up against him. Sort of a Mexican standoff. I couldn't get the file cabinet over him, and he wouldn't move. Finally, he said he'd give me $25,000 more than I'd paid the day before. I said $50,000 and nudged him a couple more times. He was tough, I got to hand him that, and we finally settled in the middle. $37,500."

The banker told a story about an oilman. "You got to remember," he said, "most independents would rather make five dollars dishonestly than ten dollars in a deal that's legitimate. I knew this one wildcatter who'd find a well already drilled. Abandoned. He'd buy up the lease on the land, then sell shares in a planned drilling operation. To sell shares, you need to find people with money, people who don't know much. What group fits this category? Doctors. Doctors have lots of cash, are inevitably greedy, and don't know what the world is like. Lawyers are greedy, too, but they're also smart. Anyway, IRS will tell you that as a group doctors lead the world in tax evasion. So they have all this cash, and they want more. Treating people in between golf games has become a bore. Along comes this wildcatter, rough hewn, and the doctors think he's another H.L. Hunt. They think *they'll* become H.L. Hunts. Two ranches to go along with the mansion they already have in Highland Park. Of course, the wildcatter, like all good con men, lets the doctors sell themselves. Offers the poison and they slurp it up. All he promises is to drill a well where experts once thought there had been oil. He collects maybe $25,000 each from some thirty doctors, spends virtually nothing *re*drilling the well — it's already been drilled — and says, 'Gee, boys, just bad luck this one didn't work out. But I've got another . . .' You'd be astounded how many doctors travel this road two, three, four times."

Gosdin drove me back to Ramada Inn at 10 P.M. It had been a day such as I had never spent, hearing about deals and more deals. The show "Dallas" and arch-villain J.R. Ewing didn't capture at all the relentless pursuit of deals, any sort of deal that might make money. As Art at Tony Roma's had proved, and Satterfield earlier, you didn't have to know about a field to invest in it. In a way Satterfield had been the most honorable of them all. He had said he would make a deal with anybody, and evidently he would.

Gosdin said he'd pick me up in the morning for the ride to L.G. Mosley's party. "You think you've seen something today," he said. "Tomorrow you won't believe."

I was just about to climb into bed when the telephone rang. *Deja vu*. I was ready for anything when I picked it up and said hello.

"Heard you were in Dallas, boy."

It was Jack Grimm. And it was really good to hear his voice. Although I'd known him less than two months, he seemed like an old friend on the phone.

"How did you know I was in Dallas?"

"Drury told me. How are you doing there?"

"I don't know. Surrounded by predators."

"The boys in Dallas are pretty rough. You be careful."

"Well, it's good to hear your voice."

"You come to Abilene when you're through there. Big television show gonna be filmed here next weekend."

"I might just do that."

"Do it, boy. And watch out for those boys in Dallas."

I was going to have to make a decision on Texas. If it were Dallas, even though I'd seen very little of the city, the answer would be no. It was probably a fine place, but I thought my first experiences with people on the make would linger too long. Abilene was small and quiet. It might be good to write a book there.

I went to sleep and dreamed about Art on a New York subway train. He was talking to a black man about writing his book, waving his thick wallet in the air, and individuals who looked like muggers got on the train at every stop.

Seven

Statues of black jockeys guarded the storybook setting, and the long rambling ranch home was fronted by four acres of green lawn perfectly manicured and reached by an elegant winding driveway. Three hundred cars were parked on the lawn, Rolls, Lincolns, Mercedes, BMWs, Cadillacs; no pickup truck crowd this one. Eight hundred people sat under the hot noon sun drinking beer around a gazebo specially constructed for the party and occupied by a lively Country and Western band. The sky was bright blue, the good scent of newly mown hay in the air. It was indeed a storybook setting, and a movie had even been filmed here. It was the sort of party you read about Lyndon Johnson giving alongside the Pedernales, except the food was probably better here, and certainly the accommodations more comfortable.

This was a national crowd, not one limited to Texans. People had come from New York, Chicago, Los Angeles, Miami, come just for this party: the common denominator, with a few exceptions, such as myself, some representatives of the media, and perhaps the Country and Western band, was the possession of a lot of money. Wherever you turned deals were being talked up, and I understood why Satterfield had been so eager to attend. If heaven consisted of doing what made you happy (Che Guevara, for instance, with an endless list of capitalist governments to overthrow, or Chase Manhattan Bank's David Rockefeller, in a world of high interest loans where everyone needed money and always repaid on time), then this had to be heaven for the deal-makers. I heard somebody selling an unraced quarter horse for $250,000. Another looked for funding for a string of catfish farms. A third searched "for the guy who's selling the airline."

We (Gosdin, his girlfriend Tillie, myself) stood in front of the 130-foot-long home and were approached by what seemed to be a teenager in shining armor. His gold and diamonds glistening in the sun hurt my eyes and made me glance away.

"Glad you could make it, Jim," he said to Gosdin.

"Wouldn't miss it for anything, L. G.," said Gosdin. "You know Tillie. And this is Bill Hoffman."

"The writer. I hear you've met some interesting people in Texas."

"How did you hear that?" Everyone, except me, knew what I was doing.

"The word gets around in a small place like Texas." He laughed. "It's good to have you here. Any friend of Drury's is a friend of mine."

I was so taken by his jewelry — his life expectancy could be tabulated in seconds if he wore it on most New York City streets — that I couldn't think of a reply. The most striking of his baubles was a long gold chain with a diamond horseshoe attached, and diamonds were in *every link of the chain.* He wore five gold rings clustered with diamonds; the rings depicted such things as a horse's head and a map of Texas.

"You like the jewelry?" Mosley asked, noticing where my attention was concentrated. Suddenly his face grew sad. "You should have seen what I was going to wear." He told us, although the words seemed to hurt, about a gold belt buckle he had intended to have inset with 100 carats of diamonds, but just yesterday the belt buckle had broken in two. "So many holes had been drilled in the gold to accommodate the diamonds," he said, "that the gold lost its structural strength."

"This is some party," I said. I couldn't think of appropriate words of solace for what clearly was a crushing loss.

"It's good to have a few friends over," he said. This time he didn't laugh, so I assumed he was serious.

Mosley was 5'8" and trim, looked sixteen but was forty. He did get his start as a teenager, however, as a roofing contractor. Gosdin later told me the whole Horatio Alger success story. The teenage Mosley, gifted with a Rich Little talent for vocal imitations, began advertising a roofing repair business. An old, mature-sounding Mosley answered the company's telephone. A young, boyish Mosley did the repairs. When a customer would come to the job site to meet the boss, young Mosley, doing the work, would tell him he was away for the moment. No one ever met the friendly but businesslike middle-aged man they assumed ran the corporation.

Mosley later became the pawn shop king of Dallas, and constantly expressed delighted amazement at the profitability of the business. Texas law allows pawn shops to charge *15% interest per month,* which to my mind took the mystery out of why a pawn shop made money. Mosley was also a trader, buying and selling horses in a boom market, and became a real estate developer. Standing in front of his big expensive home this blazing hot Sunday afternoon, he was obviously proud of what he had wrought. He had a lovely home, more money than a hundred men could reasonably expect to accumulate in their lifetimes, the respect of peers who scrambled from all over the country to get to his party, and a wife and children to whom he seemed devoted and protective. There was no indication he intended to retire and enjoy the fruits of his enterprise, although today obviously was not one set aside to turn a deal. He had brought others together for that purpose, enhancing his prestige while at the same time enjoying the role of being above it all.

And Mosley was a gracious host. All of the guests wanted to talk with him, but he was no will o' the wisp slipping frenetically from one cluster of people to another. He had time for everyone. When he told Gosdin, Tillie, and me he would see us later, to look around wherever we pleased, we took him at his word.

In back of the home was a $250,000 *barn.* We ran into Drury back there, dressed in cowboy garb, every inch the star. The man Drury was talking to, oil money I guessed, had just given him an Appaloosa horse. Drury said he had no place to keep the expensive animal, and the man said he would board him free. He was a fan of Drury's, he said, it was a pleasure to meet "The Virginian" in the flesh, and he was surprised Drury had done his own riding stunts on the TV show. He left thanking Drury for taking the animal.

"I've got to read the announcement of the J. R. Ewing Silver Piece," Drury said, "but I don't have an announcement."

"Nothing?" said Gosdin.

"Not a word."

"How would you like to write an announcement?" Gosdin asked me.

We went inside the Mosley house to find a typewriter and place to work. Hundreds of people were inside, drinking, talking, soaking up the air-conditioning, looking at exhibits. One of these had been set up for the reason that an owner was proud of his gem collection. He wasn't selling the jewelry, just exhibiting it. One item was a 72-carat Tanzanite, thought to be the largest in existence, valued at almost $750,000. The Tanzanite was mounted in a 14-carat gold and diamond setting. I knew the handling of objects like this was often controversial. No one really knew how much they were worth. What an owner usually did after buying one of the rare beauties was to "give" it away, perhaps to the Smithsonian or the Metropolitan Museum (in the case of a painting). The evaluator of the worth of the object always erred on the side of generosity (cases of an item being estimated at more than a million dollars that had cost only a few thousand were not unknown), which earned a huge tax deduction for the owner plus the nice word "philanthropist" in front of his name in news stories. Of course, no philanthropy at all was involved.

Pizarro had murdered Incas in Peru for far less gold than was on display on the wrists, fingers, and necks of people inside Mosley's house. The public often associates the wearing of jewelry with women, but at this Texas party the habit definitely had caught on with the male sex. So had weird fashion. The soles of one fellow's shoes were transparent.

Gosdin and I located a typewriter easily enough, but there simply was nowhere to put it. Every table was crowded with food and drinks or items of clothing. Finally we just set it on the floor in the midst of the big crowd and went to work.

A man who looked and dressed like a cowboy except he outdid even L. G. Mosley by wearing six gold rings on his fingers stopped to see what we were doing. The man was wiry and affable, carried a cup of beer, didn't *seem* like a crackpot.

"You boys journalists?" he asked, peering down at us. I was sitting crosslegged on the floor; Gosdin was squatting, staring over my shoulder (although Mosley's floor was immaculate, he said he didn't want to get "lint" on his pants).

"Sort of," I said. I kept typing.

"Do you have guts? Will you print the truth?"

I needed to get a better look. Yes, he seemed sane. I always expected these people to have two heads, or at the least eyes that spun like pinballs. The truth, however, was that if the fellows in the white sport jackets had to make a decision based on appearance, it would surely be me they carted off to the Laughing Academy.

"Sure we'll print the truth," I said.

"Well," he said, kneeling down so he could be close to our ears, "I've got the biggest story of the century."

"Of the century?"

"Easily. You got the courage to print it?"

"More courage than sense."

Perhaps Gosdin's sense of humor is not finely enough developed, or something, but he wasn't in the mood to listen. "Look," he said, "we're up against a deadline here, and really don't have time."

"Of course we do," I said. "What's more important, possibly the biggest story of the century, or a piece of puffery about a new bauble?"

"A piece of puffery."

"I want to hear this story."

"Oh, God."

"Do you know," the man asked, whispering, "who Jimmy Carter is?"

"Sure. Ex-President of the United States."

"No, no. Who he really is."

"I guess I don't."

"Think about it."

Maybe Gosdin had been right. "Former Governor of Georgia," I said. "Peanut farmer. Born-again Christian. Member of Rockefeller's Trilateral Commission. Nuclear scientist."

"You're way off track. That Trilateral Commission stuff is interesting, though, isn't it? But you're missing the point. Let me give you a hint. What does Carter's smile remind you of?"

"He seems to have more teeth than other people."

"Damn! You're either ignorant, or just not thinking. Try to picture Carter's smile and you'll get it right away."

"I don't want to think about Carter's smile."

"You part of the liberal/Commie media?"

"Lord!" I tried to look shocked.

"Just had to check. My friends get what I'm trying to say right away. Now, think about Carter's smile."

"Okay. I got it in my mind."

"I'll coach you along here. You're a little slow, but I think you're honest. Think about Teddy Kennedy's smile."

"Got it."

"Think about those two smiles side by side."

"Right."

"Well?"

"Well what?"

"Dammit, it's clear as a hog in your bedroom. Jimmy Carter's smile, Teddy Kennedy's smile, they're the same. Teddy Kennedy and Jimmy Carter are brothers. Couldn't be anything else."

"That's the story of the century?" I said.

"It'll knock people's eyeballs out, eh what?"

"It's the kind of stuff you don't read very often."

"Let me give you the icing on the cake. The proof. I couldn't expect you to stick your neck out without proof."

Two young women in designer jeans and swathed in diamonds had stopped to listen, and figuring he had a sympathetic audience, the man with the six gold rings no longer talked in conspiratorial whispers. "It just took a little digging," he said, "and some country common sense. The story goes all the way back to FDR. He used to vacation in Warm Springs, Georgia. One of his best friends was old Joe Kennedy, the bootlegger. Well, Joe must of taken up with Miz Lillian, because she sure is the mother of Jimmy Carter. Never hear much about Carter's father, do you?"

He must have taken my silence for approval, because he kept going. "So it's plain as can be. Joe Kennedy, visiting FDR, had an affair with Miz Lillian. Those two smiles prove they're brothers. It all fits. You have opportunity and motive. So old Joe is ambitious for his kids. He planned on making his first son president but he got himself killed in the war. He made John president, but he got himself killed. Bobby, the little Commie, got killed too. That left Teddy, and after Chappaquidick and the Kopechne girl, he was dead politically. The Kennedys wanted power, thirsted for power, but how? Why, the half-brother, Jimmy Carter! They made Jimmy Carter president and fooled everybody."

I typed a few words about the J. R. Ewing Silver Piece.

"Gonna print that story?" he asked. "Or is it too big for you?"

"I don't think anyone would publish it." I hoped he would go away. I'd made it this long in Dallas without too humiliating a scene. "The *National Enquirer* might."

"Good newspaper, the *Enquirer.*" I could tell by the tone of his voice that he wasn't the paranoid/aggressive/violent type. Just paranoid. "It's too bad," he said sadly. "Too bad for you. This story would have made you famous."

He wandered off, and I asked the two young ladies in designer jeans what they thought about the tale. "It makes a lot of sense," one of them judged. "A shame the American people don't know," said the other.

We finished the announcement — it was just a page — with only two people tripping over us, and went outside in search of Drury. I counted nine locations where you could get beer. A man named Lucky Delay, a guest, had volunteered to slice watermelons. He said Mosley had purchased three thousand pounds of Black Diamond watermelons for the party.

Barbecue trailers were pulled onto the lawn to cook the beef and pork, which were first-rate. So also were the traditional baked beans, cole slaw, potato salad, and corn on the cob. Mosley had spared no expense. A full staff of caterers made certain no one did without.

Looking for Drury, we spotted instead Satterfield, maybe 150 feet away across the crowded expanse of broad lawn. "So much," said Gosdin, "for your theory of his not showing up."

"He hasn't been exactly looking for me."

"Bill," said Tillie, the attractive blonde Gosdin had brought. She was a young, successful businesswoman who had dealt with numbers of the high-powered, fast-stepping Texas new rich. "Why not ask for more? Jim is right when he says $7,500 is nothing to these people. They might spend that much in an evening lighting cigars. It seems like a good amount of money to you, and maybe to me and Jim also, but it's an amount that doesn't even register with them. Satterfield hasn't looked you up yet today because he's got much bigger fish to fry. He'll be around, though. I really don't know how he intends to make money with this — he might just resell it — but he's got a plan, you can believe that."

"What if he won't pay more? I've already got that money spent."

"Obviously, I can't promise he will. But I *think* he will. And if he doesn't, you'll get it from somewhere else. Look around here.

Millions of dollars of deals are going down. Plenty of them would love to get in the movie business. They believe it gives them a touch of class. They've made money, but they haven't earned respect. People . . . well, you're an example. You've been on important TV shows for your books. Been written about in important newspapers. That's what they want. Recognition. They're as good as anybody, they'll tell you, but who knows that? They've made money, lots of it, and that's something. But if they ever are written about, it's usually got to do with some questionable undertaking. Investors are quoted saying unpleasant things. The reporter sticks in nasty little innuendos. This is their reward for being successful? It doesn't happen to people connected with the arts. They don't get sneered at for making money."

"What about the tax writeoff?" Having written about and known my share of moguls, albeit not the hard-charging Texas types I'd been meeting, I doubted their sensitive souls were much dismayed by carping from the peanut gallery. The bottom line was profit. If they could be loved, fine, and there were always plenty of journalists willing to say a blatant tax dodge was philanthropy. Too many of these ended up working for the very power broker they supposedly kept an eye on. Besides, if the Texas rich Tillie talked about were so concerned about image, they could give away their money to a worthy cause, no strings attached.

"I'm not saying they don't have larceny in their hearts. It's so much a part of them they can't escape it. They couldn't do something just for the pure good of it; they'd always see angles. But that doesn't mean they don't want recognition. Why do you think Satterfield picked you?"

"I don't know."

"Because he's never met an author. You could tell some of these guys you are James Michener and it wouldn't register. What mattered here was that you were invited to L. G. Mosley's party, and therefore you must be very good. And you know Jack Grimm. To hang out in this kind of company means you're pretty good."

"I don't 'hang out' with Mosley and Grimm."

"Stop being touchy. The point is, if you want to sell your movie rights, get more than $7,500 for them. Why don't you talk to Jim Drury? People here think the sun sets on him. He could handle negotiations. It would be worth more than $7,500 just to drop 'The Virginian's' name into conversations."

This was probably true enough. We found Drury in the middle of the party's largest cluster of people, signing autographs, having his picture taken, and fielding questions about former sidekick Doug McClure. Drury looked young, robust, and somehow in the one-hundred-degree heat wasn't sweating. It always surprised listeners when he told them his movie debut had been in "Blackboard Jungle."

"Here's the announcement," Gosdin said, handing him the typed sheet of paper. "Our friend Hoffman may want to talk with you."

"I don't think I do," I said. The party was a madhouse, I couldn't imagine ever getting more than a few seconds alone with Drury, and besides I didn't want to be indebted to him.

"I want to talk to you," Drury said. "I mentioned your coming to Houston. How about leaving with me tomorrow morning?"

"Told Grimm last night I'd come to Abilene. Some big anti-drug program is being filmed."

"Get High on Yourself," Drury said. "Norman Lear, the TV producer, is doing it as part of his probation. He was involved in a cocaine bust. Doing an anti-drug show is part of his avoiding jail."

"Well, I'm supposed to be there."

"You can do both. The drug program isn't till next weekend. I've got a way you might pick up some money in Houston."

Drury had told me on the *Titanic* expedition about a wealthy, very old rancher who had written a book about cowboys and the Old West. The book wasn't in publishable shape, but he thought I might get it that way. This would make the rancher very happy — he wanted to leave a book behind that his kids could remember him by — and earn some money for me also. It was a job I'd done numerous times, called "manuscript doctoring," and often worked out well for everyone concerned.

"I guess Grimm doesn't need me there tomorrow," I said.

"Good. First one who wakes up rouses the other. In Houston you can stay at my place."

"Carl Ann won't mind?" Carl Ann was Drury's wife, a charming woman about the age of the actor, and had been in Boston to meet the *Gyre* when the search vessel returned from the North Atlantic. That's when I met her. For a long time, I learned, she had been suffering severe pains in her jaw. No doctor had been able to help. Jack Grimm, picking up the bill, sent her and Drury to the East Coast where the Reverend Ernest Aingley, a faith-healer and friend of the

Abilene tycoon, was holding one of his famous services. According to Carl Ann, her jaw was much improved after the session with Aingley.

"She'll be glad to see you," Drury said. "No jokes about insurance, okay?"

One of Grimm's upcoming plans was to hold a hang-gliding championship off the top of his mountain, and Drury, who knew nothing about the sport, said he wanted to compete. Carl Ann and I annoyed the actor by encouraging his participation, and talking about the life insurance we supposedly had taken out on Drury. "Actually, Drury," I said, "you've got nothing to worry about. Grimm won't miss you. Your death will guarantee that the movie he's making will be successful. Me and Carl Ann won't miss you. Oh, a little bit, perhaps, but with all that money to spend in the South Pacific, how sad can we be?"

Our plates piled high with food, we found a table near the center of the big crowd and ate and listened. I have a friend from Wisconsin who teaches school near San Antonio, and in his opinion, "It's impossible to get good beef in Texas. I don't know why. Maybe they ship out all the good stuff. But what you get in this land of the Shitkickers is as tough and as bony as their roughnecks."

He hadn't eaten L. G. Mosley's barbecue, smoked on the spot in one of those trailers.

Many in the crowd drank a lot, and it showed, but I thought even sober the fellow who said "Charles Bronson is America's greatest actor" would have believed it. "Now Clint Eastwood's a right good boy too, but I don't think he could handle those creeps in New York the way Bronson did."

Despite the heavy consumption of beer under a burning sun, the crowd was exceptionally well behaved. The closest thing to a skirmish came when someone said "Texas drivers are the worst I've seen."

"Where *you* from?" a native bellowed from a table away.

"Ohio," was the answer.

"Well," said the native, "I'll tell you. It's you goddam Yankees who come down here who cause the traffic problems."

"Sez who?" said the Ohioan.

"Sez me!" said the Texan.

"Now, Floyd," said the Texan's wife, "let's not do anything to disturb L. G.'s nice party."

"Goddam Yankee," said Floyd. But he did sit down.

Drury didn't read the announcement from the gazebo about the J. R. Ewing Silver Piece until 4:30 P.M. After that guests started to leave. More stayed than left, however, because business knows no time clock. Those that remained, perhaps half the original gathering, had a more serious air about them. The party had been fun; now it was time to attend to the reasons why they had come here in the first place.

Gosdin, Tillie, and I had moved out of the heat to the air-conditioning inside Mosley's house. It was there Satterfield found us. He had taken a back seat to no one where wearing jewelry was concerned. But it was hard for me to keep in mind that this young, relatively unpolished individual was a very rich man.

"Ready to take care of business?" Satterfield said.

"I've been ready all day."

Gosdin groaned. Tillie looked disgusted. Both were certain, really certain, that just a minimal effort on my part would open Satterfield's wallet much wider.

"L. G. has cleared out his dining room for us," Satterfield said. "We can wrap this up in there."

I hadn't realized it was going to be a show. But that is what it was, sitting at the long dining table. People walking past could see inside the room, and a remarkable number stopped to stare. It seemed word had gotten out that a "major movie deal" was going down, and numerous guests wanted to get a glimpse of it.

I sat at the head of the elegant, gleaming hardwood table. Tillie and Gosdin stood behind me. Down the right side of the table, in order, were Satterfield, the banker, and a man in cowboy gear I hadn't met. I asked Gosdin who he was.

"Owns half of Arkansas, or someplace like that," said Gosdin.

Introductions were made. Satterfield said the banker and the cowboy were his partners in the deal: each would put up a third of the money. "But there are a few changes we'd like to make," he said.

"What are those?" I figured Satterfield had come to his senses, realized he knew nothing about movies, and now would demand provisions I wouldn't accept. That was okay. Tillie and the insistent Gosdin were close to persuading me that I was history's biggest fool.

"We want to give you $2,500 more," said Satterfield, "for the right to make the same kind of deal on your next three books. In other words, we give you $2,500 more — $10,000 in all — and on your next three books we get a chance to buy them for the same amount as this one: $7,500 a year for ten years, $75,000 if we make a movie."

"Tell him to shove it," Gosdin whispered in my ear, "and we'll get out of here."

But I was thinking differently. "My next three books?" I said.

"That's right," said Satterfield.

"Whatever those three books are?"

"You got it. The next three."

They might be cookbooks, I thought, and then where would Satterfield be? Most of the books I'd written — for example, a couple on the game of bridge — had no movie potential at all. I didn't know what the next three books would be, but it seemed a better than fifty percent chance Satterfield would be getting nothing for his $2,500.

"I can agree to that," I said.

"Good. Then just look over this contract, sign it, and we'll pay you."

"Maybe," said the cowboy who according to Gosdin owned half of Arkansas, "we should call in people from the *Dallas Morning News*. Let them get a picture of this. A story about a movie sale."

"Right," said the spunky Tillie. "I can write the caption for the picture: 'Ruthless Sharks Devour Author'."

"Who are you?" the cowboy wanted to know.

"A friend of Bill's. I hope you're proud of what you're doing here. I think it's rotten."

Of course, if these three ever entertained doubts they were making a mistake, Tillie dispelled them. Satterfield handed me the contract. There was no more talk about calling the press in.

If anything, the contract was more amateurish than the one Satterfield had shown me at the Ramada Inn. Besides the fact that it said nothing about other rights normally associated with a movie sale, such as play rights, recording rights, musical rights, etc., it was packed with even more misspellings and poorly constructed sentences than the first draft. I had doubts it was legal.

"Just sign," said Satterfield, "and I'll give you the money. You said you wanted cash."

"Bill's leaving tomorrow," said Gosdin. "I don't think he should be carrying around that much money. I'm responsible for him while he's here. I want at least to make sure he gets out of here safely. After that it's his problem."

"What do you suggest?" said the cowboy.

"Come by the Ramada at 8 A.M. tomorrow. He can sign the contract, and you can pay him, just before he heads for the airport."

Gosdin's purpose was transparent. Buying time before the sale was a *fait accompli*. But it was fine with me, also. I really didn't want to carry around $10,000 cash — $11,000, actually, what with the $1,000 for the article from Tom Taylor — even in places that seemed as relatively safe as Dallas and the Ramada Inn. I knew there had to be muggers in Dallas, but they were not lurking around each corner, as they seemed to be in New York.

Satterfield agreed to the 8 A.M. meeting, left the room, and returned shortly with a bucket filled with ice and an expensive bottle of champagne. He poured glasses all around and toasted what he hoped "would be a long and mutually profitable relationship." When I asked if he had read the manuscript of the book whose movie rights he had purchased, he said no, but that a friend had looked it over.

"What did he think?" I asked.

"*She.* She thought it was okay."

"Okay? Just okay?"

"That's what she said." It didn't seem to bother Satterfield. I thought maybe Gosdin had been right all along, that Satterfield was more interested in syndicating a movie rather than the quality of what he had bought. My vanity was also offended by the word "okay." My worry had not been Gosdin's, that I was being paid far too little, but that the book was a really good one and might be carved up by the Texas boys. I did not take it as a hopeful sign that Satterfield had not read the manuscript, and had only the vaguest notion what it was about.

I talked briefly with the rich cowboy (the Sphinxlike banker repeated his performance of the previous day — I do not believe he said a word), and learned that he joined in numerous deals with Satterfield, "who has a golden touch." The cowboy was megabucks, compared with Fred Satterfield's simply being a multimillionaire, but the two had been cutting deals together for a long time. It was some small consolation when the cowboy told me he had a Ph.D. and had read part of the book, enjoying it very much, and that the banker came from a theatrical family. When I asked what they intended to do with the movie rights, he said he didn't know. "Maybe make a film ourselves," he said.

After Gosdin backed his Cadillac off Mosley's green lawn and pulled onto the main road, I craned my neck around for one last look at the party and the people who attended it. None of those outside were standing. In the Texas twilight they sat crouched over tables talking earnestly; rich men with money and power, power to buy and to build, sought after by other rich and powerful men, not for their charm or their wit, though some possessed these, but for the chance to make more money, to put the look of respect on the faces of other men.

Eight

I was embarrassed, but the maids enjoyed themselves. Gosdin and I met Satterfield in the Ramada Inn lobby at 8 A.M. as planned (Drury was making last-minute phone calls in his room), and sat on a couch in front of a coffee table smack in the middle of the big room before God and everybody while Satterfield counted out $10,000 in $100 bills. He laid each one carefully on the coffee table. First one maid saw what was going on and stopped to watch. She called over a friend. Soon five maids were staring wide-eyed at the money, and a couple of departing guests stopped to look also. I was afraid even to wonder what they thought was going on.

Satterfield had a revised contract for me to read, and although he had shaped up some of the spelling (not all), the mention of additional rights usually associated with movies was still missing. I signed it quickly, just wanting to get out of there, but unbelievably Satterfield told us to wait. He left the money on the table and hurried back to the manager's office.

"What's this all about?" I said to Gosdin out of the side of my mouth. Ten people — five of them guests, five maids — were close around the table staring at what looked like a lot of money. Satterfield hadn't bothered to stack it, and the hundred dollar bills seemed to be a lot more than they really were.

"He's probably gone to get the contract notarized," Gosdin said. "That should be a show. The rich guy in a hurry butting heads with the do-it-by-the-book notary. He should have taken you with him. But he didn't want you carrying the cash, and he figured you'd bellyache if he still had the money after you'd signed the contract."

"You finally seem resigned to this."

"To paraphrase a prayer, have the wisdom to accept what you can't change."

"This is the way Texans do business," I heard an admiring man tell his wife. "You've got to admire these oil guys. Cash on the old barrelhead."

I thought of asking him what kind of "oil guy" he believed I was. I was once again wearing my orange tee shirt and blue jeans (why dress up for Houston when I hadn't for Dallas?), and hoped I didn't look like an oil guy, however that was.

Satterfield, I later learned, was having a verbal donnybrook back in the office. The woman notary was either unimpressed or unaware of his bank balance, and refused to plant an official stamp on a contract to which one of the chief parties was not present. Satterfield was not accustomed to being impeded, and alternated quiet reason with stormy rhetoric attempting to get his way. I'd seen Jack Grimm thwarted in a similar situation in a restaurant. He'd threatened to buy the place and fire the offending employee. I didn't think Satterfield, even with all his money and contacts, could take over the Ramada Inn chain.

A sixth maid arrived. Helen. She had been taking care of my room since my arrival Friday. She told her compatriots who I was, and they asked for autographs. No one, I'm sure, had heard of me. Some of the guests asked for an autograph. I wished Drury would show up. He was used to this, and was a real draw.

Satterfield came back, smoking mad. "You'll have to come back with me and tell them you're you," he said.

"What about the money?" I said. It looked like one of those displays in a Las Vegas casino show window.

"Keep your eye on it, will you?" Satterfield said to Gosdin.

The woman notary had me sign my signature several times to compare it to the one on the contract. Satterfield fumed. Most rich people do not suffer delays kindly. And usually they don't have to. Most citizens give them extra-prompt service, automatically, as if it's their due. The rich can accomplish more than the poor. If a poor person's car breaks down, for example, he's stuck, and has to spend time getting it repaired. The rich man has another car, and employees to handle the details of repairing the damaged one. Where accomplishment is concerned, a big advantage the rich have over the poor and the middle-class is the means to avoid necessary but time-consuming detail work and thus get on to other projects. What Satterfield found so difficult to endure with the notary is common daily fare for most individuals.

Back in the lobby we bade Satterfield good-bye — he urged me to get right to work completing the novel (I told him I intended to write the *Titanic* book first), I reminded him he would owe another $7,500 a year from today if he intended to maintain the option — and Gosdin helped me scoop the money off the coffee table into a manila envelope that was soon bulging. If I had been Satterfield, a deadline for the novel being completed would have been part of the contract; otherwise the writer would have to return the money. I think he realized this too late, and began to fear I might take ten years to write the book. Well, *he doesn't have to worry,* I thought. *It's a good book and I want to write it.* But Satterfield's concern at this last moment so delighted Gosdin that I didn't reassure the rich man.

We went to Drury's room to get him moving. The actor had enough luggage to make carrying it a sufficient chore for all three of us. Gosdin carried the lightest load. Although a tanned picture of health in dark sun glasses, polo shirt, Pierre Cardin slacks, and Timberland handsewn shoes, Gosdin said he had a bad back and shouldered only a hanging bag containing a couple of Drury's suits.

On the way to the airport Gosdin stopped at NorthPark Bank where he insisted the $10,000 be turned into a cashier's check. He was greeted as "Jimbo!" by a female executive. I had a theory that a person's solvency could usually be measured by the reaction of people at the bank where he did business. No one knew me at "my" bank in New York. On my lone visit to Abilene I had sensed people snapping to attention when Grimm entered, but that might have been imagination. The people rushing from behind desks to shake his hand had not been imagination. Regardless, the "Jimbo!" could have meant anything. Art had called him that at Tony Roma's. The woman executive was young, wore no ring, and Gosdin was handsome. He could have been Adonis, however, and if he were broke there would have been no "Jimbo!"

I had a return ticket to New York, but nothing to Houston, so that had to be taken care of at the airport. I felt sorry for Drury, but probably shouldn't have. People kept recognizing him, shaking his hand, asking for an autograph. A few made good-natured cracks about riding horses. I guess Drury enjoyed it all.

Gosdin said something nice to me. "They should ask for *your* autograph," he said.

"Nonsense," I said.

"No. I mean it."

Gosdin waited until we boarded the flight. He asked if I were going to move to Abilene to do the *Titanic* book, and I said I didn't know, a year away from New York with nothing to distract me from writing might be good. I might do *Titanic,* and the novel.

"Why not move to Dallas?"

"You're kidding." He had to be.

"Look, you saw just one side. You may go crazy in Abilene with nothing to do. Believe me, there's nothing to do in Abilene. Here you have some of the atmosphere of New York — good restaurants, theater, music — and you don't have to risk your life to enjoy it."

"Well, I'll think about it." But I knew I wouldn't.

"You'll make more money here than in New York, also. There aren't many authors here. That makes you special. You saw how people made out over you. There's nothing unusual at all about an author in New York."

I shook Gosdin's hand and promised to stay in touch. He said if I did settle in Abilene to give him a call and he'd visit. It was less than a four-hour drive directly west from Dallas. I hoped I would see Gosdin again. He had seemed sincere and concerned, a person who as a friend would wear well over the years.

Aboard the plane Drury took it for granted the decision had already been made, that I would be living in Abilene. He could see nothing negative in the move. First he talked about the highs and extreme lows involved in making a living as a writer or actor (he certainly had known both), then got around to saying — "despite what you may believe" — there was nothing wrong with financial security. He himself, he said, wanted to make enough money so he could produce and act in what he wanted, not work for other people in what they chose. Drury considered Jack Grimm nothing short of an Einsteinian genius where finding oil was concerned, and confided that he held an interest in a new well the tycoon was about to drill. "You get to Abilene with Grimm," he said, "and you'll have a chance to do the same thing. Grimm likes you. He won't lead you astray." According to Drury, I should get together $32,000 to buy a small share in one of Grimm's drilling ventures. I couldn't imagine my ever doing any such thing.

Drury was totally captivated by Grimm's persona. Looking for Titanic, for Noah's Ark, for the Loch Ness Monster were wonderful and creative ways to use one's money. Drury more that anyone else on the expedition had been in heaven out on the North Atlantic, and he talked enthusiastically about going again when Grimm went back. In the movie the oil man made of the adventure, Drury, the narrator, called the world "a better place because Jack Grimm is on it." I was with Grimm when he first saw the movie in Abilene. "Corny, isn't it?" he said, breaking into embarrassed laughter. "But I like it."

Drury was simply being positive about life. It's necessary in the acting profession. Who but an excessive optimist would even go into a business where perhaps one out of ten thousand succeed? In the long dog days of just attaining a tenuous foothold, audition after audition piling up rejection after rejection, envisioning the best was all you had to keep you going.

And there was just the possibility Drury was right. A rich man named Schliemann had found Troy. Why not Jack Grimm finding *Titanic?*

I read a magazine during most of the short flight to Houston, and came across a brief article about another wealthy Texan who it seemed might be worth watching. His name was T. Boone Pickens, he was from Amarillo (was the city really large enough for him *and* Stanley Marsh 3?), and in the months to come I would read and hear a lot more about the man.

T. Boone Pickens turned out to be like the ant of song who insists he can move the rubbertree plant. Pickens is founder, president, and board chairman of Mesa Petroleum. The next year, 1982, in what one magazine called "a wild roll of the dice," Pickens tried to take over the giant Cities Service Company. Usually when a corporation takes over another, the one doing the swallowing is much larger. Little ones are not supposed to take over big ones. Evidently no one bothered to explain this elemental principle to the ambitious Pickens, whose imagination, if not his pocketbook, was Texas-size.

The earnings of Cities Service were more than twenty times that of Mesa. Cities was the 39th largest corporation in the United States, a giant. But T. Boone Pickens almost pulled it off. He set himself up in a luxurious suite in New York City's Waldorf-Astoria Hotel, offered to buy Cities Service stock at a price well above the market listing, and proved just as daring with his personal life as with his business one: he regularly went jogging in Central Park.

A New York analyst called Pickens "a rattlesnake waiting to strike at its prey." He was featured in the "Doonesbury" cartoon strip. The *Beaumont* (Texas) *Journal* depicted him in a cartoon as a goldfish trying to swallow a whale. Pickens openly advertised that his first action as head of Cities Service would be to fire the current board of directors. They took the threat seriously enough to try to buy out Mesa Petroleum. Eventually Cities Service was taken over by Occidental Petroleum, controlled by the phenomenal Armand Hammer (he actually knew the Russian revolutionary leader, Lenin), but Wall Street insiders say Pickens came within an eyelash of succeeding. He did succeed, in fact, if making a lot of money on the attempted takeover is what counts.

Mesa Petroleum came about two decades ago out of a predecessor called Petroleum Exploration, Inc., which T. Boone Pickens started in 1956 for a mere $2,500. A $10,000 investment in 1964 recently was worth $293,485, a 2,834% increase. One of the company's secrets of success is that most employees are also stockholders, which presumably motivates them to work harder. Two secretaries, for example, have become millionaires. The company has $2 billion in assets (hardly small change, except when compared to a behemoth like Cities Service), 30 million barrels of oil reserves, and a trillion cubic feet of natural gas. Pickens owned at least $20 million in Mesa stock, and was said to hold an additional $120 million in unexercised options. At Mesa, in effect, his word is law.

The attempt to take over Cities Service would have resulted in an even bigger windfall for T. Boone Pickens had he succeeded. The average cost of finding a barrel of oil is $15, but had Pickens been successful he would have picked up Cities Service's *proved* oil reserves for just $5 a barrel. Undiscouraged, Pickens was soon trying to take over the huge Dallas-based General American Oil Company, and history repeated itself. This time the company that "rescued" General American was Phillips Petroleum, but again T. Boone Pickens turned a big profit, and did it without drilling a single well.

T. Boone Pickens, of course, had discovered the simple truth that to make huge amounts of money in the oil business it is not necessary to emulate the wildcatters of old and sweat gallons under a desertlike sun. The trick is to buy oil that is already discovered. More energy may not be produced, but large fortunes can be increased.

T. Boone Pickens was rumored to be going to the well — figuratively — a third time. Mesa started to increase its shareholdings in Houston-based Superior Oil Company, the *world's largest* oil independent, prompting a virtual flurry of controversy. "There is no apparent method to the madness," said Joseph Culp of First Manhattan Company, pointing out that Superior was simply too large for Mesa, that T. Boone should go after slimmer pickins'. "But," added Culp, "he's such a genius that he must have something up his sleeve."

The "genius" of T. Boone Pickens has garnered him homes in Houston and ultra-exclusive Palm Springs, and a massive ranch near Pampa in the upper Panhandle. His international headquarters are in Perth, Australia, and his Mesa Petroleum, traceable back to that $2,500, has a $1.5 billion investment in oil in the North Sea and the Gulf of Mexico.

Pickens, like many of the other boys of Texas, is not afraid of publicity. Reporters were able to watch much of the wheeling-dealing during the Cities Service takeover attempt from his suite at the Waldorf-Astoria, a refreshing contrast to the backroom machinations usually associated with such deals. Often the reporters openly rooted for him, the brash lightweight challenger taking on the heavyweights.

The chairman of Mesa Petroleum has constructed the T. Boone Pickens Jr. Fitness Center in Amarillo. Each day out-of-shape executives firm up at this lush exercise emporium, which features the most modern conditioning equipment. To get inside you must walk past a huge, bronze, life-size sculpture of (who else?) T. Boone Pickens.

The plane was about to land in Houston when I asked Drury if we'd be taking a cab to his home.

"A cab?" he said, feigning shock. "You think I'm a no-class guy?"

"I usually take a bus."

"Well, I don't."

We were met inside the terminal by a very old man who I imagined worked for Drury. "My chauffeur," Drury said. I assumed he was joking.

First stop was baggage claim to pick up what the actor had brought with him to Dallas, which was more than most people's entire wardrobes. The old man carried it all!

"This is embarrassing," I said. "Let's help him."

"That would hurt his feelings."

The old fellow was virtually invisible underneath Drury's luggage. To bystanders it must have seemed a small mountain of suitcases had taken on a life of their own.

"This is awful," I said. People looked at me and Drury, both relatively healthy, especially Drury, then perhaps caught a snatch of what was moving the mountain: if they did, I imagined their reaction had to be outrage. Were we living in India, where maharajahs are so lazy they insist on being *carried* from room to room? In England, where one member of royalty, to keep the hands of himself and his wife clean, had a servant to flush his toilet? In the Middle East, where harem girls still peel grapes for the master?

"Relax," Drury said. "I'm telling you."

"I don't want anything to do with this."

Intentionally walking slower, I began to fall behind. I wanted as much distance as possible between me and this ludicrous scene. I had to admire the old man, though. The luggage advanced steadily forward, never rising or dipping, and people in the terminal got out of its way. It was as if the baggage rolled along on tracks.

I don't think anything prepares a person for the heat of Houston. We came out of the air-conditioning of the terminal into what might have been an oven, except the humidity was higher. For a moment the memory of Dallas as a cool oasis flashed in my mind, and then I felt weak and dizzy. It was more than 100 degrees, muggy, a gray-yellow afternoon that ate away the eyes and sapped the spirit. The heat of Houston in August is something straight out of the bowels of hell, a phenomenon you have to feel to believe.

The "chauffeur" loaded Drury's luggage into the trunk of a car, illegally parked just as Gosdin's had been at a convenient exit. The old man wasn't even breathing hard. "I tried to tell you," Drury said. "He's strong as a Russian weightlifter."

"People seeing him don't know that."

"It's what makes the show a good one."

"Is there such a thing as the Senior Olympics?"

"He'd win, wouldn't he?"

I thought Drury's limousine might be as old as the chauffeur, and it was a class act. Actually, it was a Cadillac perhaps thirty-five years old, in mint condition and worth a lot of money. I couldn't imagine a Rolls Royce running or looking better than this venerable machine.

Riding on Houston freeways, it was immediately evident, was a risky undertaking. In New York the danger was traffic jams and getting in fist fights with angry drivers. In Houston the enemy was speed. The slowest car seemed to be going seventy, a teenager's dream. Literally everyone was in a hurry. I assumed some of the drivers were sane and would have preferred to slow down, but in this Indianapolis 500 atmosphere *that* would have been dangerous. I preferred New York. How many people get killed stalled in the middle of a traffic jam? Or, for that matter, in a fist fight with another frustrated driver?

While Drury and the driver engaged in easy banter (it was clear they'd known each other a long time), I went over in my mind what I knew about Houston. Fifth biggest city in the U.S. Super money alongside deep pockets of poverty. Oil bucks, and although the fact might embarrass Texans, most of those bucks representing East Coast money: the bigshots of Shell Oil, for instance, were not natives — in reality, though Shell tried to portray itself as an American company to avoid offending national sensitivities, its roots were in England and the Netherlands, and the powers behind Gulf Oil (the Mellons of Pittsburgh) and Exxon (the New York Rockefellers) were hardly local products.

Houston had the second highest murder rate in the nation, was grateful to Miami, Florida, for sparing it the dubious honor of being Number One. Terrible bus service; something like fifty percent of the buses didn't even run. But Houston was also a boom town, and its Port of Houston was second in the nation in total cargo handled. Houston was *alive*. Unlike New York, or most Eastern cities, where many buildings were decaying and falling down, Houston was constructing new skyscrapers. It was a city filled with optimism, not despair. It was quite a long drive to Drury's house, but everywhere were the signs of activity, belief in the future; new construction was going up all over this town.

But Houston was still Texas, as I learned as I became better acquainted with this unique state. There was the unemployed Houston mother receiving AFDC payments who had her benefits suspended after she received $500 as a reward for helping police locate a murder suspect, thus giving her more "income" than the bureaucrats thought she should have. There was R. B. Springer, a Houston police officer, who pressed an assault charge against a rape victim who gouged his hand with her fingernails when he found her screaming in a ransacked apartment — Judge Jimmie Duncan fined the woman $150, plus $65 court costs. There was Fulbright and Jaworski, a Houston law firm that billed the state of Texas $1,081,740 for legal fees for appealing a court order demanding that Texas reform its prisons. And there was Houston's Walter "Mad Dog" Mengden, Republican candidate for the U.S. Senate, who proposed the U.S. ship nuclear waste to El Salvador as a condition for that country receiving foreign aid.

Drury had one more surprise for me. When we stepped inside his big house we were immediately in a large atrium filled with bright green tropical plants of every description. It was like being in the middle of a jungle, a pleasant, cool, nonthreatening jungle. The change from the heat outside was startling. Inviting streams of water flowed from a fountain through canals constructed in the floor.

"Like it?" Drury asked.

"It's beautiful," I said.

"Carl Ann gets the credit."

"Never in my wildest dream would I have thought it was you."

Drury made a motion as if to shove me into the fountain. Then he had a better plan. "That plant over there is a man-eater," he said. "It would love raw author."

"Is it really a man-eater?"

"Sure." I never did find out if he was joking. It was the kind of thing he might own. I had a friend in New York, also an actor, who kept a large, hideous creature in his bathroom. He said it was a Thunder Lizard of Java. "Valuable in keeping the landlord away," he said. Anyway, I never felt the urge to make friends either with the Thunder Lizard of Java or Drury's man-eating plant.

It was good to see Carl Ann. She wore a flowered housecoat and gave me a kiss and hug. I reminded her we would soon be in the lap of luxury in Bora Bora, right after Drury did his hang-gliding kamikaze imitation off Grimm's mountain.

It was lovely sitting in Drury's large air-conditioned living room, blue pool glistening outside the picture window. Drury served gin and tonics. He himself no longer drank anything alcoholic, and said he was infinitely more enthusiastic about life because of it. No one could doubt his zest for living. I suspected Carl Ann was responsible for much of that. They had found each other in middle age, but they reminded me of college kids in love. Just holding hands seemed to bring out radiance in them, make them indescribably happy.

Drury said we could swim if we wanted, or just talk. Later we were going out to a Greek restaurant. He said I would meet the old rancher the next day. "I hope you get along," he added. "I think getting a book published would mean a lot to him."

We talked. Drury's politics were out in right field, but he wasn't belligerent about them, as many of that bent are. A bone-crushing super-patriot he wasn't, and he had a sense of humor I found rare in conservatives. I kidded him about being the "mouthpiece" for the National Rifle Association. Nor did Drury have a racist bone in his body, another trait too often present in the right wing.

But Drury was political, and had been for a long time. When Nikita Khrushchev visited the United States, Drury refused even to rehearse his role of "The Virginian" while the Soviet leader was watching. The actor had been made a lieutenant commander in the Navy, though he had never been in that branch of the service, because of recruiting commercials he had made. He went on numerous trips to Vietnam to entertain troops, and several times the plane on which he traveled was hit by fire.

Several friends of Carl Ann and Drury joined us at the Greek restaurant, where the food was excellent and the atmosphere more like that of a neighborhood bar. I mentioned I was interested in rich Texans known for their flakiness, and the retort was, "Which one isn't?" I then heard about Houston's John Mecom, Jr., owner of the New Orleans Saints, who converted a Cadillac into a station wagon so his wife Katsy would feel more comfortable on shopping trips, and who bought the airplane that once belonged to shipping magnate Stavros Niarchos; Melvin Lane Powers, whose aunt, Candace Mossler was also his lover, and who owned a 100-foot yacht formerly belonging to Coco Chanel; Robert Shelton, King Ranch heir (King Ranch is bigger than Massachusetts and Rhode Island combined, has 2,000 miles of fence, 60,000 head of cattle, and more than 2,700 oil wells), whose home features a 500-foot-long swimming pool; and Bill Brosseau, who keeps busy by traveling from one to another of 100 oil wells in a limousine driven by his chauffeur, who doubles as chef.

I would learn that Texans take care of their pets. At a "pet resort" near Fort Worth, animals have their own suites, complete with Hawaiian, Mexican, or other exotic themes, and are provided a den where they can watch TV. I would discover that the town of University Park, where Southern Methodist University is located, considered buying a Mercedes Benz as a police car. And later I was delighted to discover that one of the leaders of Odessans for Decency, a citizens group concerned with what we read, see, and do, was found asphyxiated in his car next to a lady of the evening.

"Know what the motto of rich Texans is?" a friend of Drury's asked.

"No, I don't."

"Too much isn't enough."

The next afternoon I met with Drury's rancher/novelist friend. He was perhaps 75 and accompanied by his 50-year-old son. I'd read the novel: it was very poorly written, filled with misspellings and grammatical errors (which, contrary to belief, are not the editor's job to correct). The story was based on a true incident which occurred in turn-of-the-century Texas, and involved a cowboy who singlehandedly faced down a gang of dangerous outlaws, eventually killing them all. The plot contained a further minus in that the cowboy could not possibly have consumed the mind-numbing amount of alcohol with which he was credited and still have been able to kill anything, leastwise experienced gunfighters.

The rancher wanted his book published — some of the characters in it were evidently ancestors — primarily to leave something tangible, besides money, for which he would be remembered.

"What do you think of my manuscript?" he said.

"I don't believe it can be published as it is. Given a free hand with editing and rewriting, I think I could make it publishable."

"How much money could I make?"

I had been through many sessions before with people wanting help getting a book published. Usually they thought only of the thrill of seeing their names listed in print as authors. Such was not the case with this man, nor with other well-to-do Texans I later met. They'd spent their lives making money. Money was always a prime consideration. The rancher wanted to be remembered, but if there wasn't a profit in it, well, he'd look for something else.

"I don't know what the book would earn. I don't even know if you'd find a publisher. I think you would, and I'm usually right about these things, but I couldn't promise."

"What would you want?" He was used to getting to the point, a trait in Texans I found admirable.

"Two thousand dollars. It generally would be a lot more, but you're a friend of Drury's."

I could see my thinking didn't make sense to this horse trader, and I felt I'd made a mistake. Drury later confirmed the fact. "Keep friendship out of these things," he said. "Makes people suspicious. I introduced the two of you because you both might find it profitable. You're a professional. Get paid what you deserve."

"How does getting paid on a book work?" The subject of money again. This almost always was the farthest consideration from a fledgling writer's mind. I had come into the meeting hoping to *like* the old man (Drury would scoff at this sentiment), to meet an admirable specimen of advanced age who had slaved over a manuscript, no matter how poorly done, because I knew writing any kind of book was a terribly hard feat.

"You get paid an advance from a publisher," I said. "This can vary from a few dollars to a million dollars. My guess is you'd get $5,000. This is a first book, and no one's heard of you. Then . . ."

"I've got a lot of friends," he said. "I'm well known to them, and in the ranching community also. I'd sell a right lot of books just there."

"I doubt it. Experience shows that friends buy *one* book, then pass it along for everyone to read. Anyway, you'll get royalties if the book sells, after the advance is repaid out of royalties. You'll get 10% of the retail hardcover price of the book for the first 5,000 copies sold." This was going to get a bit complicated, but I could tell this rich rancher had no trouble with dollar figures. "You get 12½% of the retail price on the second 5,000 copies. Fifteen percent after that. Paperback rights generally sell for a lump sum. You own fifty percent of these; the hardcover publisher owns the other fifty percent. You own 100% of foreign rights, which are not to be sniffed at. You own 100% of movie rights. There are other rights, such as magazine serial, which usually are less important, especially with a novel."

"Could I make a million dollars?" he wanted to know.

"It's more likely the Sahara Desert will flood."

"*Could* I?"

"Sure. But don't spend the money yet. Look, the American people are not having a love affair with books. Especially hardcover books, which are expensive and most people can't afford. The average first novel sells maybe 1,500 copies."

"Why not sell this one to paperback?"

"You could, but you'd probably make even less money. The big payments in paperback are for books already reviewed, publicized, and made successful in hardcover."

Here we were still talking about money. I wanted to mention that a hardcover book *looked* better, had the good feel of solid furniture (at least to the author), and was something that would last for his great-grandkids to read. I could have mentioned it, but I didn't think he would be impressed.

"Well," he said, "I think we might get money for a movie."

"That's a possibility."

"You ever write books with other folks?"

"Often. It's called ghostwriting. I write someone else's story, but my name doesn't go on the book."

"That a pretty common practice?"

"More than you'd think. A lot of times the person you think wrote a book had very little to do with it."

"How does that work financially?"

"Fifty percent, fifty percent. Usually."

The rancher grew silent. A leathery old man, a tough customer at one time, I imagined, his Number One quality now — or at least vying with monetary concerns — was suspicion. This time he came at the subject obliquely.

"You think if you worked on my book, it would sell to a publisher?"

"I do. I can't guarantee it."

"You think it's a good subject?"

"Yes. It's just not handled right."

"You think it might make a lot of money?"

"No. Well, it *might*. Who knows? I'd give big odds against it."

"But it might?"

This was tiring. I'd expected to meet a nice old man doing something worthwhile with his latter years; instead I was confronted with a rich rancher still chasing a buck, even on something that supposedly was "a work of love."

"Anything might happen," I said. "Former Governor Connally *might* give a speech criticizing the oil companies. Probably won't."

Again he cogitated. His son, a beefy specimen, had scarcely said a word. It was clear he thought Daddy was able to make sound decisions on his own.

"I'll tell you what I'll do," the rancher said. "I'll let you go fifty-fifty on my book. You do whatever it is you do, get the book sold, and we'll split everything right down the middle."

"I won't do that."

"All you're offering me is the chance to give you two thousand dollars. No guarantees. For all I know, that's all it is: giving you money."

By this time I didn't want to work on the manuscript anyway, and welcomed this opportunity to wriggle out. The trick was to avoid bluntness, and thus not offend a friend of my host, Drury.

"I've already agreed to more than I should have," I said. "I'm not going to work on speculation. I stopped doing that a long time ago."

"Why is that? You're pretty sure my book would sell. You'll make more than two thousand dollars."

Yes, I thought, *and a lot of headaches I don't need.* The rancher would not be easy to work with. He was unconvinced the writing in his book was bad, and would surely scrap tooth and nail over every change. Most important, and this was difficult to explain to any writer whose ego was involved, if I wanted to ghostwrite another book — getting no public credit for the work — it would not be one whose popular potential was limited at best. The books to ghostwrite, to throw yourself into over a long period of time, were ones involving important events or people. The rancher also failed to understand that a good ghostwriter did not have to spend time on Western novels. It was my fault, in my desire to help a friend of Drury's, that I neglected to mention I didn't need the work. I'd been willing to help if the emotional and personal involvement could be kept to zero; in other words, off by myself, if I could do whatever I thought was necessary to turn the manuscript into a good publishable book.

"It's best we just forget about it," I said.

"I guess it is," said the rancher. "I'd think you were pulling some kind of fast one — taking two thousand dollars from me — if Drury hadn't vouched for you."

"Well, no hard feelings."

"None at all for my part. But you'll see. You've lost out on quite a deal. I'll just send the book on to a couple publishers the way it is. Bet they snap it right up."

How *much* do you want to bet? I was tempted to say. But it was best to let it go.

Drury later said he was sorry it hadn't worked out. I told him I wasn't, and that it had been enjoyable visiting him and Carl Ann. I said I'd better get on to Abilene the next morning — Wednesday — and he said he might see me there. He'd been invited to appear on the anti-drug show.

"Say hello to Jack for me," Drury said.

" I sure will, boy."

Nine

Grimm's all-purpose man, B. J. Billing, Grimm himself, and I were in my room at Kiva Inn. Somehow it had fallen on Grimm to coordinate the arrival — and even the acquisition — of stars for Norman Lear's television *mea culpa,* "Get High on Yourself," and B.J. was doing the detail work. Now he was giving Grimm an update.

"That TV producer we wanted," B.J. said. "He said he'll only come if we can guarantee him a beige room."

"A beige room, you say?" Grimm's voice was low, his eyes dark. A man of near-perpetual motion, he had stopped pacing to try to digest this unpalatable information.

"That's right. It's an easy enough request to . . ."

"What is he, boy? One of *those?*

"I don't know, Jack," said B.J. "Some of these Hollywood people are spoiled. But I think every room in this motel is beige."

"We don't need him, boy. Tell him not to come."

"Right. Now about Ted Nugent, the singer. He's called a couple of times. He *wants* to be here. Thinks it's a good cause."

"Nugent? The loud guy with the bam-bam-bam music?"

"Right. Very popular with young people."

"The one with the hair down to his ass?"

"That's the one. He . . ."

"The one with the tube up his nose?" Grimm would have made a good prosecuting attorney.

"He says he doesn't take drugs any more, Jack."

"Ridiculous. Of course he still takes drugs. Just look at him. This is an *anti*-drug program, B.J."

"Kids will listen to him, Jack."

"I don't want him, boy. Might as well have Dean Martin telling people not to drink."

Other people making guest appearances on the TV show met with more friendly reactions. Morgan Fairchild, Lou Ferrigno. A couple of the Dallas Cowboys Cheerleaders. Roger Staubach. Charley Pride. Cathy Lee Crosby, a former champion Oklahoma tennis player and star of "That's Incredible," would host the TV extravaganza. Grimm said we were having lunch the next day at the Petroleum Club with Cathy Lee.

"Anything else for me?" Grimm asked. He was usually on the go. Poker game with his buddies. Out in the hinterlands checking his oil wells. Rounding up his herd of buffalo, which frequently broke out of its enclosure and went marauding across the land of neighbors.

"That preacher called," B.J. said. "He said God came to him in a dream last night and told him you were going to give him a Lear Jet."

"Well," Grimm spluttered, "God didn't come to me in that dream." With this he was gone, slipping sideways out the door to his Cadillac. I'd detected a pattern to his arrivals and departures. They occurred when you least expected them. He came unannounced and seldom said good-bye. He was just there; then he wasn't.

B.J. drove me in his big van — handy for carrying heavy movie equipment needed for Grimm's film projects — on a tour of Abilene, one much more complete than the one I'd had on my first visit. There were three colleges — Abilene Christian, Hardin-Simmons, McMurry — which meant library facilities would be good. No tall buildings; the highest was an old hotel, maybe twelve stories. Very few parking meters downtown. Later I told a New York friend about the absence of parking meters, which I thought was good. "It's bad," he said. "Means they don't care about raising revenue for poor people."

"*Not* having parking meters is bad?"

"It is in Abilene."

There were a few rundown areas of town, but not many. Certainly no slums to compare to the South Bronx, which for years had looked as if an air raid had just struck. I didn't even see a lot of American flags; Dallas was champion in this area. It wasn't that there were so many flags in Dallas. But the ones you saw were just huge.

Plenty of churches. Big, handsome churches. Tiny churches in disrepair. Much of the religion in Abilene was fundamentalist. B.J., a bulky Vietnam vet, said he was a born-again Christian. He spoke in tongues. He told me he could do it just about any time he wanted and I asked for a demonstration. What came out of his mouth was like nothing I'd ever heard before.

The church B.J. belonged to believed success in business was a sign of God's approbation. Individuals got ahead by giving themselves to Jesus Christ and then asking Him for help. Through the Bible, B.J. believed, you could tell which way the world was going. The State of Israel, he said, was fulfilling many of the prophecies. He said Israel would fight Russia and Israel would win.

We drove past such Abilene landmarks as the home Billy Sol Estes lived in when he wasn't in jail and the home of relatives of actor Robert Redford. "Whenever he comes here," B.J. said, "he tries to keep it a big secret. But word always gets out. You should see the mob scene outside the house."

Set on the grass divider of one of Abilene's main thoroughfares was a glistening white sculpture, evidently someone's idea of art. It resembled a hand with perhaps eleven fingers jutting into the air. Its name, I was told, was "Multiple Erections."

There were plenty of places to buy and drink liquor, and I told B.J. this surprised me. "Thought you fundamentalist folk would keep the area dry," I said.

"It was until recently," he said. "You had to go to Impact to buy booze."

"Impact?"

"A little town outside Abilene."

"Sounds like a rough place."

"It is. Stay away from there."

Impact, Texas. It had a ring to it, sort of like a good John Wayne-type fist right to the chops. I learned of other names that might be warning sensible people away. Bangs, Texas. Deadwood. Bleakwood. Cut'n Shoot. Scurry. Cheapside. Nixon. Muleshoe.

Slide. Tow. Cost. Cyclone. And Crabb. On the other hand, there were Fair Play, Comfort, Utopia (I doubted this), Security, Jolly, Loving, and Pep.

"I guess muggers aren't much of a threat here," I said.

"They're very rare," said B.J. "The big danger here is not getting robbed, but getting killed. Lots of guns around. Pretty tough crowd in some of the bars."

"Who are they?"

"Roughnecks, mostly. They're wild when they come in out of the oil fields. Roustabouts. They're a cut below roughnecks in pay and prestige. But everybody, really. People believe in carrying guns here. Unfortunately, they sometimes get gassed up and use them."

In a sense I really didn't care what Abilene was like. I wanted a quiet place to work, without distractions, and Abilene certainly wasn't any Entertainment Capital. I thought it would be interesting driving Grimm's pickup to the grocery store every day or so.

Besides, it would just be for a year. It would be good to get away from the reality and memories of the East for a while. I had been divorced for two years — after twenty years of marriage — and had four kids, three in their upper teens, one in his early twenties. My only daughter (second youngest of the brood) was living with me in New York and working there. Oldest son had a job in California. The two youngest boys were nineteen and seventeen, and the nineteen-year-old, just graduated from high school, would probably like to come to Abilene on one of those scholarships Grimm had promised as part of the inducement for the move. I suspected my daughter might prefer staying in New York, which she had loved at first sight, and where she had a good job and was planning to attend night school. She could get a roommate or two and take over the apartment.

I spent the evening watching TV in my Kiva Inn room, enjoying the rest, shuddering when I thought of the Dallas boys, imagining all the work I could get done in this small, slow-pace town. Grimm was on the 10 P.M. local news, greeting some celebrity or other at the airport. I laughed out loud when I saw the familiar sideways walk.

The Petroleum Club each lunch hour throws an excellent buffet, $7.50 I believe, and you can eat all you want of steamship roast beef, baked ham, fresh baked fish, fruit, vegetables, warm rolls, salad, and dessert. Or you can order from the menu. Cathy Lee

Crosby and Penny Tower, daughter of Senator John Tower, were at the table with Grimm, B.J., and me; only Grimm had ordered from the menu.

Penny Tower's job was hard to describe. She seemed to be a go-fer for Cathy Lee, learning about the TV business while generally making herself useful.

Cathy Lee Crosby was always "on." Cheerful, a big smile never leaving her face. This wholesome former tennis player radiates sincerity. She said she was "thrilled" to be doing "Get High On Yourself," because years before she'd had a problem with drugs. Cathy Lee was clear-eyed, fresh-faced, scrubbed, an All-American girl it was impossible to believe ever had a problem. She resembled Chris Evert Lloyd, another tennis player, though Cathy Lee's features were cleaner.

Diners kept coming to the table for introductions and autographs, and Grimm knew them all. His face would light up in a grin, then he would introduce them as "R.R." something, or T.M., or F.P. Most of the oil boys went by initials. Their roughnecks or other oil field workers had two names: Jimmie Joe, Fred Bob, Billy Ben, etc. Jimmie Joe graduated to J.J. if he struck out on his own and succeeded.

They were all Grimm's friends, and he was happy to see them. The scene kept repeating itself. Smile spreading across Grimm's face, hearty handshake and how are ya, and then an introduction to Cathy Lee. Her way of saying hello made a person feel she had been waiting for this instant her entire life. It made you feel good.

Most of those who came to the table were oil men, though there were bankers also. In New York businessmen dressed like bankers. In Abilene, bankers dressed like oil men. I thought it said something about who was running this lashup.

The meal was almost finished when Grimm's face broke into the biggest smile of all. This had to be someone important, I thought. His friend Nelson Bunker Hunt, visiting the provinces? Maybe Senator John Tower, lending his presence to his daughter's cause?

"One of the Winset boys," Grimm said proudly, leading him over to Cathy Lee. She was alert, smiling, obviously delighted to meet this notable, but the name hadn't set off bells.

"Biggest gun dealer in America," Jack clarified. His face shone with happiness. Cathy Lee's did also. I looked hard, but couldn't find a trace of disappointment behind her eyes.

Jack Grimm is a man easily bored. Looking for the *Titanic* might be enough adventure for most men in a lifetime, but it wasn't even enough *at the time* for Grimm. He had B.J. and that religious group stirring things up in China while he searched the North Atlantic, and from the ship's radio kept track of his considerable fortune, a task which by itself would be too much for most people. In short, Jack liked to keep a number of balls in the air at all times. Even his frequent gambling in Abilene and Las Vegas could be classified as business: he was such a skilled, shrewd gambler he seemed seldom to lose.

Jack hated for people not to be busy. Especially did he dislike it when someone was living off him, as I was on this trip to Abilene. He was shouldering the bill at Kiva Inn. He had heard me say I thought B.J.'s China adventure, which he was lucky to survive, passing out Bibles as he had right under the noses of Red officials, would make an interesting book. When we left the Petroleum Club, he asked if such a book would make money.

"Sure," I said. "It could have B.J.'s impressions of China. One of the first Americans to visit there since the revolution. Meeting John Denver doesn't hurt. Plenty of adventure. Then Tibet and Tenzing Norgay. Finally, trying to get out of China without a twenty-year layover in jail. Plenty of good material for a book. B.J. took some beautiful pictures. They'd help."

"How do we sell it?"

"You write ten or twelve pages telling what the book will be about, how exciting it is. Emphasize how much money the publisher will make. Literature, as the saying goes, can wait. Send the pages to my agent. He'll try to get an editor interested."

"Why don't you write this book?"

"It's B.J.'s story. Besides, I've got *Titanic* to do. And a novel."

"Do three books, boy. Make something of yourself." I'd heard this last line from him before.

"I don't want three books hanging over my head. I guess I'll just keep plugging along."

Grimm grew thoughtful. We were standing between two battered pickup trucks in the Petroleum Club parking lot. I could tell he was disappointed in my lack of ambition.

"Think B.J. could write the book?" he finally said.

"Why not?" I said. "He's a bright guy. He knows the story. No one's written a book until they've written one."

"Would you do those ten or twelve pages you talked about?"

"I guess so." Besides the cost of the motel, I had been running up a healthy tab on food. "We could do it in my room at Kiva."

"You're a good boy, boy," he said affectionately. "B.J.," he called out. B.J. was standing over by his van, waiting for us to conclude so he could drive me back to the motel.

"B.J.," he said, "I want you to do some writing with Bill this afternoon. We're gonna make you an author."

"How's that?" He didn't seem excited by the prospect. Or maybe he was simply leery of Grimm's promises. After all, a pledge to put him "on top of the world" had meant not money or prestige but a dangerous trip to China and Tibet.

"You need to work with Bill," Grimm said. "About the China trip. He's going to write something we'll try to sell to a publisher. If we do, you can work on the book itself later."

"I've got a lot of arrangements to make for incoming people," B.J. protested. "Also, ones who are already here. They expect you to plump their pillows for them. Hold their hands. Prove you love them by being at their beck and call. I've never seen such an insecure bunch."

"Do it from Bill's room, boy. Use his phone. Use your legs if anybody needs something. Everybody's staying at Kiva Inn, right?"

"Right." B.J. wasn't at all happy with developments.

"Well, men," said Grimm, "get on with it." This was a surprise. He seldom addressed people as "men." You could be 100 years old and still be "boy" to him. Women, in the same vein, including two 80-year-olds I saw in his office, were "girls." When Grimm started using the word "men," it meant money was involved.

B.J. had to round up a typewriter, paper, and correction fluid, and it was 4 P.M. before we were in the room ready to start. A book outline, as the ten or twelve pages are called, is very difficult to write, because it has to be just about perfect. You're trying to persuade a publisher to advance money on the project, and especially in the case of a new author like B.J., there is very little on which to judge his ability. Thus the need for the outline to be excellent. I told B.J. if the book were sold and he had trouble writing it, I would help, but that I was confident he could do it on his own.

Anyway, we set up the typewriter and started to work. The process was slow, and not speeded any by B.J. having to be on the phone performing his regular chores for Grimm. Normal air transportation, even first class, wasn't good enough for a number of the stars. They insisted on a private jet or they wouldn't come.

The process was also hard. The writing and the story had to capture an editor's attention immediately. Numerous beginnings were started and rejected.

Grimm came into the room unannounced at 7 P.M., walking fast but sideways. I was hunched over the typewriter. B.J. was next to me, trying to remember if the head of the Praise the Lord Construction Company, who was along on the China trip, was also a minister.

"Finished yet?" Grimm asked.

"Finished?" I said. We had scarcely started.

"Don't get excited, boy," Grimm soothed. "You said ten or twelve pages. I thought you might be done by now."

"Well, we're not."

"Fine. Just stay after it. B.J., how are we coming on guests?"

"It might be cheaper to pay them. Everyone wants to travel in Louie the Fourteenth splendor. Private jet. Air fare and accommodations for girl friends. Limo service while they're here. The whole nine yards."

"Louie the Fourteenth didn't have jets and limousines." I could see Grimm was growing hot.

"That's what they want," B.J. said. "If *we* want *them,* that's what we'll have to provide."

"Damn," said Grimm. "Reminds me of a boy who used to work for me. Sent him to New York to negotiate a movie deal. He was staying in this big room cost a hundred dollars a day. I called him, said I never stayed in a room cost more than thirty. And I'm the boss. 'Get your ass out of that room,' I said. He said he had claustrophobia. Needed a big room. I told him, 'I'm not paying for your claustrophobia. Have claustrophobia in a smaller place.' Told him to get out of that room or find someone else to work for. Claustrophobia, he said. Can you believe that?"

Jack didn't wait for an answer. Thinking about the celebrities and beige rooms, that claustrophobic employee, and perhaps the cost of my motel room, he was gone as suddenly as he came. He had been pacing back and forth, to the door, to the typewriter straight back from the door, back to the door. Once when he paced to the door he simply opened it and kept going. To the airport, I guess, because he was on the 10 P.M news again.

"Grimm always worried about details?" I asked.

"When money is involved," B.J. said. "He can be wildly generous, like those scholarships he's offered your kids, or buying a lot of scientific gear for Columbia University. But he can be tight, too. I was at a convention in New York with him. You had to pay $25 to get a badge to go onto the convention floor. He bought one for himself. Wouldn't buy one for me. He said I could wear his, go onto the floor when he wasn't there. The next day a lot of people thought I was Jack Grimm, because I'd been wearing his identification."

We were still working at 11 P.M. when Grimm came in again, looking over his shoulder as if he were being followed. "Finished yet?" he said.

"No!" I said. "And it doesn't help for . . ."

"Cool your water, boy. I was joking."

Not completely, I thought. Grimm wanted things done in a hurry. For a moment I felt sorry for that sculptor who was going to be hanging from the side of Jack's mountain, carving that sculpture four times the size of Mount Rushmore. "Finished yet?" I could hear Grimm shouting up to him through a bullhorn.

"Just came by," Grimm said, "to find out if you knew what is in back of your room."

"An army of armadillos?" I said.

"Not far wrong. Come on. I'll show you."

In back of our wing of the motel, one after another in a long fearful line, stood perhaps one hundred huge tanks. Mammoth tanks. I couldn't imagine their having gotten here without our knowing it. The one directly behind my room was perhaps fifteen feet from the back wall.

"Abilene expecting the Russians?" I asked.

"They'd have a helluva time taking this town, wouldn't they?"

"Why are these here? The boys trading in their pickups for these? Or have you just bought your own tank brigade?"

"We've got a military base here."

"I thought it was Air Force."

"Well, boy, I don't know why they're here. Just felt you'd like to see 'em. Make you feel secure."

"I felt secure *before* I saw them."

Grimm ignored this. "I gotta be on my way," he said. "But don't worry. I won't forget you're here."

"What does that mean?" I asked B.J.

"It means he'll keep visiting till that outline's done."

"Does he think his stopping by helps?"

"It probably does. Don't you want to finish so he'll stop asking if you're finished?"

"You've got a point. But he won't be happy later if we've finished in a hurry and the thing doesn't sell."

We worked until almost 1 A.M. I slept soundly, woke at seven, checked and was pleased to learn the tanks had left as silently as they'd arrived, and was eating a room service breakfast when B.J. arrived at eight. He told me he'd stopped by Cathy Lee Crosby's room, which was the hub around which the entire TV show wheel revolved. "She was eating breakfast in bed," B.J. said. "Charley Pride was sitting there, strumming a guitar and singing."

We went back to work. B.J. tried to keep his telephone calls to a minimum, and word by word the outline began to take shape. "Like pulling teeth," B.J. said, an apt analogy. My back was hurting, always a sign I'm working hard, and I had the good concentration that indicates something readable might come out of all this.

Jack Grimm came in at 11, in a hurry as usual, but this time his demeanor radiated concern and earnestness.

"How's it going, men?"

"Jack," I said, "it would be better if you didn't stop by so often to check."

"I'm just interested, boy. I can see you're a perfectionist."

"It will be done when it's done," I said.

"How many pages have you got?"

"Jack, we'll show it to you when it's finished."

But he had already snatched up what was completed. Shock and dismay registered on his face.

"*Three pages?* You've only got three pages?" You could tell he was trying to figure out what was wrong.

"It will get done," I said. "Leave us alone." But even as I talked I knew he had another solution.

"Type faster, boy," he said.

"Jack . . ."

"Why, my secretaries type faster than you do."

"Get your secretaries to write this outline," I said.

But he was gone. Out the door to a poker game or an oil well or somewhere. He'd solved the problem. Type faster.

"Can't you see this guy with Shakespeare?" B.J. said. "He'd ask, 'Does this play *Hamlet* have to take so long to write, boy'?"

"Grimm means well," I said. "I suppose he does."

We stayed after it until seven that evening, my typing speed increasing slightly, but the outline still wasn't completed when Grimm once again broke our momentum.

"B.J.," he said magnanimously, "it's Friday night. Why not go home and enjoy your family? You and Bill can start up again in the morning."

"We're going to dinner, boy," he said to me after B.J. was gone. "Royal Inn. They have right good food there. Taking Cathy Lee and Penny Tower and my wife Jackie along."

Royal Inn was only a couple hundred yards east of Kiva, but Grimm drove it very fast. The waiter showed us to a table, and we were in the *process* of sitting down when the oil man offered his menu preference: "The fried catfish looks good to me, boys."

The fried catfish was the least expensive item on the menu at $3.95, though Grimm later swore that had nothing to do with his recommendation. Regardless, the three women — Cathy Lee Crosby, Penny Tower, Jackie Grimm — who had just been called boys, ignored the tycoon's dining tip and ordered meals in the $12-$15 category. Grimm and I ate catfish, which could not be confused with the lobster on Cathy Lee Crosby's plate. The next evening, Saturday, Grimm paid for dinner at another restaurant, *sans* menu recommendation. That evening was notable because we met a young lady outside the restaurant who clearly was unhappy — it turned out she had been stood up by a date — and although he had never met her, Grimm invited her to eat with us.

On Saturday morning B.J. and I finished the book outline. It was still 24 hours to the filming of the TV show on a big spread called the Perini Ranch, and another 24 hours after that until I'd be back in New York. B.J. had everything as "sewn up" as he could where the celebrities were involved, and left for an outing with his family. I figured Grimm would show up and was right. He came through the door at 1 P.M.

"Do you know a bookmaker?" I asked. Of course he knew a bookmaker.

"I might. What you got in mind?"

"The football game tonight." It was a preseason exhibition, the last before regular play began, for "the championship of Texas" between the Houston Oilers and Dallas Cowboys. Dallas was favored by 6½ points in the Astrodome. I figured Houston would be "up" for the game against its more famous rival. Besides, "the championship of Texas" sounded like a close, hard-fought game that wouldn't be decided by more than 6½ points.

"What team do you like?" Grimm said. His attention might wander on other subjects, he might in fact just leave, but gambling was an important matter for which he always had time.

"Houston," I said. "With six and a half points."

His face, expressive under any circumstances, took on the look of someone who might just have heard his best friend was committing suicide.

"I like Dallas, boy," he said.

He was touting me onto Dallas. Well, I thought insanely, that's good. What does he know? I was still irked at the pounding he'd administered at poker on the Titanic expedition.

"That's what makes a horse race," I said foolishly.

"I'm betting on Dallas, boy," he said.

Good, I thought. *It will be sweet to win while you lose.* Actually, the Mad Hatter was rational compared to me. Here was one of the best gamblers in the world — he had proved it finishing second in the World Series of Poker — giving me a tip, and I was sneering at him. "I think it will be a close game," I said. "My hunch is as good as yours." Even at the time I wondered if I could really be saying this.

"I talked with Roger this morning," Grimm said. I assumed this was former Cowboy quarterback Roger Staubach, in town for the TV program. "Roger says the Cowboys are ready."

"Why are you telling me all this?"

"I like you, boy. I want you to win. Bet on the Cowboys."

"I'll stay with Houston."

"Well, boy, I always say if someone wants to throw money away, you might as well stand in the way and catch it. Why don't I book the bet for you?"

"I don't want to win money from you."

"Don't worry about that."

"I'd rather bet with a bookmaker."

"I can't change your mind? About the bet, that is. I'd like your stay in Abilene to be a happy one. I'm telling you, the Cowboys will be rougher than a corncob on a bare behind."

"We'll see," I said.

And of course we did. The Houston Oilers, except for the heroic Earl Campbell, were terrible. The Cowboys scored early and often that Saturday night, and sitting alone in my Kiva Inn room there wasn't even the *hope* of a last minute rally to overcome the point spread. Midway through the third quarter I walked in disgust over to the Kiva Inn lounge and drank beer.

I told the story later to a New York friend of mine who previously had thought moving to Abilene would be a mistake. "Go," he now said. "Go right away. *You* may hate it, but *I'll* love it. Here's all you do. Pick a football team you like. Really like. You're hardly ever right. Then see if Grimm likes the other team. He's hardly ever wrong. If he likes the other team, the combination should be unbeatable. Call me and tell me about it. I'll be rich."

Everything went wrong at the TV extravaganza at the Perini Ranch. Someone who was not thinking — I believe it was Cathy Lee Crosby — decided the press could not attend. Now this was a big event for Abilene. Stars everywhere. I had been a newspaperman, and I knew what banning the press meant: reporters would find a way to sneak in, but their stories would not be leavened with any kindness to the whole affair. Even heavy police or private guard security, which obviously the TV network did not want to employ, would not have kept enterprising reporters out. As it was, anyone who wanted to get in got in, but not in the mood the promoters of the affair would have liked.

The Abilene *Reporter-News* ran the toughest story. The writer pointed out that an anti-drug program was well and good, but what kind of example was set, he asked, when many of the stars — urging youngsters to stay off drugs — were bellying up to the bar in the beer tent.

That Sunday evening was spent at Grimm's house. He cooked steaks for me and another friend, Jackie and himself, and when it came time to serve them he was so engrossed talking about the *Titanic* expedition — he was convinced he had photographed a propeller from the mighty ship — that he carried the steaks over to the table *with his bare hands* and dealt them onto our plates as he might a deck of cards.

I kept looking at him curiously throughout the meal. "What's the matter, boy?" he finally asked.

"Don't your hands hurt?"

"Why should they? You think I'm making too much money?"

"That's a different subject," I said. But evidently his hands didn't hurt. And he didn't seem to be aware, just as he wasn't when he was always finding money on the ground, that anything was out of the ordinary.

Jackie Grimm read a lot, a habit she surely hadn't picked up from Jack, and we talked about books that night. Grimm, impatient, kept leaving the room for forays into his backyard. A couple times I heard the car start and he drove off briefly on unknown missions. I thought that one night it might be interesting to follow him. See where he went.

The next morning he drove me to the airport. I had a ticket for Dallas to New York, but none from Abilene to Dallas. Grimm insisted on paying for it, and asked if I were going to move to Abilene. I said I probably would. I had to go to Tampa, Florida, I told him, to help someone with a book, but after that I suspected I'd be back.

"That's good, boy," he said. "We'll be waiting for you. We'll make a Texan out of you, just like I promised."

Ten

Once I started telling friends of my intention to move to Texas, I began hearing and being shown stories about my home-to-be, some of them funny, all of them weird. My own impression of the state after my ten-day visit was confused. I hadn't liked a lot of what I'd seen in Dallas — the frantic, nonstop hustling, the preoccupation with getting and spending — but surely I hadn't seen the entire picture. Most of what I recalled of Houston — besides Drury's good company — was heat and sapping humidity. Abilene, which would be most important, was Jack Grimm, a one-of-a-kind I didn't think I'd get tired of watching. And quiet. Quiet was what I told myself I could use a year of.

Everybody had a Texas story. A Lyndon Johnson hater told me the departed president's real campaign song had been "Sweet George R. Brown," a reference to the Houston construction king who bankrolled much of LBJ's political activity and was rewarded with fat government building contracts, particularly in Vietnam.

Lyndon, to be sure, had been something else. He once had a telephone conversation with the black chauffeur of insurance magnate Gus Wortham, a man named Lester. "Do you know who this is?" Johnson asked. Lester said he did not. "This is the President, Lester," Johnson said. The chauffeur seemed unimpressed.

"Lester," said Johnson, "what does it feel like to be talking to the President of the United States?"

Another friend, a lover of grandiose schemes, told me of a plan favored by the Texas rich and their politicians to bring the Mississippi River to Texas. It was to be diverted from Louisiana, and with John Connally serving as co-chairman, an illustrious Committee of 500 was formed to bring the plan to fruition. No one bothered to ask Louisiana if it had objections, but the final shock came when voters refused to approve the necessary bonds.

My agent, a native Texan, had subscribed to *Texas Monthly* magazine for several years, and from its pages came an idea of the Lone Star State's endemic whackiness. There was U.S. Congressman Dale Milford explaining Russian Roulette: "One loads up the cylinder of a revolver with bullets in all cartridge holes but one." State Representative T.H. McDonald, who objected to switching capital punishment from electrocution to lethal injection because he didn't think criminals should get off with a slap on the wrist. Mayor Woodrow Glasscock of Hondo, who, when his town was turned down for federal aid because there weren't enough unemployed, asked President Carter for 180 "welfare-collecting loafers" he could get to move to his town. In Corpus Christi, the city council sued every resident of the town because voters had placed a limit on the tax rate. A San Antonio company marketed a game called "Slick," which contained "authentic Mexican crude scooped off of Texas beaches," with instructions to pour it into swimming pools. Alpine police chief Ace Moseley resigned, saying he was disgusted with courts that released drug dealers, then was indicted for possession and conspiracy to sell marijuana. The city of Waco decided to reduce its crime rate by reporting fewer crimes to the FBI. State Representative Clay Smothers, worried about funding abortions for rape victims, wondered if hysterectomies couldn't be used instead. Cleveland, Texas, wanted to throw a New Year's Eve party, but couldn't decide on a date. When Governor William Clements heard that skin diving could damage a fetus, he wondered if the sport might be a good means of birth control. State Representative Bill Heatly, arguing for a $53,000 elevator in a two-story National Guard headquarters, said "Those generals are the only thing between us and Khrushchev." An El Paso florist's Valentine's Day billboard: "GET YOUR SWEETIE SOMETHING FOR VD." And the Public Utility Commission staff recommending that the phone company receive a higher rate increase than it requested.

Actually, I thought, where the venality of politicians, servility of bureaucrats, and greed of the rich were concerned, Texas probably wasn't worse than anywhere else; the state was just more open about it, had less to fear from an alert press. The Texas boys had not yet found it necessary to hire slick public relations firms to put a smooth face on whatever they did. After all, wasn't Texas almost a separate country?

The state was an independent republic from 1836 to 1845, when it joined the union. Texas would be even larger than it now is if in 1850 it hadn't sold all or part of what is Wyoming, Colorado, New Mexico, and Montana to the U.S. for $10 million. By constitutional provision, Texas can divide itself into five separate states, and has the right to maintain its own Navy. This independence, perhaps more imagined than real, contributes to a we'll-do-it-our-way attitude less restrained than in other areas of the nation.

The Texas landscape, I knew, was no feast for the eyes, but that was not a consideration in my decision to move. Pretty scenery, despite popular conceptions, can distract a writer as much as it can help. Yet Texas would be stark. Before the Civil War, the U.S. Army attempted to use camels in arid West Texas, but the terrain there, unlike Mideast deserts, was too rugged for them.

Arrangements had to be made before I was free to move. First I had to go to Tampa where I was being paid a fee plus expenses to see if I could shape up a manuscript about a sea disaster that had recently occurred. The Coast Guard ship *Blackthorn* had gone down in Tampa Bay with an appalling loss of life, and a member of the commission investigating the disaster had written a scathing account of Coast Guard negligence. He'd heard about me from Jack Cosgrove, one of the cameramen filming the *Titanic* movie. Other members of the movie crew in Tampa included Mike Harris, Nik Petrik, and my blackjack-playing buddy, Bobby Blanco.

"Have you met the boys yet?" Bobby wanted to know.

"Not the ones Grimm refers to," I said.

"You're really moving to Abilene?"

"You think it's a mistake?"

"It's a disaster. Every penny you make writing, and then some, will go into Grimm's pocket in poker games."

"No chance. Besides, I couldn't afford to get in his poker games.

He bets more on the turn of a card than I bet in a year. He just played us to keep from getting bored."

Bobby had decided that this fall he would make his fortune wagering on football games. I told him about losing the Cowboys/Oilers game, and he called me "mucho" crazy. "You got a tip from Grimm, Mr. Bucks himself, and bet the other way?" Bobby shook his head sadly. "If that pirate would give me tips," he said, "I'd hock everything I own."

"I'm looking to get even," I said. "What team are you betting this weekend?"

"You'll listen to me, but not Grimm? You need a psychiatrist, not a bookmaker."

"Look," I said, "leave me alone. What does Grimm know that we don't? We're smarter than he is." I remembered this being said several times before, always to my regret.

Bobby finally told me he was betting on the Oakland Raiders, giving 1½ points to the Minnesota Vikings. He agreed to get my wager placed, and said we could watch the game at the home of a friend of his, Arnold. I remembered Arnold. He had to be a good friend of Bobby's. He had flown from Florida to Massachusetts to greet Bobby when the *Gyre* docked in Boston, bringing a case of liquor, smoking a big cigar, and passing out a business card that said he was available for clearing out bars and assassinations.

"Can't we watch the game somewhere else?" I said.

"Arnold likes you," Bobby said.

"I'm glad of that."

"He's all right, and we'll have a good time. You'll get back the money you lost in Abilene."

The work on the *Blackthorn* book took only a day, but Mike Harris, chief of the movie crew aboard the *Gyre,* called the motel to say he wanted me to visit "a lawyer who represented Hoffa. He knows stuff about Hoffa you wouldn't believe."

It was a story, I thought, that might really be worthwhile. You never knew. But certainly it was worth a visit. It wasn't a Western novel written by a retired rancher.

Cosgrove, Harris, and I went to the lawyer's house, a big place in an exclusive area of Tampa, swimming pool, expensive furniture, and I recognized him immediately. His picture had been in *Time* magazine, and he had been surrounded, I recall, by people the press called "mobsters." That was all right, if he had a good story. My sister, the Notre Dame nun, did not know what had happened to Hoffa.

For several years now the lawyer had been suspended from his practice of law. I wondered, but discreetly didn't ask, how he afforded his plush residence. That didn't worry me. I did get a little edgy when he mentioned he had represented Santos Trafficante, reputedly known as "Concrete Shoes" for the way he allegedly deep-sixed competitors in Tampa bay. Trafficante, a friend of Meyer Lansky, was not a person with whom to trifle.

But it all must have been a mixup. The lawyer, alluding frequently to his friendship with Hoffa, wanted a screenplay, not a book, and he also wanted to know how to raise money for a film. I told him he should go for a book first, then a movie, but he swore up and down that he knew "the order should be reversed. Everybody will read the book, then no one will want to see the picture." There is no arguing with a person who is not right but is sure. I didn't try very hard. The story might be a good one, but the mere mention of the name Santos Trafficante dampened my enthusiasm.

I stayed in Tampa two more days, going to a party with Nik Petrik, to dinner with Bobby Blanco (at Busch Gardens — Bobby once had been its manager), and to Jack Cosgrove's home to see the underwater photography he hoped to make into a book. It was good to be with "normal" people. Except for the lawyer, there had been no continuous chain of odd characters, such as encountered in Texas. I'd like to have seen Fred Satterfield, for example, or Art the Oil Man, cutting a deal with Santos Trafficante.

Arnold, of course, was different. He too lived in an expensive house, and said his job was to train guard dogs. "The more vicious the better." The dogs guarded the houses of rich people, and Arnold used them to provide security at rock concerts. His pride and joy, which kept growling at me, lived in the house.

"Can't you put him outside?" I asked.

"He won't hurt you unless you upset him."

"What if I upset him?"

"Don't."

The dog got upset when I cheered an Oakland touchdown, and Arnold stopped him, seemingly in mid-air, as he was about to attack. "Let's get out of here," I whispered to Bobby the first time Arnold left the room.

"It would hurt Arnold's feelings," Bobby said.

Oakland rolled up touchdown after touchdown, but an observer might have thought I was losing the bet, so much was I determined to maintain silence and not disturb the German Shepherd — named Cuddles — which was at least the size of a full-grown wolf.

Back in New York there were important arrangements to be made before the move to Abilene. My daughter was delighted to be getting her own place; I made her promise to get a suitable roommate, preferably two, or she'd never make it in that apartment. The rent was typically New York outrageous, and Con Ed, the light company, has the highest rates in the nation. During the summer when the air-conditioning is running, the amount of the electric bill more resembles what people in most other parts of the country pay for rent. Con Ed was a sore point with me anyway. While doing an article about the company, I discovered it was able to get *millions of dollars* in tax refunds *despite not paying taxes*. The New York Public Service Commission, like the one in Texas, like the ones everywhere, was simply a rubber stamp for the utilities.

Incidentally, after I moved to Texas, a move was afoot to *elect* members of the Public Utility Commission. One major newspaper was shocked. "This is too sensitive a matter," the paper editorialized, "to leave to the whims of the voters." Right. So for that matter, I guessed, was the election of a president.

My son Joe, professing to love small towns, wanted to come along to Abilene and take advantage of Grimm's scholarship offer. Joe was 19, a tall husky youngster, a good athlete, and it was good to know I wouldn't be completely alone. So eager was he to leave that I sent him on ahead. Grimm said he would look after him until I got there.

Acclimating my agent to the fact that I would be a thousand miles away was important to accomplish before I left. The opinion expressed in F. Scott Fitzgerald's will, asking to be cremated and for ten percent of his ashes to be thrown into his agent's face, and comments about the only thing being smaller than a flea's navel is an agent's heart, did not really apply to my literary representative. What I had to do was make sure he could handle my business while I wasn't there. In New York, if an editor wanted to know something about an article or book, I could go see him. Obviously, this wouldn't be possible in Abilene, though my agent assured me there were phones in Texas.

"Don't be a wise guy," I said.

"You act like you're going to another planet."

"I was down there. I saw."

"I *lived* there," he said. I had forgotten that.

"Well, I just want things to keep going as if I were here."

"If my clients don't make money, I don't make money."

"Just work hard," I said. Already I sounded like Grimm.

I had some people I wanted to see before leaving. One was Alan Sontag. I'd written a couple of books with Alan. He is one of the best bridge players in the world, holder of numerous national and international championships, and makes a very fine living indeed doing nothing but playing and teaching bridge. Often he had visited Dallas to practice with that city's great bridge team, the Aces.

We met for lunch at the Bedford and I sat on a chair John Steinbeck often had used. The waiters were old and for some reason liked me, and I always heard Steinbeck stories at the Bedford. He and Robert Capa, the photographer, did books together. Capa was responsible for the best war pictures ever taken. He would photograph the GIs in battle, capturing images of what combat really entailed, which irritated some of his bosses. "Can't you ever get a picture of a general?" they would ask. Capa, always taking risks, was killed by a land mine in Vietnam.

Sontag was a born-and-raised New Yorker. Civilization ended for him at the city's borders. He had a great apartment, in the building used for George and Louise in "The Jeffersons," and hated leaving it and the city for bridge tournaments, though it was necessary to maintain his world-class status in the game.

"Texas," he said. "Tell me it isn't true."

"No muggers," I said.

"No fun," he said.

"Muggers are fun?"

"No. Texas isn't. You can't write in Texas. You need mental stimulation, people with whom you can knock around ideas. Texas has oil types and cowboys."

"They wouldn't like you, either."

"Good. I'd be doing something wrong if they did. Look, Hoffman, this will pass away. I'm going on a bridge cruise. The Caribbean. I get paid for giving bridge lessons a couple hours a day. The rest of the time is take it easy in the sun. Come with me. I can swing it so it's free. Pretty girls. Ocean air. Your mind will clear."

"I was on my cruise for the summer."

"Looking for the *Titanic?* Cold water and icebergs? Come on."

"Well, I'm going. Just thought I'd tell you I won't be seeing you for a year."

"I give it a month."

Sontag was no help at all. I caught a cab uptown to Central Park, to Tavern on the Green, where I'd asked Marty Reisman to meet me for a beer. Marty was a good friend. He had been perhaps the greatest table tennis player of all time, for four years gave exhibitions at the halftime of Harlem Globetrotter basketball games, and was much better known in Asia and Europe, where the game is very popular, than in the United States.

Many times I had stayed until early morning in Marty's ping-pong establishment, watching a dazzling array of characters come and go. Tennis player and hustler Bobby Riggs would drop in for ping-pong lessons; he had a money match scheduled for somewhere, and came to Reisman to be prepared. Bobby Fischer, former world chess champion, liked to gamble in Marty's place. He would spot opponents a rook, or a rook and a knight, and then play with them for money. Every sort of hustler came to Reisman's. If there was anything you thought you were good at, you could find someone to gamble with on it. Trouble is, the person being played was probably among the best in the world. There were sharks at gin, pool, poker, Scrabble, pinball machines, penny tossing, drinking beer fast, and horse race handicapping. And especially table tennis. The best players in America lay in wait to take your money. If the stakes were particularly high, Reisman himself might emerge from some dark corner, spot an opponent eighteen points in a game to twenty-one, and annihilate him.

Reisman's table tennis emporium represented a genuine subculture of people in New York. Like Sontag, Reisman had written a book with me. I spent a lot of time in his place, and continued to visit when the book was completed. Actor Art Carney was another who found the atmosphere irresistible. He was too smart to bet with anyone. Walter Matthau was different. He played in marathon poker sessions originating from Marty's.

Reisman, of course, was the ultimate gambler. I would like to have seen him against Grimm. Probably the two would avoid each other. There were too many easy marks to waste time butting heads with an expert. Reisman was also a hustler *par excellence*. Hustling was in his blood. He had plenty of money, the fruits of years of betting on himself at ping-pong and running a successful business, but he couldn't resist a well-timed scam. One of his favorites was standing on a New York sidewalk next to some furniture that had just been discarded by an apartment dweller. Invariably a passerby would stop to ask the price of the furniture, and Reisman would sell it to him, but not until first establishing a fair price.

Marty was sitting at a table wearing a beret. He was perhaps the slimmest man I'd ever known, and the most graceful. He could hit a ping-pong ball more than a hundred miles an hour, play the game with his feet and defeat most opponents. He was about fifty years old now, with a bad complexion from having spent his life indoors, but was in far better shape than most men.

"Today ended a terrible ordeal for me," Marty said.

"You lose a bet?" Nothing terrible ever happened to Marty.

"Be serious, will you? I still can't believe it happened."

"Tell me." The story was bound to be a good one. The only trouble Marty ever had came from dealing with a world that didn't revolve around table tennis or gambling. With anything else he couldn't cope.

"You know my place got broken into a couple months ago?"

"You told me."

"It was worse than I said." His face was so sincere that I had to discipline myself not to laugh. Although surely the story was not funny to him, I was certain it would be to anyone else. And I didn't know what the story was yet. I did know Marty.

"What happened?" I said.

"Well, the day after I was robbed, I had to leave the place on an errand. Two cops were walking past the door. I told them I'd been robbed the night before, and asked if in the course of their rounds they'd keep a special eye out. They said sure. I was grateful and handed one of them three dollars. Whooom! Bam! Next thing I know I'm up against a wall and the handcuffs are on."

Giving a New York cop money is so common that I figured their captain must have read the riot act to the two patrolmen, demanding that some token arrests be made to mollify the press. That they were honest I really did not consider seriously. Serpico was so rare as an honest New York cop that a movie was made about him. But my analysis, leaping ahead of Reisman's story, was wrong.

"They drove me around Central Park. One said to the other, 'This clown must think we come awful cheap. Three dollars! I ought to shove that three dollars up his ass.' And the other cop says, 'We could just shoot this cheap bastard and dump him in the park. Nobody would be the wiser.' I want to tell you, Bill, I was scared. These guys were tough. So I said, 'Listen, I'm not really cheap. I made a mistake with you fellows. I've got a lot of money in my wallet. I'll give you $50. $100. $150. You don't even have to watch my place'."

Now the story was taking shape. I had for years been amazed by Marty's incredible sophistication as a gambler, hustler, and athlete, and his inability to grasp most other areas of life.

"The cop said, 'A hundred and fifty dollars, that's more like it. We'll have to check it out with the sergeant, of course. He's part of any deal we make.' I breathed easier. Figured I'd saved my life for $150, a bargain. We drove to the back of the police station and one of the cops got out and went in to talk to the sergeant. I was still handcuffed. After a long time the cop came back. He said the deal was on. He said he would take off the handcuffs, and I was to walk around to the front of the police station and make the payoff. The sergeant would be there. I'd recognize him."

Good old Marty. I was sure what had to happen could only have happened to him.

"So I met this big guy out in front. It was real bright out there, plenty of light. I gave him the money. Whooom! Bam! I'm back against the wall with the cuffs on. Now they had me on felony bribery charges. The $3 was just a misdemeanor. Those damn bright lights: they filmed the whole transaction. My goose was cooked."

"Sounds like they solicited you to commit a crime," I said. But I knew that in New York this sort of reasoning was naive.

"Sure they did. But they didn't tell the story the way it happened. They had me. I was trying to bribe a cop. The whole mess finally was settled this morning. My lawyer knew the judge and got the case kicked out."

"You should be happy."

"Happy? The lawyer charged $2,500. I start out paying a lousy $3, and end up losing $2,500. More, actually. Had to pay a bondsman to bail me out that night."

"Live and learn," I said. What could I say?

"Why does it always happen to me? Remember when I took the karate lessons?"

How could I forget? Marty, razor thin, had thought he'd better toughen up in case he had to throw an undesirable out of his establishment. For years he'd had no trouble, but when word got out he was taking karate lessons, it seemed the entire neighborhood wanted to challenge him. After a while he decided it was time to show what he could do. Facing off against a particularly rough specimen, he turned himself into a human pinball, preparatory to delivering a devastating kick. Marty missed his opponent and shattered his leg against a wall.

"I wanted to tell you," I said, "I'm moving to Texas for a year. Won't be around your place for a while. I'll miss it."

"Texas. I once beat a guy out of a lot of money there."

"I don't want to hear about it."

"Texans think they're great gamblers. A few of them are. But the easiest mark at my place would clean up in Texas."

"I'm not going there to gamble, Marty."

"Of course not. What are you writing?"

"A story about the search for the *Titanic.*"

"There was plenty of gambling aboard that old ship."

"Stop talking about gambling. I just wanted to say good-bye for a while."

"Everything's a gamble," Marty said. "But you'll get along fine in Texas. Tell them you're from somewhere else. Don't mention New York. And, Bill, don't say I said it, but I'll miss you, too."

That night I called Jack Grimm to find out how my son Joe was doing. He was staying at Grimm's house, which had to be unlike any he had known. There was furniture taken from a turn-of-the-century Nevada house of prostitution. An old slot machine. A 16th Century desk. A Victrola. That wood purportedly from Noah's Ark. And of course the Picasso prints.

Grimm was a bit concerned. He kept saying Joe "was a good boy, a handsome boy, All-America type kid," but I could tell something was wrong. I asked to talk to Joe.

"I think he's upset," Joe said, "because I'm not driving his Cadillac."

"What?"

"He woke me up this morning. 'Up and at 'em, boy,' he said. 'Greet the glorious Texas morn.' Then he asked if I had a driver's license. I said yes. He threw me the keys to a Cadillac, said I should check out Abilene, and left. It was strange. It was almost as if he disappeared."

"I know."

"Well, I don't know how to drive a Cadillac. He asked if I had a driver's license, and when I said yes he tossed the keys to me. I didn't have time to tell him I couldn't drive it."

"Tell him now."

"I'd rather not."

"Why?"

"He's rich, Dad. He makes me nervous."

I knew what my son meant. Rich people made me nervous too, and I'd had far more experiences with them than my son had. The rich were different. They tended, for one thing, to see the state of the world as pretty good. What could be the matter with a planet that treated them so well? And money made many of them arrogant. Other people might think twice or three times about whether a feat could be accomplished; the rich never doubted it could.

Art the Oil Man was an example of arrogance, and possibly of why currently there are so many bad movies on the market. It may never have occurred to him that filmmaking was an art. He saw it as a means to make quick money, like drilling an oil well, and never wondered whether this was desirable.

Grimm had a sense of humor, and was amusing to me, because he was a genuine eccentric, so I felt little discomfort with him. But I could understand how Joe felt. Grimm's "Drive the Cadillac, boy," was like his "Type faster, boy," and if you didn't do it, somehow you felt diminished in his eyes as a *man*. I figured Jack didn't know the difference between typing and writing. Joe figured maybe it was better to crack the car up than admit he couldn't do something Grimm expected. Wouldn't a younger Grimm, the rough-and-ready wildcatter, have done precisely that? The difference between my attitude and Joe's was purely one of experience.

"Well," I said, "tell him if you want, but don't drive the car. I wouldn't worry about what he thinks."

I talked to Jackie Grimm. She had guessed immediately what the problem was. She had seen Jack's "Just do it, boy" method of operating ever since they had been sweethearts in college. Jackie thought, and I believed it was true, that the two would be getting along fine in no time at all.

I left for Abilene two days later, with one suitcase and a shoulder bag. Furniture for our place — what would it be? — I could buy when I got there. If Joe stayed on for college, he could keep the furniture when I returned to New York.

At the layover in Dallas I bought a big cowboy hat, boots, and Dallas Cowboys tee shirt. Grimm and Joe were going to meet me at the Abilene airport, and I figured I would show them I was in the proper frame of mind.

Eleven

"Grimm thinks I should take petroleum geology," Joe said.

"What do you think?"

"I want to take history and journalism."

"That's what you should do."

"Grimm won't like it."

"I don't think he'll mind. But don't worry about what he likes. His geology helped him make a fortune. I doubt if it's what you want, or would be good at."

It was my first night in Abilene, and we were sitting on the floor of our new apartment. Grimm had just gone ahead and rented the place, putting down the deposit: "You can take care of the rent in the morning, boy."

Jack had done a good job, and I was grateful. Our apartment was in a big new complex. Had central air. Free cable TV hookup. Two big bedrooms. Two full bathrooms. Kitchen. Dining room. Large living room. Drapes. Wall-to-wall carpet. Automatic dishwasher. Patio. The apartment complex itself featured a miniature golf course, tennis courts, and four swimming pools. It was new and modern and cost less than half what I'd paid in New York.

"It's great, Jack," I said, when he showed us in.

135

"Glad you like it, boy." He had driven us straight in from the airport, was fixing to leave so Joe and I could be alone. At least that was part of it. I suspected also he had a card game to attend.

"Who wouldn't like it?" I said. "I can already see myself lounging at one of those pools after a day at the typewriter."

"Plenty of pretty girls, boy."

"Right, Jack."

"Know the best part about this place?" he asked.

"The liquor store across the street?" I had opened the drapes and was looking through the picture window.

"No. It's that you're only five blocks from me, boy."

Good grief, I thought. I remembered how he kept checking on the proposal I'd done with B.J. at Kiva Inn. Would he come over just as frequently for a whole book?

"Well, boys," he had said, "I'll leave you to yourselves." He tossed a key to me. "That's for the pickup I promised you could use. The big green Chevrolet down in the parking lot. It's tougher than iron. All set if you want to go ripping around."

So Joe and I sat on the floor of the apartment watching the gathering twilight of an Abilene evening. The only furniture was a small couch Grimm had brought over earlier. We would have to sleep on the floor for a night, but that was all right. The electricity was on. We could turn on the overhead lights that came with the apartment, and store groceries in the icebox.

"I think Grimm has a lot of people on scholarships," Joe said.

"That's good."

"I mean *a lot.* Why do you think he does it?"

This was my son. I'd taught him to be wary of rich people, both in personal talks and books I'd written, but now was the time for a slight balancing of the picture.

"Maybe he's just a good guy," I said. "It can happen, you know."

"Think it's a tax write-off?"

"Joe, it might be. But I doubt it. There are loads of rich people spending their lives looking for tax write-offs, and they find them, but when they do nobody else ever benefits. I know Grimm gives a lot of scholarships. That's good. You could go to most rich people and ask them for help and they'd laugh you out. I think Grimm, despite his eccentric ways, wants to do some decent things in his life. Other people have just as much money as him, or more, and just sit on it."

"He said he'd pay for as long as I wanted to go to school."

"Good. Forget journalism and become a doctor."

Albertson's Supermarket was less than a quarter-mile east of us and we decided to put some food in the refrigerator, and at the same time get a look at where we'd be doing most of our shopping. Wearing my cowboy hat and boots — probably fooling nobody — I drove the pickup to the store. It was sturdy, I could agree with Grimm, and drove like one of those tanks I'd seen parked behind Kiva. I couldn't imagine this pickup ever breaking down. We sat high in the air riding in it, and getting out was like climbing down a ladder to the last rung, then having to jump.

Albertson's was Texas-size. Perhaps as big as two large supermarkets in Ohio, five in New York City. Prices, of course, were much lower than in New York, and there weren't guards and TV cameras in every aisle. I didn't see any guns for sale, but later learned there were other supermarkets in Abilene where you could purchase them right along with your groceries. One store, advertising its weekly specials, instead of luring customers in with a good deal on butter had a sale on guns. A criminal wouldn't even have to buy a gun to rob the place. He could walk in, pick up one of the guns for sale, and then stick the store up.

The supermarkets didn't seem to get robbed in Abilene. The convenience stores, always close by, did. Joe had a theory the convenience stores, whose prices were much higher, were owned by the supermarkets, and their sole purpose was to give a holdup man something to rob. Better a small store than a big one.

We bought a lot of staples, canned vegetables, sugar, flour, etc., because somehow it made me feel permanent. I didn't want to just up and leave when something went wrong, a definite possibility. Joe could stay in a dorm. Grimm had offered to pay *everything* connected with school. Yes, I could leave, go back to New York and my friends, and Joe would be all right, but that was not my intention. We ate terrible hamburgers and passable French fries from a nearby Jack in the Box and went to sleep on the floor early. I woke up only once, about 1 A.M. Across the street beyond the liquor store was Gramm's Central Station, a dance hall, beer hall, and club for young people. The apartment was fairly noise-proof, but the squeal of tires and the wail of sirens came through, as did the flashing red lights of the patrol cars through the drapes. It would be a scene repeated almost every night. The young, many of them teenagers, never caught on that the time for their A. J. Foyt imitations was not at 1 A.M. outside a popular watering hole, nor did the police, eager to show their alertness and chalk up traffic tickets on the big score card that was their record, ever weary of chasing them down. Teenagers versus cops: the contest was never even close. The police didn't have to bother to position their cars behind buildings to remain unseen. The hotblooded teenager in muscle shirt and cowboy hat, his girl in blue jeans, would lurch straight for their beat-up car, no muffler, and *go*. The cops were shooting fish in a barrel. The amount of arrests they could make was limited only by their numbers. A hurtling car, reminiscent of those seen on television at the Bonneville Salt Flats, would streak by another car already stopped by the police.

Gramm's Central Station was a very large club, but compared to what? Even bigger was Gilley's, made famous in *Urban Cowboy,* located just outside Houston. I'd met Mickey Gilley, who'd been in Abilene for the "Get High on Yourself" show, and he was quite an entrepreneur. He even sold *Gilley's* beer and put out a *Gilley's* magazine. Some five thousand people a night flock to his honky-tonk, which in looks has been compared to an airline hangar.

Another drinking spot built for Brobdingnagians was Billy Bob's in Fort Worth, which has live bulls inside. It also has phone booths where lying to your boss or wife is made easier. Depending on the circumstances, you can pick out a telephone at Billy Bob's and the background noise your listener will hear is that of an airport (planes zooming overhead) or an office (typewriters, ringing phones, etc.).

In fact, you have to see Texas bars and honky-tonks to believe them. Towering over your head at Texas Swing in Nederland, Texas, is what is advertised as the largest wagon wheel in the state, which surely means it's the largest in the world. At other bars you can ride a bucking armadillo, sit at tables built in the shape of Texas, shoot down alien spacecraft from your bar stool playing a giant video game, and arm wrestle with a mechanical monster. At one bar in Abilene you can play poker with a machine that insults you when you lose.

Grimm was at the door at 8 A.M., pounding loudly. "Things to do, boys," he said, bristling past me into the apartment. "Furniture to buy. Groceries. Gotta get soap and stuff like that so you can live."

"We got the groceries and soap last night," I said. "We can look around on our own for the furniture."

"You don't know where to look. Come on."

Joe drove the pickup truck — "need it to carry furniture" — and I rode with Grimm. I agreed with the oilman's assessment that it was unusual he could drive the truck and not a Cadillac.

Grimm did exactly what I feared. He drove to one of the best furniture stores in Abilene. "Here we are, boy."

"You may be here. I'm not. Jack, I don't want to spend a lot of money on furniture."

"You want the place to look nice, don't you?"

"Yes. But I want to keep costs down." I didn't want to tell him I wasn't buying furniture for the place where I intended to spend my remaining days.

"Well, let's go in. You probably won't be able to resist what you see."

"I can resist anything with a high price tag."

The manager of the store literally tripped over his feet when he saw who was coming into his store. Visions of big bucks danced in his head. "Jack Grimm!" he said. "What an honor!"

"Aw, it's no big deal," said Grimm. He was blushing.

And it wasn't. It wasn't any deal. It took a while, but I convinced Grimm I wasn't going to spend a fortune on furniture. The manager, I think, kept hoping Jack would step in with his wallet, but he was wishing up the wrong oil rig.

Shopping with a rich person is one of life's most terrible experiences. I've had them several times, and another was awaiting me several months down the line. It occurred at Neiman-Marcus in Dallas, trailing behind a Mad Shopper, the wife of an oil man, who went from aisle to aisle grabbing up top-of-the-line merchandise. She kept urging me "to get something nice" for my son. "You love him, don't you? He deserves it, doesn't he?"

Many rich people have no idea others live on a budget. The woman, a bad and bored poet whose husband thought I might help her writing, probably spent more money just on nail polish than most citizens earned in a year. But unless an individual is very thick-skinned, he has to feel guilty not buying a present for a worthy offspring, or at least to believe somehow he himself has been a sluggard in the game of life. Why else could he not afford that gold studded (in the form of bulls) $600 tee shirt?

Which brings up Neiman-Marcus, which has expanded into

other states but is rightly thought of as Texan. For $3,500, Neiman-Marcus would sell a custom-designed mousetrap that trapped mice alive in a miniature ranch. Along with the ranch came a personalized branding iron ("using a special indelible ink so you won't traumatize your herd") toddlers could play with as they prepared for real life. Other gifts available from Neiman-Marcus were a 106-carat opal, which was said to have been described by Pliny, for $150,000, and a submarine for almost a million dollars.

Sakowitz of Houston vied with Neiman-Marcus for offering the most expensive gifts. For slightly under $1 million, Peter Duchin would teach piano, Mark Spitz swimming, Jimmy the Greek gambling, Jean-Claude Killy skiing, and Larry Mahan bronco-busting. Thrown in was the opportunity to talk with Truman Capote, a dubious gift. I wondered if you learned broncobusting from Mahan if Duchin's piano lessons would still be of value.

We went to a less costly store for the furniture, Grimm and I in the Cadillac, Joe straining to follow in the pickup. Jack wheeled through church parking lots to avoid traffic signals, careened around corners, was oblivious to potholes and bumps. He drove the Cadillac the way I imagined oil field roughnecks drove pickups.

The next store was my kind of place. Inexpensive. I bought two double beds, dressers, dining room table and chairs, sofa and easy chair, a couple of coffee tables, assorted odds and ends. It took less than an hour, and Grimm was impressed; not by the cost of the furniture, but by the speed with which it was purchased. Jack didn't like wasting time. I later often saw him pushing a shopping cart through Albertson's. He could maneuver in a store as well as anyone, grabbing generic brands off the shelf with one hand as he kept the cart moving with the other.

Grimm said he would meet us at the apartment and sped off while Joe and I loaded furniture onto the bed of the truck. It was immediately apparent we'd have to make several trips. While I was inside explaining this to the store owner, I heard a loud crash. Hurrying out the door to the sidewalk I saw that my son had backed the pickup smack into the side of a yellow coupe. The coupe had been going by on the road when it was broadsided. Not much question which driver was at fault.

It was Joe's first accident in three years, and time for me to remember how worried I'd been when I'd had my first. My father had remained cool when I'd expected him to blow up, and it taught me a lesson. There was no good to be accomplished criticizing someone who already felt terrible. I told Joe that Grimm had insurance, and we should wait until the police arrived.

No one was hurt, though the coupe had been smacked pretty good. The pickup, of course, had no damage whatever. I figured this green monster would come out first in a fight with a building.

We talked with the driver of the yellow car. He was about Joe's age, nineteen, short and thin, ultra polite, spoke very quietly. His car, however, was a bright flower display. Flowers were painted all over it, on the doors, roof, hood, trunk, even the windows. There were hand-painted messages also, innocuous enough in New York (but guaranteed inflammatory in Abilene, I guessed), calling for controversial ideals like peace and love and brotherhood.

The police took twenty minutes to arrive. The cop was young, not much older than Joe or the displaced hippie kid from the Sixties, and he started to take down the routine report. Like I had been that day Grimm first talked to me in New York, the cop was not prepared for the scene that followed.

Jack wheeled up in his Cadillac. He had gone to the apartment, grown impatient waiting, and figuring we were lost decided to initiate the search from where he'd left us. Now, looking at the accident, he sized the situation up in seconds, hopped out of his car and came sidling over. "What's up, men?" he asked.

"Nobody hurt," I said. "I'm sorry about the insurance claim you'll be getting."

"That the other driver?" Grimm asked, nodding at the hippie who was standing apart.

"Yes. He's a little nervous."

Jack, employing his sideways walk, approached the cop. "Good morning, officer," he said cheerily.

The cop didn't look up. He just kept writing.

"Nice day, isn't it?" Grimm persisted. He was Mr. Charm.

"It's okay, I suppose, if you like the heat," the cop said, glancing at Grimm, then back at his report.

This, as the comic strip character would say, was a revolting development. The cop hadn't recognized Grimm. He had to be the only policeman in Abilene who didn't know the town's most prominent citizen. I imagined his chief would be embarrassed. Surely Grimm was a generous contributor to the policemen's ball, or whatever passed for such in Abilene. Maybe the cop was newly arrived from the East. Texas towns had been recruiting police from the East.

"I own the pickup truck," Grimm said.

This interested the cop. "Got insurance?" he asked. "You got to have insurance."

"Of course I've got insurance . . ." Grimm spluttered to a stop. He had been about to call the cop "boy." The oilman quickly gathered himself together and turned on the charm. "I'm Jack Grimm," he said, holding out his hand to shake. The cop accepted the proffered hand without looking up.

Jack figured the cop might recognize the name, if not the face. But he didn't. The man who searched for the *Titanic,* for Noah's Ark, a millionaire many times over, was cast in the role of average citizen. Well, he could handle that. He hadn't always been rich. He hadn't had a dime when he'd come out of the University of Oklahoma, rawer than the crude he sought, and he'd gotten by. Prospered. He could handle this kid cop.

"Officer," Jack said, "it's pretty clear to me what happened."

I had come over to join what mostly had been a one-sided discussion. "Jack," I whispered, "I think it was Joe's fault."

"Stay out of this, boy."

"But . . ."

"So what do you think happened?" the cop said. He was partly amused, but part of him perhaps advised that here was a person to whom he should listen. Rich, powerful people generate a confidence that tells others they are rich and powerful. It can't be faked, except possibly by a very good actor. Whatever, the cop wanted to hear the version of what "clearly happened" from someone who had not seen the accident.

"This boy in the flowered car," said Grimm, "was going too fast. Otherwise he could have swerved out of the way. He should get a ticket for speeding."

"No evidence of speeding," the cop said. "Were you speeding?" he asked the hippie.

"You going to take his word for it?" Grimm asked. "Look at the physical evidence. He didn't swerve."

"The boy in your pickup," the cop said, "could have pulled right out into him. That's the way it looks. He got him right in the door."

Not only did it look that way; it had happened that way. But Jack wasn't giving up.

"Can you believe that car?" Grimm said. "A moving florist's shop. Why, there are flowers on the windows. He couldn't have seen the pickup pull out if he'd been looking. Which he wasn't."

The cop scratched his head.

"Give him a ticket for driving with obstructed vision," Jack urged. He waved his hand at the coupe derisively.

"I can't rightly do that," the cop explained. "No law against paintin' your vehicle. Seems to me if he was payin' attention, there's enough glass there to see through."

The young cop just wanted to write his report and get it over with. It was a minor accident, both cars insured, the insurance companies could fight it out. And it was hot. A good sun to get out of and back in the air-conditioned patrol car. On the other hand, the guy who was so eager for him to write out a ticket seemed like a bigshot, and just might be. He had better be careful.

Grimm was pacing in small circles now. Finally, he decided to bring out his heavy artillery. He stopped, his face sincere, his voice reasonable. "Look, officer," he said. "Look at those two boys." With a sweep of his hand he took in both of them. "I ask, if you didn't know them, which one would you think responsible for this unfortunate collision?"

The hippie was thin, bearded, had hair down to the middle of his back. Joe was 6-2, 200 pounds, with short hair (it would have been long also, but I'd told him to cut it before coming to Texas). The hippie looked like Charles Manson. Joe might just have stepped off a football practice field.

Jack thought the case was clinched. A little smile of satisfaction curled on his lips. It was a look Clarence Darrow might have had after delivering a knockout closing argument. Any good Texas cop could look at these two and quick as a jackrabbit see which one was at fault. The verdict had to be for the husky kid in the pickup over the sissy in the coupe.

The young cop wavered but didn't break. He told Jack he wasn't going to give the hippie any ticket; he was just going to write up the accident report and let the insurance companies decide. I gave the young officer a long look. It was not the smallest victory I had ever witnessed. Probably in a year or so, when he knew more, when cynicism took hold, his decision would be different. That, or he'd be in a different line of work. I didn't think patrolmen became lieutenants and captains and chiefs in Texas (or anywhere else) siding with hippies against oilmen.

Back at the apartment with the first load of furniture inside, I asked Jack why he'd made such a fuss with the patrolman. "Didn't you see that hippie, boy?" he said. "He was to blame for the accident, that's why I spoke up. Why, he couldn't see his windshield wipers, there was so much paint on the windows. He's a menace in that car."

I believe Grimm had convinced himself the hippie was at fault. Though maybe he didn't realize it, the length of the kid's hair and the peace messages were probably what did the convincing.

I thought about the cop during the three more trips required to move the furniture. I imagined it was hard to be honest in a state where fast-dealing and corruption at the top were taken for granted. The former gubernatorial team of Ma and Pa Ferguson was an example. Pa Ferguson served one term and was elected to a second. After seven months of the second term, however, the state of Texas decided that that was enough, and impeached Pa. Eight years later, Ma Ferguson was elected governor and promptly set a record for number of pardons granted. The deal was, to make it legal, the criminal had to buy a mule for $2,000 from Pa Ferguson. Or so the story went. Then there was Representative Bob Davis, of whom a fellow legislator said, "He wouldn't use a pay toilet without asking a lobbyist for a dime." Another legislator, Clay Smothers, described as "a black Archie Bunker," said, "I am against blacks, Mexicans, women, Indians, and queers talking to me about their rights."

So much was whacky about Texas. The president of an El Paso smelting company said acid rain could be good for the state. A guy in Austin made news when he refused to pay for his wife's birth control pills because he'd had a vasectomy. Dallas Power & Light Company patted itself on the back for setting aside $20,000 to help poor people pay their electric bills, then admitted the $20,000 would probably be added to the bills of other customers. Cullen Davis, previously mentioned in these pages, walked to the front of the First Baptist Church in Euless to give himself to Christ with the loudspeaker announcing, "The son of Stinky Davis has found the Son of God."

For a long time things had been bigger than life in Texas. For example, the "Monster Wreck," which was supposed to be the most sensational train crash of all time. It was scheduled for September

15, 1896, the brainchild of the aptly-named William G. Crush of the Missouri, Kansas & Texas Railroad, and 50,000 people paid to see the event at an out-of-the-way stretch of track near Waco. A pair of six-car trains, each going ninety miles an hour, collided head-on and the engine boilers exploded. Two people died and there were numerous injuries.

We did not yet have a television, so after the furniture was safely in the apartment, I looked around for something to do that evening. I read the Abilene *Reporter-News,* and it was clear the main activity in town was going to church.

Why not? I thought. See the natives in their favorite after-hours place. Learn something about the people who were my neighbors. Brother Billy Ray, whose topic was "Finding Success Through Christ," was appearing in the main meeting room of a local motel. Billy Ray was advertised as "humorous," "insightful," "able to show you the way to spiritual *and* material success."

"Want to hear a preacher tonight?" I said to Joe.

"No," he said.

"That was clear enough. But what else is there to do?"

"Read. I think I'll read."

As a writer, this should have made me happy. But I wanted to go out, and I didn't want to do it alone. I imagined once I started the *Titanic* book, which would be soon if only to avoid Grimm viewing me as a loafer, I wouldn't be much interested in the flavor of the town.

"Brother Billy Ray," I said, "will show us how to be spiritually and materially successful. At least he says he will."

"Is he like Uncle Andy?"

We had heard Uncle Andy on the pickup's radio that afternoon. His message, if nothing else, was to the point: "God's broke, folks! He's flat out of money! The till is empty! The coffers are cleaned out! So send your money to God care of Uncle Andy!"

"I don't think he's like Uncle Andy," I said.

"How do you know?"

"Dammit, I don't. Where's your spirit? Let's go see Brother Billy Ray. Getting out, the fresh air will at least blow the smell off us. Get us out of this stuffy apartment."

This wasn't going to work. The apartment's air-conditioner worked beautifully. If any place was stuffy, it was outside, where the temperature was stuck on 100 and what breeze there was only stirred up the dust. I had to try a different tack. "I guess I could go out and find a bar," I said.

"You'll get in trouble," he said. I could see this ploy was working. "You'll start criticizing Texas and get punched out."

"I'd keep my opinions to myself."

"No, you wouldn't. Good grief, what a choice. Brother Billy Ray or letting my father get in trouble."

"I suppose you have to make a choice. Decisions like this are called growing up."

"Hallelujah, then," he said without enthusiasm.

It cost five dollars apiece to get in, but that included food, which meant Brother Billy Ray, or whoever was behind the meeting, was showing an immediate loss where we were concerned. Joe eats like a horse. Things like a half gallon of milk a meal, or two chickens. "Let's get out of here," he said, after he'd gone through the buffet line four times.

"I want to see what this is all about," I said.

Four long tables, holding perhaps fifty people each, sat lengthwise in the meeting hall. The speaker's table and podium were in front. All ages of faithful were present, from infants on the bottle to citizens who must have been in their nineties. It was a richer crowd that I expected. Wealthy people, in my experience, urged others to attend church, but assiduously avoided it themselves.

The first speaker, the master of ceremonies, opened the proceedings with a prayer. He was pastor of a local congregation, and said how honored we should be that Billy Ray would soon be talking to us. A financial report was read, and then the collection plate was passed. Joe and I were sitting in the back, near the door, and tried to look invisible as we deftly glided the plate to the person next to us.

First on the agenda was standing up and holding hands. Nothing was said. We held hands and thought of what Christ had done for us this day. I felt embarrassed. Joe leaned over and whispered in my ear, "Let's get out of here."

Next came singing, while we still held hands. It seemed the singing might lift up the roof, so joyous and full of feeling it was. Several people in the gathering of two hundred or so did their own thing; faces enraptured, they broke away from the masses holding hands and delivered individual renditions of the songs. Three or four others shouted messages of thanks to Christ.

Who can tell what's in another's mind? Some of those doing the shouting looked like showboats grabbing for attention. Others seemed genuinely overcome in the midst of a religious service. I suspected both types were present. It didn't hurt business chances in Abilene, I learned, to be carried away by fundamentalist ardor.

A new preacher took the podium and talked about a building fund. He, like the first man, like every preacher I saw, appeared to be without a care, smiling, radiant. Like the Mormon kids in their blue suits who used to knock on the door. For a time I used to enjoy arguing with the Mormons about their church's treatment of blacks and women, but that became tedious.

The collection plate was passed for the building fund and it was wish-you-were-invisible time again. If I were in a giving mood, I thought, I could think of so many better causes, but I was sure there were two hundred people here who would argue that point.

"Let's get out of here," Joe whispered. I wished he would stop whispering that.

The worst came next. Another preacher, an expression on his face so joyous I had seen its equal only once (on a fellow who had just won on the New Jersey lottery), asked everyone who had recently found Christ to come up to the speaker's table and join him in a prayer of thanks. The line started as a trickle, but soon they were going in threes and fours. Half the gathering was in front of that table.

"I know," the preacher said loudly, "I just know there are more of you out there. At least two more of you. Come on up, brothers, and praise the Lord!"

He was looking at Joe and me. I was sure he was looking at us. I lowered my head reaching for a napkin to wipe my mouth with, and kept it lowered. Maybe he couldn't see me now.

"Two more! The two of you know who I mean. Come on up, and we'll thank the Lord together!"

I lifted my eyes. The preacher was a long way away, but I imagined he was looking at us. Of course he was.

"Let's . . ." Joe started.

"I know, get out of here. Well, we made it this far and we're staying to the finish." But I'd have gotten out if I could. We couldn't leave now, with everyone staring at us.

And that's how it felt. Everyone staring at us. I could feel two hundred pair of eyes on my lowered head (maybe they would think I was praying?).

"We're not going to continue," the preacher said, "until the two of you come up."

We'll be here forever, I thought. *How could you get yourself in this situation?* I asked.

"You've really gotten us into a situation, Dad," Joe said. His chin also was nearly touching the table.

"Why don't you go up?" I suggested. "It won't hurt you, and maybe that will satisfy him."

"You go," Joe said.

This wasn't going to get us anywhere. I felt like an idiot staring at the tablecloth, everyone else looking at me. I wasn't going up there, I resolved, I was sure I hadn't found Christ and wasn't going to say I had. But a part of my brain said, *Why not? Go on up. You can't sit here for eternity, which is what he promised.* Still another section of the brain (the same brain which hadn't been working when I'd talked Joe into coming here) piped up. *He's bluffing He won't wait forever.* But I couldn't be sure. The last time I'd looked he had a big welcoming smile on his face, and he probably admired Job.

"All right, brothers and sisters, here they come!"

Could it be true? I chanced raising my eyes but couldn't see the action. I lifted my head but it would have to come higher. I might have to look someone in the eye. I brought my head all the way up and immediately had a strong urge to praise the Lord. Two young boys, not more than eight years old, were shyly making their way to the speaker's table. The congregation broke into song.

"See," I said. "He wasn't looking at us."

"Sure seemed like it."

The collection plate was passed again before the featured speaker — Brother Billy Ray — took the podium. I gleaned that Brother Billy was much in demand on the Bible Circuit, that he was a super-rich rancher who gave full credit for his success to God. I couldn't find out if the Ray in Billy Ray was a last name or middle name. I guessed it was middle. Regardless, he was a big shambling man who would have looked more comfortable in overalls than the wrinkled 1950s suit he wore.

"As a boy," he said in a smooth voice that had just enough rough country edges, "I was so dumb I thought penmanship was somebody's boat. I didn't get thrown out of school, though, until I started to shave — I was in second grade. I graduated first grade because the teacher liked me: I was dating her."

Brother Billy then covered his teen years. "I got married early. First thing I learned was why God made man first. He didn't want advice on how to do it. Decided to enroll in the Army but flunked the entrance exam. In those days you passed if you knew what shoe to put your foot in."

Billy Ray's topic was "finding success," and he got around to it in his own good time. You could tell he wasn't the sort who hurried, and besides the audience was so happy cracking up at his jokes that it would have been a crime to rush. A couple more examples of Brother Billy's humor: know what the liberal said when he was asked about the Indianapolis 500? 'They're innocent.' And the liberals keep whining that the CIA tried to kill Castro. That's terrible, isn't it? I'd take the CIA to court and sentence them: to six months of target practice."

At last came Brother Billy's own success story. "One day I was leanin' on this fence lookin' at this old field, scratchin' my head, a straw between my teeth, the sorriest most pitiful individual you ever did see. 'What's gonna become of you, Billy Ray?' I asked. 'You're dumb, and you can't do nothin'. You're the most worthless creature in God's creation.'

"So I stood lookin' at this field. And all of a sudden it came to me, not out of a burning bush, what I'd heard an old preacher say. 'The Lord Jesus Christ will give you anything you ask for.' Well, now, I decided to give it a try. I asked the Lord Jesus Christ to give me this old field, and He did.

"But a couple weeks later I still wasn't nothin'. I had the field, but what good was it? So I decided to try again. I asked the Lord Jesus for a tractor to till that old field, and wouldn't you know He gave me a tractor! You see before you a flesh and blood witness that you can come back to Jesus, time and time again, and He'll give you whatever you ask. All He wants is for you to ask, and to worship Him. I mean to tell you, and you can see I'm not much different from that dumb kid who got thrown out of second grade, I'm doing pretty well these days. And all I had to do was give myself to Jesus and ask Him for help."

Brother Billy Ray chronicled personal success after personal success in a soul-stirring climb to the financial top that would have brought tears of joy to Horatio Alger's eyes. Each personal triumph was larger than the previous, and told matter-of-factly with a sense of humor. Never was there a mention of begging bankers for loans, long hours spent on the job, hard wrangling over a sale. Brother Billy asked something from Christ and it became reality.

Although the meeting was open to all denominations, and numerous were present — Brother Billy Ray was an entertaining speaker, a top draw — the prevalent theology was a hard Calvinist predestination. Success on earth was a sign of God's favor. A thing to be sought. Brother Billy put it bluntly: Jesus Christ wants you to be rich.

The preachers, if not the audience, were very political. No hesitation at all in telling the congregation how it should feel about abortion, school prayer, punishment of criminals, foreign aid, foreign wars, welfare, school busing, the entire gamut of social issues. Disaster was just around the corner if good Christian people didn't wake up.

The collection plate was passed a final time. I thought this round drew the most generous response of all. You felt almost a responsibility to thank Brother Billy Ray. He had no church, no congregation, was just a layman "witnessing," none of this went in his pocket. He had received an *ovation* when he finished.

Abilene, I would learn, deserved its name "Buckle of the Bible Belt." One of the most popular shows on television was a quiz game called "Bible Bowl," in which the Gospel Girls competed against the Bible Boys answering scriptural questions. The moderator, whose bias for the Bible Boys was obvious (they usually lost), was more enthusiastic than any network game show host.

"What did you think?" I asked Joe when we were in the pickup.

"They passed the plate too often," he said, "but I kind of liked Brother Billy Ray. He has *chutzpah*."

"Yes," I said. "He has that."

"Do people really believe what he was saying?"

"I don't know," I said.

Twelve

Very quickly I found plenty of things to like in Abilene. The phone company hooked up service in a day. Try to get that in New York, or any other big city. At Albertson's where we shopped, they welcomed my personal checks, despite the fact that because my account was new they contained no printed name or address. In New York you could have a check signed by David Rockefeller in his own blood and not get it cashed. The man at the gas station checked the pickup's oil without being asked, and the cost was less than at stations in the East that advertised the misleading and misspelled "Self Serv." The landlord didn't arbitrarily cut off the apartment's hot water because he decided his fuel bill was too high.

A small-town trust existed in this dusty West Texas city that reminded me of my own Wisconsin childhood. I didn't entirely buy Jack Grimm's "A Texan gives you his promise" speech, but there was an assumption here that people should be helped, that they had a purpose in life other than to be harassed and exploited. The electric utility, undoubtedly a profit-gouging monopoly, nonetheless did not insist on a deposit. In New York you not only had to fight your way to the busiest section of town to give Con Ed a deposit so you could be a customer, but had to stand in an endless line to pay it.

It occurred to me again and again. Things work in Abilene.

Things that should work everywhere, but don't, and you begin to think that the malfunctioning of people and equipment is the norm. At the bank where Grimm had his offices, the elevator was always working, never a long wait. In New York you would stew for what seemed ages, then become involved in a cattle-drive push to get aboard, and finally be treated to a stomach-turning adventure as the elevator creaked and groaned and threatened to plummet to the basement. The "close door" button on most elevators in New York, I suspected (and later had it confirmed by an Otis man), was merely a placebo. When the door wouldn't close, which was often, they wanted frustrated riders to push on the button rather than kicking dents into the wall.

Early on I was with a newspaperman from the Abilene *Reporter-News* when his car broke down. In just a few minutes no less than five motorists stopped to ask if we needed help.

Little things. The daily delivered newspaper wasn't swiped every other morning.

But the ease with which checks could be cashed was the most important to me. Occasionally I would receive royalties from a publisher. My agent would deduct ten percent and send along his business check, written on a New York bank, for the remainder. The bank in Abilene cashed the out-of-state check without question. It hadn't been that way in other places where I'd lived. In San Diego, for example, the Bank of America wouldn't let you cash a check unless you had equivalent funds in your account, and those funds were frozen until the check cleared. The bank said this took fifteen days, the check going to New York, the funds coming back, but a newspaper *(Wall Street Journal)* reporter I know said this was absurd. "The bank can find out right away if the check is good," he said, "and the other bank can transfer the funds. It's a major ripoff. What the bank does is use your cash for fifteen days. You're not Daddy Warbucks, of course, but when they can use the money of thousands of people like you, it comes to a tidy sum."

Once I took a cashier's check to Bank of America and couldn't turn it into money. The banker said he couldn't tell if a cashier's check was any better than a personal check. He had to wait for it to clear. I asked him what good a cashier's check was, why anyone should pay money to get one, and he claimed its value was purely psychological. People thought it was good. I asked him if his own bank wasn't taking money under at least an implied false premise (people did *think* they were getting something) when it sold cashier's checks, but he'd already written me off as a troublemaker and merely shrugged his shoulders.

In any case, many of the hassles of big city life were missing in Abilene. I even got to know the people in neighboring apartments.

My second day in town I bought a big used color TV and was looking for a good used typewriter when Grimm got wind of the search. He told me to come to his office. He'd lend me a typewriter.

The typewriter was a huge, slick, modern electric with more symbols on it than I knew existed. It erased automatically, which I could appreciate, but had keys in strange places and exotic devices I couldn't understand. Immediately I began to miss my old Facit, which I'd long ago started to think of as a friend. I *talked* to the Facit, which probably meant I was a bit crazy.

Four times I tried to type a single paragraph on Grimm's razzle-dazzle super deluxe, but I couldn't do anything right. The machine seemed smarter than me, and likely to poke fun if I made an error — it reminded me of a taunting high-IQ wise guy. It was spanking clean and bristling with sophisticated playthings, and it was so big I felt it was in control.

"I think I'll get something more simple," I said.

"You're living in the modern era," Grimm said. "You can't keep using Stone Age tools."

"I like to feel the typewriter does what I tell it. This thing has a mind of its own."

"Use it, boy. Go first-class."

We were in Grimm's offices on the third floor over the First National Bank Building. He showed me some of the letters he had received from people who wanted to search for the *Titanic*. A few were dillies. One woman sent a picture of herself wearing a bikini, and said she was a scuba-diving instructor. She said it long had been a goal of hers to scuba-dive on the *Titanic*.

No fewer than 28 psychics wrote saying they wanted to come along, they "knew" where the *Titanic* rested, and each gave a different location. An elderly man claimed he should be included on the search because he knew more about the *Titanic* than anyone else alive. How did he acquire this knowledge? "I made four round-trip crossings on her before she went down."

Perhaps the zaniest individual to apply for passage identified himself as "Metatron, Chief Archangel of the Presence of God of the Holy Kabbalah of Israel," and said he was the first Old Testament prophet. If Metatron was not allowed aboard the search ship, he contended Grimm could still become "the most famous and rich man on the face of the Earth" if he would finance an expedition to Agharta, "the subterranean world located on the inner surface of this planet, Earth. . . . I should be able to get you exclusive mineral rights to all the natural resources to be found on the interior surface of this planet. The Inner World Government of Agharta does not use crude oil," this last being a fact revealed to Metatron by "God the Father." Further, Metatron said the world is hollow, that flying saucers emanate from a huge hole in the North Pole, and that the U.S. Government is hiding all of this vital information from its citizens.

No fewer than fifty marine engineers wrote with plans explaining how the *Titanic* could be raised, which instead raised questions about the quality of their educations. Raising the *Titanic,* of course, was patently impossible given the current state of technology.

Still another correspondent was an Englishman who was not so much interested in accompanying the expedition as he was in preventing Grimm from making it. The man from England said he already owned everything aboard the *Titanic.* He threatened to "seize the *Gyre*" if Grimm persisted, a potentially unwise move since the search ship was owned by the U.S. Navy.

Grimm showed me the letters as "background" for the *Titanic* book, but once he got involved in rummaging through correspondence he went further. He handed me letters from people who wanted him to invest in projects that clearly were absurd. A machine that turned water into oil, for example, and a method of photography to film the distant past.

"What do you do with this mail?" I asked.

"If the idea is crazy enough, I refer the writer to Bunker."

"Bunker Hunt?"

"Right. I tell the person I don't have any money right now, but Bunker does. I give him Bunker's private telephone number."

"What does Hunt think of this?"

"He loves it. He gets crazier requests than I do, of course, and sends the nuttiest to me."

"Seems like you both lose."

"It's fun, boy."

After going through just a small portion of Grimm's crank letter files, I staggered to the elevator with the typewriter, and down to the pickup. In the lobby of the bank building, the newspaper, cigarette, and candy concession stand was run by a blind man. He couldn't tell a $5 bill from a $50. He had not been robbed once, and was rumored to have been there as long as the building.

Robbery appeared to be no particular problem in Abilene. But as I started reading the daily newspapers, mass murder, in Texas, began to seem as popular as football.

Just reading the Texas newspapers, I counted five mass murders — the fewest killed was four people — *in a single week* in the state. The mass murders occurred in small towns and big cities, in the most remote country areas and on busy, crowded streets, in private places like homes and churches and public ones such as stores. The thing was, the murders kept happening, week after week. I counted at least one mass murder per week for three months, and then wearied of the exercise.

I wondered why this slaughter, seemingly unprecedented except for wartime or revolutionary situations, wasn't more publicized. Anyone coming to New York City, for example, either knew about the danger of muggers or had been living in isolation for a century or so. There were so many reports of muggings one began to suspect that muggers would soon run out of victims and start assaulting one another. In truth, I remembered there had been an instance of a mugger mugging a mugger. But except for a sensational incident such as the Texas Tower shootings in Austin, where a madman named Charles Whitman began sniping at anything that moved, who thought of Texas instantly when the subject of mass murders was mentioned, as one automatically thinks of New York City and muggers.

The press didn't appear particularly alarmed. If the murders were as commonplace as they seemed to me, the attitude was understandable. One doesn't get upset at the norm. But was this normal? I decided to do a little checking.

I couldn't find statistics on mass murder in my cursory check, but where just plain murder was concerned, Texas lived up to expectations. Only Nevada had a higher homicide rate. I sort of expected as much from Nevada. Hard-eyed casino owners versus crossroaders, a special breed of individuals who try to make their living cheating gambling establishments. Not that this was the only type of murder making Nevada Number One; gambling, prostitution, and drugs helped. Still, I'd heard plenty of stories of crossroaders being buried in the desert where no one goes to look.

But why Texas for murder? Texas, home of strait-laced Baptists and Bible-thumping fundamentalists. Pretty, docile girls and courtly, fair-minded men. Houston and Dallas/Fort Worth I could understand, but why Lubbock and Wichita Falls? Of the thirty most likely cities in the U.S. to be murdered, nine were in Texas.

I never did figure out the reasons. There were ghettoes in Texas, breeding grounds of violence, but surely not as bad as the ones in the East. And poverty, but again not so widespread and concentrated as elsewhere.

The ultimate mass murder (but can this really be said with certainty to be true?) surfaced long after I'd left Abilene. A deranged killer, released from a mental home where he spent time for killing his mother, was arrested in Montague County, Texas, and confessed to murdering *156 women*. The man's name was Henry Lee Lucas, he was described as a "drifter," and most jurisdictions just decided not to prosecute. There was no sense to sentencing him over and over again to life in prison.

Perhaps the high murder rate is related to the *macho* image of Texas and Texans, or to the state's fairly recent rise from a frontier economy. We may never know.

One day shortly after my move, B.J. Billing, Grimm's all-purpose man, came by to see how life was going in Abilene. I was writing. B.J. wanted to talk football. Everyone in Texas wanted to talk football. B.J. had played football in high school, but was far from his physical condition of those days.

My oldest son, William, was visiting, he would end up returning to Abilene and staying for more than a year after I was gone, working for the *Abilene Reporter News*. William was almost as tall and husky as Joe.

Billing was determined to keep me from writing, so I decided to challenge him to a game of touch football. It would be William, Joe and I against B.J. and "any two others" he could find.

B.J.'s first selection for his side was the son of one of Jack's secretaries, a strong young man who had worked in the oil fields and been an all-conference college linebacker. "Good," I said to B.J. "He's probably slow."

"The other guy I'm trying to get isn't."

"With you and the linebacker, you'll need some speed."

"My third man runs the hundred in nine point six."

"That's not fair," I said. "Nine point six is too fast. That's close to championship speed."

"You said I could get anyone I wanted."

"Not a nine point six sprinter. Promise me you won't get a nine-six sprinter, or the game is off."

"I promise."

B.J. must have taken courses at the feet of the master, Grimm, because he kept his word and still found a player who almost singlehandedly won the 48-42 game for them. The new man didn't run the hundred in nine point six either. He did it in *nine point one.* His nickname was Cat, I first suspected he was a ringer when he arrived at the same time as the ball in the opening kickoff, and the next time I heard about him after our touch football game, he was returning punts and kickoffs for the New Orleans Saints.

As the weeks passed Joe and I settled into a routine. He had arrived a few days late for the fall semester, so would have to wait until January to begin college. Grimm was willing to swing his weight around and get the school to make an exception, but we felt four months wouldn't matter. Grimm hired Joe as a roustabout — maybe being out in the field would convince him of petroleum geology's value as a major — so he was gone every morning about seven. What he and the two others he worked with mainly did was rattle from one of Grimm's oil wells to another, making repairs. Since the wells were far apart, much of the day was spent in the pickup. "It's hard when you're working," Joe said, "but you're not working that often."

I had started the book, and although progress on it wasn't fast enough for Grimm, I was satisfied. A book is always slowest at the beginning. Jack came by almost every day, no pattern to his arrivals. He called me a "good boy" if I happened to be at the typewriter and looked perplexed if I were reading or watching television. He wanted the *Titanic* book on the market.

Just to upset him I told stories of other authors.

"You know Jack, a lot of authors take years to finish a book."

"Did you say years, boy?"

"In fact, there's an author in New York who's been writing *one* book for almost forty years."

"You pulling my leg?"

"No," I said, suppressing a smile. "Writing a book is a labor of love. You can't rush it."

"Well don't love this one so much, boy." Grimm turned and strode quickly toward the door. Then he stopped and turned back toward me. "And remember, type faster."

Thirteen

I was being interviewed by Johnny Carson on the "Tonight" show about a blockbuster bestseller I'd written when my son Joe shook me awake.

"It's for you," he said. "The phone."

"Male or female?"

"Male."

"Probably Grimm. Wants to know if I'm working. Tell him I'm sick. I'll call him later."

"I know Grimm's voice, Dad. It's not him."

"Well, say I'm sick. Take a message." I rolled over and tried to feign sleep.

"It's long distance, Dad."

Better whoever it was pay for the call than me. I slipped into a bathrobe and headed for the phone in the living room.

"Bill, it's me, Cherrier."

"Cherrier!"

Jim Cherrier was the longest-lasting friend I had. I'd known him since we were three years old. We went to kindergarten, grade school, and high school together in Prairie du Chien, Wisconsin, a little town on the Mississippi River where we'd been born. Cherrier had attended my wedding, had helped me write a book on Queen

159

Juliana of the Netherlands. We had gone drinking dozens of times, fishing hundreds of times — our shared memories numbered in the thousands. We might not see each other for years, but when we were back together it was as if no time at all elapsed. Cherrier had worn well over more than four decades. He always would.

"I'm calling to see if you can come visit tomorrow," Cherrier said.

The *Titanic* book was coming along nicely — I had been hammering hard on it, though not up to Grimm's speedy standards — and I figured I deserved to take a break.

"You still in Lytle?" This was a tiny town some thirty miles south of San Antonio. Cherrier taught at a nearby elementary school. I imagined he was a very good teacher.

"The same. Can you make it?"

"What's the occasion?"

"Do friends need an occasion?"

Cherrier is much smarter than I am. As boys we heard there was treasure buried in the bluffs overlooking the Mississippi River. *I* was the one who scaled the cliffs while Cherrier stood below supervising. Another time, repairing a barn for a farmer, we crashed through a wall, causing serious damage. *I* had to tell the farmer. As adults we lost money in a business we thought was can't-miss. *I* had to break the news to our wives. Yes, as good a friend as Cherrier was, I wanted to know the occasion.

"You just want to hoist a few?" I said hopefully.

"Something like that."

"What else? Tell me."

"We'll hoist a few."

"That's it?"

"Stop being suspicious. We'll relive old times."

"I'll be there."

"Start early. Meet me at the school. You can sit in on a class or two. I've told the kids you were out looking for the *Titanic,* and they'd love to hear about it."

"Fine."

"Bring Joe along."

"Why should I bring Joe?"

"What kind of father are you? Spend some time with your son. It's touching. Father and son arm-in-arm."

"We're together too much as it is. I get on his nerves. Besides, he just started school a month ago. He'll be glad to have the apartment to himself for the weekend."

"He needs a break. I know he needs a break."

"How do you know what he needs? He didn't even recognize your voice when you called. You never stay in touch."

"That hurts me. I've always cared about Joe."

"Why don't you just tell me the truth? Why do you want him along?"

"I know he'll enjoy himself. I'm concerned about him."

"Since when? You never remember his birthday."

"Only because the occasion can become crassly commercial. I'd love to send him a present, but he himself wouldn't want the businessmen who've invented this whole idea of birthdays to profit from his."

"You're talking crazy."

"No, you are. Your son loves you. He wants to share things with you. Give him a chance to make this trip."

"I'll ask him. Okay?"

"Don't take no for an answer."

"I told you, I'll ask him."

"We'll have a great time, Bill."

"It will be good to see you."

"Well, I'll say good-bye. See you tomorrow."

"Good-bye, Jim."

"Don't forget to bring Joe."

I fixed a cup of coffee, retrieved the newspaper from in front of the door, and sat down to catch the news before going to the typewriter.

"Why do you read the news, and watch it, at the same time?" Joe asked. He was doing push-ups prior to going to class. I never exercised before starting to write. Figured I needed all the energy I had. Youth was wonderful. On the other hand, when I was Joe's age and going to school, I hadn't exercised before class either.

"That was Cherrier," I said.

"Could tell it was."

"He wants me to visit him in Lytle."

"Great! I'll have the place to myself?"

"You don't want to come along?"

"Why would I want to do that? With you gone, I can play my music as loud as I like."

"I thought you might enjoy being with me. Father and son doing things together. Sharing. Getting to know each other better."

"Aw, come on, Dad."

"I'll have to take the pickup."

"Fine. I'll jog to school. It will be worth it. You gone. The place all to myself. Whoooeee!"

I got started at 6:30 A.M., going a roundabout route through Austin. The Paris of the Southwest, Austin was called. I knew the state capitol building was the largest in the nation, constructed of pink granite, just slightly smaller than the national capitol building in Washington, D.C. The LBJ Library was in Austin. Lyndon Johnson's entire career, from his first "landslide" electoral victory — the winning votes being cast just as the polls closed, and everyone in the critical town voting in alphabetical order — to his later lavishing of contracts on Brown & Root, cried out for investigation. I doubted if people getting libraries to house their papers filled them with incriminating evidence, but what did I know? Important revelations had come from scholars burrowing among dusty shelves at the Truman, Eisenhower, and Kennedy libraries.

The Governor's Mansion in Austin was reportedly the finest house in Austin, which I found surprising. Even the White House is a shack if compared to the residences of certain Rockefellers and DuPonts. The best housing arrangements, I'd learned, were reserved for the rich, possibly as a reminder to politicians about who really is in charge.

I had to admit Austin was lovely. Green and hilly. Plenty of water. Park land. I wanted to look for a place to live, get out of dusty, hot Abilene and do my best book here. I had to remind myself that Austin was packed with all shades of politicians, some of them almost paleolithic in their ideas.

But how bad could it be here? A courageous writer named John Henry Faulk lived in Austin. Faulk had been nearly ruined during the witch scares of the 1950s by zealous right-wingers. He couldn't find work in New York City, but could in Austin, which said something about stereotyping. And of course the great short story writer William Sydney Porter — O. Henry — had lived in Austin. His home was a museum now open to the public.

Leaving Austin behind, I ground along toward San Antonio in Grimm's pickup. It was an indestructible brute. I have had terrible

luck with cars: new ones, old ones, in between. Planned ob-
solescence was not just a phrase to me. How else could the auto industry be kept humming along, unless people *had* to keep buying
something new? Most cars were simply designed to break down. I
wondered if the same were generally true of pickups. I suspected so,
but someone had goofed up making this 1975 Chevy pickup, and it
would run on and on.

San Antonio. The Alamo. This most famous shrine in Texas was
of course a former mission church where 186 white settlers — including Jim Bowie and Davy Crockett — were killed in 1836 by
Santa Ana's soldiers, after having held out for thirteen days. It was
said Texas would never split into five states, as its constitution
allowed, because none of the new entities would allow another to
have the Alamo. Of course, if Texas did separate into five states,
the area would have ten U.S. Senators, a prospect that would have
to be happy for big Texas corporations interested in fat government
cost-plus contracts. The Alamo, incidentally, had been the Number
One tourist attraction in Texas until recently, when it was replaced
by Six Flags Over Texas, an amusement park with dangerous-
looking roller coasters situated between Dallas and Fort Worth.

I learned that many Texans really did revere the Alamo. When
rock singer Ozzie Osborne urinated on the Alamo wall in a display
of odious bad taste, his performances were banned from public
facilities in San Antonio. Ozzie Osborne is perhaps best known for
biting the heads off live bats during concert appearances.

I knew San Antonio was famous for its beautiful River Walk, for
La Villita, and for HemisFair Plaza, site of the 1968 World's Fair.
It too seemed a good place to visit, but I drove on. If I had been going to stop anywhere, it would have been Austin, where I had an invitation to visit Dale Chayes. He had been the radio operator
aboard the search ship *Gyre,* and had provided glowing accounts of
places to eat in Austin. But I was growing eager to see Cherrier —
it had been two years now — and reach the school where he taught
before the students were let out.

I almost didn't make it. As soon as I got off the main highway, I
was on blacktop and then dirt roads. There weren't even houses or
farms in sight, just a twisting narrow road that would be a
nightmare when it was dark. The man at the gas station had warned
me that the school would be hard to find, but he didn't tell me I
could drive through the town of Lytle and not know I was there.

Cherrier taught sixth, seventh, and eighth grade, mostly Mexican kids classified as slow learners. I didn't think the school district could find a more dedicated teacher than my friend. He was the very rare person who possessed an A-1 mind, yet he had the patience to be with children, listen to them, teach them. This was well into the school year — begun in September — and I couldn't believe the so-called fast learners, whoever they were, any longer were ahead of Cherrier's youngsters. They were quick of mind and curious, and seemed to love their teacher, who clearly was very proud of them. Cherrier also coached the junior high school basketball team, which was undefeated.

I talked for fifteen minutes about the search for the *Titanic,* and when the bell rang to signal school was out, they wanted to listen longer. It is not that I am a good speaker. They were just fascinated by the great ship that sank, and the odd Texas millionaire who looked for it. One little girl asked if Jack Grimm would come and talk to them. I said he might. Jack had paid for a long-distance hookup to a small town in Colorado and talked to a third-grade class there for an hour.

"How about a beer?" I said to Cherrier when we were walking towards the pickup and his car.

"Just what I had in mind," he said. "I've got a six pack iced up for you. Follow me to my apartment and we'll drink it there."

"How about a nice bar on the way? I'm hot and my throat's dry."

"My apartment will be better."

Cherrier lived on the second floor of a twelve-unit complex near Lytle, and a woman was waiting at his door when we arrived. She was my height, 5'8", husky, perhaps thirty years old with short brown hair, and she wore jeans and a work shirt.

"Marcy," Cherrier introduced, "this is my friend, Bill."

"Marcy," I said. "I guess that's for Marcia."

She smiled, shook my hand firmly, and we followed Cherrier into his small apartment. I knew immediately why he'd wanted Joe to come along. Joe, who was 6'2" and more than 200 pounds.

Everywhere on the floor were boxes and crates, all set to be moved. This wasn't so bad. I sighed when I saw the refrigerator, the same refrigerator he'd had when last I saw him in California.

"Father and son should spend time together, huh?" I said.

"Bill, I wasn't thinking of Joe helping with the move. You did know I was moving, didn't you?"

"How could I know that? You don't write."

"I thought I told you. Got a nice home in the country. Away from everything. Cows come right up to the bedroom window every morning."

"Good for you. Have the cows help you move."

"Bill . . . we're friends." He laughed. "Why, I think you believe I asked you to visit so you could help me carry my stuff."

"Why would I think that?" I didn't think it. I knew it.

"Good. Because that would have been an underhanded trick. No, I was just thinking of the beautiful country home I'm moving into, and I realized — came to me like a flash — who better to help break in my new home than my oldest friend, good old Bill Hoffman."

"Well, I'm here. Give me the directions to your house, and I'll meet you over there when you get the stuff moved in."

"And lose precious time we could spend talking together? I won't hear of it. We see each other little enough any more as it is. You just make yourself comfortable, tell me how you're doing, let me know everything that's happening with you, and I'll enjoy listening while Marcy and I do the moving."

"All I have to do is watch?"

"What else? And before we start, I suggest we relax and have one of those cold beers I talked about. You and me and Marcy. We'll sit right down and have a cold beer together."

Cherrier headed for the refrigerator, and I gave Marcy — Marcia — a closer look. The word "hardy" came to mind. "Healthy." "Strong." She caught me studying her and shyly smiled back.

"Damn!" I heard Cherrier exclaim from behind me, at the same instant snapping his fingers. "I thought sure I'd remembered to get that beer."

"The old I-forgot-and-have-to-go-out-and-get-the-beer trick, eh?" I said.

"Bill . . . Bill . . . Bill . . . What happened to the trusting, see-the-best-in-everyone friend I knew as a boy?"

"He almost broke his neck on a cliff looking for treasure while you were on a safe ledge issuing orders."

"That old story," he scoffed. "You don't remember it right. You've exaggerated it in your mind."

"I remember it exactly. I broke my fall with my wrists, one of which was shattered in three places."

"I've felt bad about that ever since it happened. I've often wished it had been me who fell."

"Sure you have."

"Let's not dwell on moments that are unpleasant to me, Bill."

Unpleasant to *him? I* was the one who broke my wrist.

"What we want to do," he continued, "is enjoy our reunion. Two good friends back together again. A perfect time to enjoy a beer, look back at all that's happened since Prairie du Chien, look ahead to what's left to be done."

"Come off it, Cherrier. You just wanted help moving."

"How can you say that? To prove you're wrong, I'll go get a six pack while you and Marcy talk. When I get back, we'll enjoy a beer, then Marcy and I will do the moving."

"I'll go get the beer. Where's the store?"

"You can't get there from here."

"Ridiculous. You can get anywhere from here."

"I mean, you couldn't find it. A lot of tricky turns. No landmarks to guide you. You'd be lost for sure."

"Nonsense. Tell me where the place is and I'll find it."

"No, I can't let you get lost. I don't want to go. I'd rather talk to Marcy. And I'll only go under one circumstance. That you promise you won't move anything."

"I'll promise that."

"Fine. I'll be back." Cherrier started out the door.

"Wait a minute," I said. *"When* will you be back?"

"Soon," he said, and was gone.

I couldn't think of anything to say to Marcy, so after a few minutes I began to pace. She seemed to pay no attention to me, but I couldn't help but be aware of her. Other words came to mind. "Sturdy." "Solid." The word "hefty" didn't fit. She just had a lot of muscles.

Ten minutes went by. Marcy rose from her sitting position, lifted a box, and carried it out the door and down the outside stairs to a waiting van. I stopped pacing, cursed Cherrier, and sat on the floor. He wasn't going to do this to me. I refused to feel sorry for this woman — who looked like a shorter version of Cowboy tackle Randy White, anyway — and help her. I didn't know why she was doing Cherrier's work, but it didn't matter. I hadn't come all the way from Abilene so he could save a few dollars in moving expenses.

Of course, no man, regardless of how callous — and this day I felt I was right up there in this respect — can for a long period of time watch a woman do heavy work and not volunteer to help. I told myself it was chauvinist of me to think this way, Marcy was perfectly capable of handling the work, I had a duty to the women's movement *not* to help. Fleetingly I even thought Cherrier might be paying her to work, but my rational mind forced me immediately to abandon this insane thought.

I knew perfectly well what Cherrier was doing. He was in a friendly local tavern drinking cold beer.

It was impossible to hold out. Marcy had carried perhaps fifteen boxes down the stairs, and although she didn't look in the least winded, I figured she had to be tired. Cherrier reads a lot. Those boxes were surely packed with books, and books are heavy.

I began to work. What else could I do? Stay seated on the floor? The boxes were as heavy as expected, and several times I feared I would pitch forward down the stairs and break my jaw. But I kept at it. Foolishly I believed I should match Marcy box for box. I hurt an ankle, a knee, and my right hand — my typing hand, damn Cherrier! — when I didn't do what I should have, which was drop a box containing his dishes; instead I laid it gently on the floor of the van, and got my hand stuck underneath.

Why did hope keep rearing its ugly head? I didn't even complain carrying chairs, or helping Marcy with desks and the dining room table. I could stand anything, I thought, except that refrigerator, and surely he would be back in time for that onerous task. But deep inside I knew he wouldn't. He would show when, *if*, we got the refrigerator onto the van.

Well, he would have to stay away a long time, I thought. The refrigerator would be the very last thing we moved. But then I realized that was no punishment at all, making him stay away. He was having a good time. I felt like Mr. T. had been pounding on me.

The refrigerator began to assume mountainous proportions in my mind. Why didn't we just leave it, anyway? It was older than Cherrier himself. What could it be worth? Maybe a lot, I feared, it might have been one of the first ones made. It would serve him right if we wrecked it. I didn't know how you wrecked a refrigerator, especially one that seemed as indestructible as a bulldozer.

I was still trying to think of ways to avoid this last, heavy indignity when the remainder of Cherrier's apartment was emptied save for the refrigerator. I sat exhausted on the floor watching with despair as the indomitable Marcy came trudging through the door pulling a dolly behind her. I rose wearily, went to the window, looked out. No sign of Cherrier. Marcy had the dolly in front of the refrigerator.

I held the dolly. Marcy went into a deep knee bend, her rear nearly touching the floor, her broad back straight, eyes concentrated, bulging in anticipation, and *she lifted the front of the refrigerator onto the dolly.*

We exchanged places, me moving to the back of the dolly (the end you *push,* the one that means you're on the top of the stairs while your partner is going down), she to the front, the end you *pull,* making her the one the refrigerator, if such was the will of the fates, would tumble on and crush.

The pushing was easy only in comparison. I thought at first the stairs would collapse under the weight, and each step we went down I feared would be Marcy's last. I held the dolly back as best I could, but Marcy's life was in very weak hands. I thought it would be heaven when the refrigerator was finally safe on the van to lie down in that empty apartment and sleep forever. But I knew there wouldn't be time even to get back up the stairs, much less lie down and rest, before Cherrier came zipping back into the parking lot. In fact, I emerged from the semi-darkness of the van expecting to see his headlights.

Actually, it was ten minutes before he arrived. I'd prepared myself for the car-broke-down story, but he claimed instead that he got lost. It was a clever sort of lie. It was so unbelievable, so unlikely, that you tended to believe it. Cherrier, as mentioned, is a bright person, and could have spun an elaborate tale, or produced a bill from an auto repair shop. Telling a story that was fantastic — how could you get lost in a town that, as the joke goes, has a sign with "Welcome to Lytle" printed on both sides? — was just the right touch. If it's not true, you think, why didn't he come up with something better?

Cherrier, Marcy, and I sat on the stairs and drank a beer. At least he'd bought a whole case, and it was ice cold. Which meant he lolled away time in a bar first, then bought the beer.

He and Marcy went to the van, talked for a minute or so, and then she drove off. "Let's head for the house," he said, when he returned to the stairs.

"One more beer," I said. "I need another beer before I can go anywhere."

"Drink it in the pickup while you're following me."

That's right! I thought. One of the more questionable laws in Texas made it legal to drink *while* you were driving. As long as you weren't legally intoxicated, you could zip down the highway waving your drink at the cops, and they couldn't arrest you. They *could* stop you, and would, but if you passed the breathalyzer, you were okay.

"You have a lot of nerve," I said. "I break my back three hours humping your furniture — why don't you junk that refrigerator, by the way? — and now you want to hurry me over so I can do it again."

"I like that refrigerator. My folks had it in Prairie."

"Your grandfolks had it in Prairie."

"Well, I like it. It's a scientific impossibility, you know. A refrigerator can't last as long as this one has. I mean, this refrigerator . . ."

"I don't want to hear about your refrigerator. I'm telling you, I'm not moving another thing."

"I wouldn't think of asking you."

"I can't believe you're going to help Marcy. She's strong, but even she can't handle that refrigerator on her own."

"Fear not. A couple of acquaintances will move the furniture in on Monday. You'll be safely away by then."

"We're sleeping in an empty house?"

"Sort of like old times, eh? Like when we were out on the islands on the Mississippi."

"We were twelve years old. I'm staying in a motel."

"There isn't one. Not unless you want to drive to San Antonio."

Following Cherrier in Grimm's pickup through the Texas night, expecting at any moment a cowboy or teenager to come head-on at me doing one hundred miles per hour, I thought about the twists people's lives take. Grimm, his home in the middle of a dusty desert, searching the North Atlantic for the most famous ship that ever sank. Satterfield, the deal-maker, by his own admission devoid of any ideas about movies, suddenly finding himself in the business. And, yes, I thought about Cherrier and myself. I had many friends as a boy, but I couldn't even remember some of the names now, and certainly couldn't tell you how their lives turned out. Anyway, it was something, I thought, Cherrier and me, Northerners, forty-three years later, driving in tandem over these deserted Texas roads.

Of course his electricity hadn't yet been connected by the power company, so his house was darker than dark. It seemed a nice place, what I could see of it, the guest home of a widow whose husband had left her large chunks of land, including the big ranch on which the house was set. We sat out on the steps of the house, the Texas sky as usual bright and star-filled, and I could hear the mooing of the cows Cherrier said came to his window in the morning, and birds and crickets and other night creatures. We drank the entire case of beer, talked until early in the morning. I was so tired even that blanketless floor appeared inviting.

"Know what we've got planned tomorrow?" Cherrier asked, when we were sprawled out ready for sleep. "I mean, tonight. It's 4 A.M."

"What?" I said, sleepily.

"A double date, old friend. Bet you haven't been out in quite a while."

"That's nice," I said.

"Want to know who you're going with?"

"Sure."

"Marcy."

"She seems like a good person."

"She is. And a lot of fun, too."

"Doesn't say much. In fact, I can't remember her saying anything." It was true, I realized. We had been together more than three hours, and she hadn't uttered a word.

"She'll loosen up," Cherrier said. "You've just got to get to know her."

"Good night, Jim."

"Good night, Bill."

Cherrier was right about the cows coming up to the windows to moo. But they did more than that. They butted their heads against the windows, which were barred on the outside. They made a terrific racket, and seemed to be practically on top of me when I woke up and saw them. A whole herd was out there.

"Cherrier! What the hell is this?"

"Don't get in an uproar. Go back to sleep."

"Those are wild cows out there."

"They're just hungry. The guy who used to live here paid his rent by feeding them. Go out and feed them and they'll quiet down."

"I'm not going to feed your cows."

"They're not my cows. Chase them away if you want."

"I'm not going to chase them away. I'm afraid of them. I'd probably cause a stampede."

"Cows don't stampede. Go back to sleep. They'll leave after a while."

But it was impossible to sleep. I had a terrific headache and it was only 7 A.M., which meant I'd had three hours of sleep. I got up and went to Cherrier's stove, without really much hope, and the gas was plugged in. I was twice-blest. On an otherwise empty shelf I found a jar of instant coffee. Who said he didn't provide his guests with amenities?

I drank coffee and slowly came awake. There was something charming about those cows peering through the windows. If only they weren't so insistent. They banged their heads against the bars but Cherrier was impervious. The volume of his snoring increased.

What had he told me last night? Something about Marcy. I had a date with Marcy. And he had a date. I realized everything about this smelled even worse than his ploy to get me to move his furniture.

"Wake up!" I said, shaking his shoulders. "Wake up!"

"Leave me alone. It's morning."

"I want to talk about this double date." I was still shaking him. He opened his eyes and rubbed them.

"You didn't fix coffee for me?"

"Of course I didn't. I want to talk about the double date."

"I can't talk until I have coffee."

I made his coffee. "I'm sorry I don't have the eggs and ham too," I said.

"It's okay. You could have put more sugar in the coffee."

"What about this double date?"

"Stop shouting. Haven't you ever taken a woman out? You're going out with Marcy. I've got a date. That's it. No cause to start brutalizing me before dawn."

"What's Marcy like?"

"You met her. She's fun. She likes you."

"How do you know that?"

"She told me so before she drove off. Said you were a good worker."

"What does she do? Besides work for you for nothing?"

"Is this the Spanish Inquisition? I fix you up with a date, you probably couldn't get one on your own, and you come on like a prosecutor."

"What does she do?"

"She's in transportation."

"What does that mean?"

"She drives a truck. She's a worker."

"What kind of truck?"

"I don't remember."

"What kind? I swear, I'll pour this hot coffee on your head."

"An eighteen-wheeler."

"Well," I said, "I guess that's all right. Is there anything else I should know?"

"Nothing."

"What about your date?"

"Just a girl."

"Good looking?"

"So-so."

"What does she do?"

"She teaches."

"Where you teach? That's nice."

"Actually, at a college. In San Antonio."

"She's a professor?"

"I guess you could say that. Look, would you leave me alone."

"Don't give me that, Cherrier. Not after last night."

"Yes, she's a professor."

"Of what?"

"English Literature."

"Got a Ph.D.?"

"I suppose. Will you stop this third degree?"

"So I'm dating a truck driver and you're going out with a Ph.D. How did that come about?"

"Just happened that way, I guess."

"Tell me the truth, Cherrier."

His face took on a look of desperation. "You've got to help me, Bill. I really like my date. Been trying to get her to go out for months. I told her about you. Naturally, she's interested in authors.

Said she'd love to meet you. I said, 'What a coincidence, he'll be visiting soon. He has a date. Why don't we double date?' You need to help me on this."

"Why should I help you?"

"We're friends." After last night it was remarkable he could keep a straight face.

"Let me get this straight," I said. "The professor wants to meet me. But you're taking her out."

"Right."

"You're low, Cherrier."

"I know it. But I really want to take this girl out."

"Well, I'll do it. Not for you. For me. I could use a good time, and if Marcy is as fun as you say, it should work out."

"Oh, she is."

"Why did you pick her?"

"She's the only other woman I know."

We drove around San Antonio that afternoon, stopping at two Mexican cafes for glasses of wine, and promptly at 6 P.M. Cherrier was knocking at the door of a nice condominium.

Cherrier had called her "so-so," but she was a twelve on a scale of one to ten. Five-feet-five. Blonde shoulder-length hair. Green eyes. Perfect complexion. Perfect features. A figure most women would kill for.

And she was smart. Not quick-smart, or one-liner smart, but someone who had thought things through. She was a kid from Maine whose earlier work with Chicano groups had brought her to San Antonio. Her favorite author was Dostoevsky. Of course, she said, she also liked Tolstoy. Her name was Janet.

I could have killed Cherrier. Janet should have been my date. It was me she had wanted to meet. Anyway, maybe later. I would talk with her. Show I was a really bright fine fellow. The problem was, she and Cherrier were in the front seat, I was in the back, and the radio was playing and he was talking, something I had to admit he did well. But since when had he been a fan of Mozart? His tastes ran to Pete Seeger and Judy Collins.

We stopped and got Marcy in Lytle. She wore a soft pastel angora sweater and a grey wool skirt.

"Good to see you again, Marcia," I said.

"Nice to see you again too, you old peckerwood." Her voice was soft and surprisingly pleasant to the ear, but she punctuated her greeting by delivering a bone-crushing blow to my shoulder. Was this the same Marcy?

Cherrier grinned at me from the front seat. "See, I told you Marcy liked you."

I swallowed the pain and smiled at my date. "Ready for a night on the town?"

"You bet your sweet ass I am." She said in her mellifluous voice. Stars swam before my eyes as Marcia dealt my already mangled shoulder another "love tap."

From the rear seat of Cherrier's car I tried to stare a hole into the back of his head, but he was too busy changing the tape to Beethoven and pretending to Janet to possess a culture I knew he didn't have.

"Well, gang," I said, "where would we like to eat?"

"There's a lovely Mexican place," Janet said, "halfway between here and San Antonio. It has the best *fajitas* in the world."

"What are *fajitas?*" I said stupidly.

"Highly seasoned strips of skirt steak," Cherrier said, now in the role of gourmet. He only knew this because he taught Mexican kids. "They're cooked over charcoal or mesquite. Wrapped in a flour tortilla with guacamole and hot sauce. They trace back to . . ."

"I get the idea," I said. "How does that sound to you, Marcia?"

"Just dandy, Billy, just dandy." She threw her huge arm around my shoulders and literally lifted me off of the seat in a show of affection. It was like being loved by a python.

Marcy sat close to me, holding my hand. I noticed Cherrier was holding Janet's hand. He was talking about Zen and collecting books on the *I Ching,* and such exotic subjects as the essentiality of trigrams and hexagrams. I knew he didn't care a zit about any of these things. But Janet was impressed, particularly when he said he'd read all of Carlos Castaneda's books. I could have piped up that I thought Castaneda's books were fakes, he probably imagined the events while on drug trips, but that would have scored no points.

"Do you enjoy driving a big truck?" I asked Marcy.

Her sweet voice purred. "Does a wild bear shit in the woods?" This was followed by another life-threatening hug.

My God, I thought.

Dinner was as good as Janet had promised. The meat was tender and the mesquite over which it was cooked imparted a special memorable flavor. Cherrier played the role of charlatan to the hilt, pretending to be well-versed on a dozen subjects that interested Janet. She, by the way, grew more beautiful as the evening passed. When, merely to be polite, she asked me about my writing, Cherrier was ready with a *bon mot* to deflect the conversation. I thought I'd be sick when he started to talk about his French ancestors. I knew for a fact one of them had been a notorious swindler and extortionist.

I finally got him alone in the men's room. "Marcy's a lot of fun, is she?" I said menacingly.

"Give her a chance. She's a great dancer."

"I don't want to dance."

"Well, tell that to Marcy. I promised we'd go dancing after dinner."

"A truck driver with the voice of an angel, the body of King Kong, and a vocabulary that would make a roughneck blush! Cherrier, this is the worst ever."

"Don't laugh at her. She's strong."

"Dammit, I know she's strong. I don't want to laugh at her. I want to cry. For both of us."

"I think she's kinda cute."

"I don't. I ought to . . ."

"We can't keep them waiting. How do you like that Janet? Is she something? Don't I have good taste?"

"Even rats appreciate steak. Listen, I . . ."

"Tell me later. I want to get back to Janet."

We went to a loud country and western club on the outskirts of San Antonio. The place had a huge dance floor sprinkled with sawdust and smelled of beer and smoke. I thought Cherrier had made his first mistake, taking the classy Janet to a dive like this, but it turned out she was delighted. "I've always wanted to sit and watch this sort of thing," she said, hugging his arm and putting her head on his shoulder.

The key word was "watch." But Marcy didn't want to watch. She wanted to be out on the floor where the action was. The dance was some variety of the bump, now infamous as slam-dancing, where the object evidently is to body-block your partner hard against a wall. It wouldn't have been bad if I'd been dancing with Cherrier. I could have bumped him right *through* one of those walls. But Marcy, as has been observed, was strong. She bumped me bowling ball-like through a crowd of dancers, followed me on tiptoes, casually tossing the dancers, both men and women alike, out of her way, caught me just as I was sliding gratefully to the floor, and swung me around once in a sort of dancing-bear two-step.

The next bump sent me reeling against a table filled with cowboys and I knocked over a pitcher of beer. Luckily for me, Marcy cowed them properly before they had the opportunity to destroy what was left of my body.

After one of the dances when we had sat back down with Cherrier and Janet, Marcia spied someone she knew walking past our table. He was like a house with a beard, and Marcy's face just lit up. She grabbed his arm. "Hey, Ben Bob, you old bastard, you wanna arm wrestle?"

Ben Bob was a truck-driving buddy. He sat down and I couldn't believe it. He and Marcy arm-wrestled. Marcy won. Janet cuddled closer to Cherrier, her eyes wide with amused wonderment, and I could tell she was thanking him for bringing her to this delightful place.

Ben Bob was a gentleman. He asked if I minded if he danced with Marcy. I said that was fine, since they were old friends.

Marcy came back perhaps an hour later. She laid her hand on my shoulder, lightly this time, looked straight into my eyes. "Listen, Billy," she said, softly, "don't take this wrong, but I was wondering if you would mind me staying with this old sheep raper?" Marcy clapped Ben Bob on the back with her other hand, a blow that would have felled a Clydesdale. Ben Bob stood, unmoved. His lips parted in a smile. He had a total of three teeth.

"That would be okay, Marcia."

She leaned over and gave me a fine kiss.

"Have a good time," I said.

"See ya around, you old peckerwood."

By now Cherrier and Janet were nose to nose, talking intimately, kissing once in a while, little affectionate pecks that promise more. I stuck *my* nose into my beer mug and took a deep swallow. Then I listened to the loud music and watched the sweating, writhing dancers batter one another. Janet was right. It was something to see, this slice of Texana.

Fourteen

It was 10 A.M. of a cloudy, humid mid-November Sunday, and I had just parked the pickup truck in the sprawling lot of Albertson's Supermarket. As I walked towards the front entrance I tried to imagine what wonders awaited. The invitation had come in a simple enough form: a phone call the previous night from Grimm.

"How would you like to meet some more of the boys tomorrow?" he asked.

Jim Gosdin, calling from Dallas to see how I was, had no clue to the identity of *these* boys — "Probably the reprobates Jack runs around with," Gosdin guessed. Joe predicted they would turn out to be Grimm's poker playing buddies. I simply didn't know. "The boys" in the broadest sense to Jack were every male in Texas, in a more specific way were other Texas millionaires, especially his brethren in the oil business. But this was Abilene and the ones I was to meet were *the* boys.

This was clearly the highest I could rise in Jack's opinion. He had welcomed me into his home, encouraged his family to show me every consideration, even had me as a guest numerous times at the Petroleum Club. But this was the summit, the final gesture to seal our friendship.

"Albertson's?" I had said. "The boys are going to be at Albertson's?"

"Right, boy. Ten A.M."

"How do I recognize them?"

"Look for me. I'll be eating breakfast."

I had been in Albertson's dozens of times, but didn't know you could eat breakfast there. It had to be in the deli section.

It was. I spotted Grimm right away, wolfing down eggs and biscuits, talking animatedly with seven other men. Next to Grimm was a shopping cart. It was packed with generic brands. He had been doing his shopping prior to breakfast.

The men were seated at one big table, each eating eggs and biscuits, and drinking coffee. One of them was in his forties; the *youngest* of the others must have been eighty. They were all dressed in worn, dusty jeans and work shirts with holes in them, except for Jack, who wore khaki pants and a white shirt. Grimm spotted me, waved me over, made introductions.

"Bill, this is T.J. Bill's a writer from New York. Bill, T.J. is in the oil business."

"Bill, this is R.T. Bill's a writer from New York. Bill, R.T. is in the oil hauling business."

"Bill, this is C.L. Bill's a writer from New York. Bill, C.L. is in the oil equipment business."

And so on. All of them were in the oil business, all, except Grimm and the "youngster" (they called him that), seemed older than Texas itself. And all of them had initials instead of names. No one appeared to mind my being there. If Grimm said I was okay, that was enough for them.

"Why don't you get yourself some breakfast?" Jack said. "Just go up to the counter and tell them to fill your plate."

The woman behind the counter filled my plate with eggs and biscuits, told me to help myself to the coffee over by the window. She then moved along behind the counter to the cash register. I handed her a five dollar bill.

"I'm sorry," she said. "I really don't have much change right now. Not many people in the store at this hour. Most folks are in church."

I handed her four one dollar bills. She looked at them, smiled, sighed, and handed them back. "Don't you have anything smaller?"

"Change? You want change?"

"I'm sorry. Please. If you have it."

"How much is this meal?"

"Twenty-one cents. The coffee is free."

"Those guys over there are eating twenty-one-cent breakfasts?" I waved in the direction of the boys.

"Oh, yes. They eat here every Sunday morning."

"Well, your prices are right."

"They think so. Especially since they can drink all the coffee they can hold."

The boys seemed barely to notice my presence. *So this is how it's done*, I thought. My friends in New York imagined the oil barons cooking up their sinister deals, arranging their complex cabals, and plotting to lower wages in plush board rooms and executive suites, on lavishly appointed jets or in soundproof lushly carpeted private clubs. But no. The scheming that doomed average citizens to lives of penury were made in an empty, cavernous supermarket deli over a breakfast that cost twenty-one cents. *You're a reporter,* I told myself. *It's your duty to listen closely.*

F.A. was talking. He was probably $20 million on the hoof, though he could have passed for a hobo in those old jeans and tattered shirt. "Hard to get intelligent help these days," F.A. said. "I was out at one of my wells the other day. Had to yell at this boy to be heard over the noise. Now that I've got a little age on me" — I guessed he was at least ninety — "I don't like to have to raise my voice. Anyway, I said, 'Goddammit, I told you to put in two.' That's a simple thing. Two. But he couldn't get it. So I yelled louder, clear as I could, 'You idiot, that's two! Two! Two, two, two!' Still didn't get it right. Gotta spell things out for people. I shouted as loud as I could. 'Two, you fool! That's two, Two, TWO! Two, you dumbbell, T-E-U, TWO!' "

"F.A.'s good at finding oil," Grimm said.

"I hope so," I said.

"Am," said F.A.

D.O. was talking about his upcoming birthday party. It evidently always was one of the social events of the Abilene winter season, and this year, D.O. said, he was going all out. "Gonna have a top country band," he said. "I mean top."

"Why not a rock group?" Grimm said, snorting into his sleeve.

"Can't stand the noise," D.O. replied seriously. "Gives me the worst headache. Besides they all got that long hair, they take drugs, and they dress funny."

"You're right about that," said J.M.

"Now these boys I got coming in are real sharp." D.O. was warming up on the subject of the party. "Wait'll you see the band I got. They wear red western outfits that got their names spelled out on 'em with sequences."

"What are sequences?" asked J.M.

"You dummy. Why everyone knows that sequences are those shiny things like Liberace and Buck Owens have on their clothes."

"What's so special about sequences?"

"You're a no-class guy, J.M. They kind of jazz things up, make 'em pretty. The only thing you think is pretty is that waitress at the Abilene Club."

R.T. was smoking a cigar that seemed as big and round as an oil pipe, and kept flicking the ashes into his water glass. The smoke from the cigar was so thick it could have been used to flash Indian signals to tribe members waiting on an opposite hill. T.J. kept looking at R.T., and for a few moments I thought it might have something to do with the cigar's aroma, or the fact that it befogged the entire table.

But it couldn't be that. T.J. was angry, and getting madder by the minute. R.T. didn't notice, but T.J. was close to exploding. Finally he let it come out.

"R.T., we've known each other a long time."

"That's right, T.J."

"Your trucks have been hauling my oil for a long time."

"Right on twenty years, T.J."

"I just learned something."

"What's that, T.J.?"

"You've been stealing five thousand dollars a week from me. Been under-reporting how much oil you've hauled."

"I'm glad you found out, T.J."

"You are? Well, I'm damn upset about it."

"What are you going to do?"

"Get me somebody else to haul my oil, that's what."

"You could do that, T.J."

"Damn right. It's what I'm gonna do."

"Know what will happen, T.J.?"

"Yep. Your thievin' hands will be out of my oil."

"You'll get somebody new. Somebody who's not your friend like I am. That new guy will steal twenty thousand dollars a week from you."

T.J. thought it over. Slowly enlightenment dawned. He made up his mind in a hurry.

"You're right, R.T. I took leave of my senses there for a minute."

"Well, you don't have to apologize."

"I want to, R.T. I owe you an apology."

The two men shook hands across the table. I thought I saw moisture in T.J.'s eyes. Certainly remorse. How could he have been upset with his friend? But it was all right. R.T. understood. He patted T.J. on the shoulder and spoke a few consoling words.

L.K. had a problem to air out in front of the boys. "It's my wife," L.K. said. "Wants a Lincoln Continental, and I don't see how I can turn her down. She was hot about my last Vegas trip. Then I bought me another plane."

"Pay your money and buy your peace," said C.L. He was the one in the oil equipment business.

"But, geesus, the cost of a Continental!"

"It's called keeping up with the Joneses," said C.L.

"Goddammit, *I am the Joneses,*" said L.K.

Several of the boys got on C.L. He wasn't really one of them, they said. Not a gambler like they were. They put up their money and took the risk, and the odds favored a return of zero. C.L. got paid no matter what. He couldn't lose.

C.L. seemed hurt. "Haven't I given you credit when you needed it?" he said.

"No," was the simultaneous judgment of several.

There was still no clear purpose to this get together. All of them had finished their breakfasts and were making frequent trips to the free coffee dispenser. It didn't seem likely this was the only time they had to meet, since a couple of them seemed to be in one of Grimm's card games, and others were partners in various business ventures. The common denominators were big bankrolls, the oil business, and advanced age (with two exceptions).

"You ought to slow up on that coffee," T.J. told F.A. "You're beginning to look older."

Beginning to look older? I thought. He had wrinkles deep as canyons and a Father Time beard.

"I'll have a shot or two of whiskey when I get to the club," said F.A. "It'll put a little color in my face."

He already had color: grey. He was a tough old buzzard, and despite how he looked, I figured he might outlive us all.

"You should go to one of those health food places," said T.J. "Get yourself some wheat germ and carrot juice."

"Shit," said F.A. "I've never seen anybody who looked healthy in a health food place."

The conversation shifted to a replay of the previous night's poker action, indeed an important subject but still, I suspected, not why eight millionaires chose each Sunday morning to have breakfast with one another. Maybe all of them simply appreciated a bargain: twenty-one cents for breakfast. For another dime they could have had sausage patties, but none availed themselves of the deal.

Specifically, they talked about a newcomer in the card game. He'd played three or four times, and the question was whether to permit him to continue. On the plus side was the fact that he was rich and an atrocious player. He bluffed every hand, and never ceased to be amazed when someone stayed to call. In the minus column, he drank a lot, and there was fear he might be a disruptive influence. In addition, he seemed to have the social graces of an alligator, and a temper that grew as his bankroll diminished. He must be a real slob, I thought, if the boys objected to him. Most of them would not have been at home having tea with Queen Elizabeth.

"Well," said R.T., "we've got to make a decision. He's not a very good poker player. Piss poor, to be frank about it. I say that outweighs everything else. I say he stays."

"He does pay his bills," T.J. said approvingly.

"Never asks to write out a check," added C.L.

"Not a bad dude at all, really," said R.T.

"I kind of like him," said T.J.

"The salt of the earth, in some ways," decided C.L.

The man was about to be eulogized when F.A., the *oldest of the old* — a sort of leader, I imagined, because of his venerable age — interrupted with the announcement that his great-granddaughter was entered in a beauty contest. "Well, she'll win," R.T. said. "A real little beauty."

"Yep," said F.A. "I sure do enjoy bouncing her on my knee."

"You do?" I said. I had said virtually nothing up till now.

"Yep. Cutest little six-year-old you'll ever see."

"Six? And she's in a beauty contest?"

"Right, boy." He was the second person from Texas to call me boy. "We like our beauty contests here."

It turned out the competition was the Texas National Little Miss, and that Texans did indeed enjoy their beauty contests. There was a Watermelon Thump Queen, who presided over seed-spitting contests while dressed in a gown with a train covered in sequined watermelons. There was the Rice Queen, for which Texans, not hypocritical, require absolutely no talent. Miss Cavalcade, another straight beauty competition unsullied by singing, dancing, or the playing of a French horn. The Tyler Rose Queen — H.L. Hunt's daughter once held this title — the winner being determined by whose father gives the most money to approved causes. Miss Black-Eyed Pea, with the winner having to swear she loves the vegetable and prove it by consuming large quantities. And Miss Cow Chip Queen, who parades in front of judges dragging a burlap bag filled with dried cattle manure, the theory being that anyone who can look good doing this must be a genuine beauty. Miss Cow Chip Queen also serves as a judge in cow chip throwing contests, an activity almost as popular as chili cookoffs, rattlesnake hunts, and armadillo races.

Texas entrants do extremely well in national beauty competitions, probably because they often start early and it can be a full-time job for them years before they make it to something like the Miss America or Miss Universe Pageants. Three former Miss Americas from Texas were Phyllis George of Denton, Jo-Carroll Dennison of Tyler, and Shirley Cothran, also from Denton. The beauty contest entrants from Texas also get special help from professionals, often financed by a rich person, not available to contestants from other states. Recently there was a mini-scandal when a wealthy man was discovered having paid for a beauty queen's cosmetic surgery. Texans are interested in beauty contests, want to win them, with a fever almost equal to winning football games.

The interest in football was evident everywhere in Texas, and the boys in the Albertson's deli were no exceptions. All but the youngest of them was far too old to have children in school, but they knew the names of every high school player in Abilene, down to the least of the scrubs, and had considerable knowledge of players in other towns. They knew who was "coming up" from junior high and grade school also. Unbelievably, the practice of red-shirting — keeping a student back so he would be eligible for an extra year of football — controversial at the college level, was used occasionally in *junior high school*. Still, it reached its absurdity in college. Texas Tech, a Southwest Conference School, would have *56* redshirts on its team. Many schools don't have that many players.

It was just past 11:30 A.M. according to the big clock in Albertson's' when F.A. looked at his gold watch and said, "It's just past 11:30." He had been alerted, I think, by the influx of customers to the supermarket. Families, brightly dressed, had gotten out of church, and were stopping for last-minute items for the big Sunday dinner. An assistant manager briskly stepped from checkout counter to checkout counter to inspire his workers. It had been a sleepy morning — certainly the store wasn't going to get rich on the boys — but now the store's very purpose was about to be fulfilled.

The boys came alive too, and I doubt if I will ever see anything like it again in my life. For a few seconds, so lulled had I been by the everyday aspirations of millionaires, I was simply not aware what was occurring. Then it became clear. Speaking quietly but quickly, rushing but not in a hurried way that invites mistakes, the boys in less than a minute carried out the transactions that had brought them here. And large transactions they were.

They bet on the Sunday NFL football games. They wagered amounts I imagined you could buy some small countries for, and it was carried out with virtually no haggling. A point spread would be offered and either accepted or rejected. If rejected, another game was brought up. A good deal of preparatory thought must have gone into this Sunday morning meeting, and they might have been produce clerks talking with a customer. "Do you want apples? No? How about oranges? Not oranges either? Here's some lettuce you might like."

Bets made, the boys one by one ambled out. As they edged past shoppers to the door, I wondered if the shoppers even knew who they were. I guessed they did not. The boys, through their money and influence, probably determined much of the quality of life in Abilene, but few even knew their names.

Since they had arrived before the supermarket came alive, they had been able to park right in front of the store, and through the big front window I could see them getting into their pickup trucks. Even F.A. the Eldest drove a pickup. I saw him hop spryly into the cab. Grimm, I guessed, was the only one who came in a Cadillac. He had loaned me his precious pickup.

The boys probably wanted to get where they were going by noon. Abilene was on Central Standard, which meant the televised 1 P.M. games in the East would soon be coming on. Also, the Cowboy game in St. Louis was scheduled for noon. The Cowboys had by far drawn the most action in the betting.

Only R.T. and T.J., the two involved in the discussion about the missing oil, Grimm, and I remained. R.T. and T.J. *were* hassling. T.J. wanted the Cardinals and seven points. R.T. was offering 6½, which was the official line.

"Dammit," said T.J., "can't you ever give me a little room?"

"What Jimmy the Greek says is good enough for me," said R.T.

"He doesn't make the spread any more. Besides, what do those hotshot Vegas boys know? The fair point spread is seven. What game do you know of that was decided by six and a half?"

"Now don't get your water hot, T.J. You know as well as I do the reason for six and a half."

"I'm just asking for a half-point."

"It's not right, T.J. We're friends, and I'd be happy to give you that half-point, but if you won that way, you'd feel bad. You'd think how you'd taken advantage of your friend. You'd have a sour taste in your mouth, T.J., I know you would."

"What are you talking about?"

"I'm talking about your basically decent nature, T.J. You don't want to win a bet that's not on the up-and-up."

"Bullshit," said T.J.

"Well, I'm sorry to hear that. But I'm not giving you seven points. We'll just pass for the week." R.T. got up as if to leave, and a look akin to panic fluttered briefly across T.J.'s face. He couldn't live through an Autumn Sunday afternoon without a football bet.

"Sit yourself back down," T.J. said. "You can't just play God." He mimicked R.T.: " 'Take six and a half points, or leave it.' "

"That's the official point spread, T.J. God didn't make it, but He might as well have."

"That wasn't your attitude when you got a couple extra points from me last week."

"I felt bad about that, T.J."

"Well, return the favor. I'm only asking a half-point, dammit."

"Made a promise to myself I wouldn't do that again. It's not right. I want to do what's right, T.J."

"What's stopping you?"

"There's nothing I can do." Again R.T. rose to leave.

"I'll tell you what," T.J. said. "Give me six and three-quarter points."

R.T. hesitated in mid-step. He thought it over solemnly. "All right," he said. "Because we're friends. I'll make an exception and give you that."

Hands were shaken and R.T. was gone, off in his pickup to watch on television his money at work. T.J. gathered up his Marlboros and eyeglasses preparatory to exiting.

"There's no difference," I pointed out foolishly, "between six and a half points and six and three-quarter points."

"There is to me," T.J. said determinedly. "First time in twenty years he's conceded anything, even if it was nothing."

I waited in line with Grimm while he finally checked his cart filled with generic brand cans through the pay counter. Almost everyone passing by recognized him and gave a greeting. His well-publicized searches for *Titanic* and Noah's Ark, his second-place finish in the World Championship of Poker, and his involvement with fund-raising for charities made him a highly visible person. No one had noticed him earlier sitting with the boys in the deli section. That gathering, which perhaps typified him more than did the public's perception, must have appeared to passersby as a field trip by members of the Sunset Home ... except retired people would have dressed better.

"Want to watch the game at my place?" Grimm asked when we were in the parking lot.

"Love to," I said. He was always fun to watch, had a big fancy television in his living room, and his wife Jackie could be counted on to serve pecans picked from the backyard trees.

"Bring Joe along."

I watched Grimm amble to his Cadillac, slide into the driver's seat, and speed away as if starting the Firecracker 400 instead of going five blocks to his home. I didn't think it was hard to picture him, thirty years from now, seated over that twenty-one-cent breakfast, *primus inter pares* — as F.A. currently was — among the boys.

Fifteen

The days of my Texas year began to pass quickly. I finished the *Titanic* book in April, 1982, much to Grimm's relief. He had begun to think it would never be completed. Under optimal conditions he is not a patient man, and in this instance — chafing at the bit to see the story of his expensive and historic search in print — he had used every inducement he could think of to move the project along more rapidly. When urging me to "type faster" hadn't worked, his exhortations took the form of frequent visits to the apartment to check on the progress of the manuscript. I understood and sympathized with his concern, which was to get the account of his considerable efforts into a published record, but there was no explaining to him that books took time. One of the single most necessary qualities needed to write a book, patience, he did not possess. In short, he was constitutionally incapable of sitting for a long time.

The day the book was mailed to the publisher Grimm stopped by to invite Joe and me to dinner.

Grimm was upset this day with the publisher of the *Titanic* book. We had gotten word that the title had been changed to "Beyond Reach: The Search for the Titanic." The "Beyond Reach" hadn't been there before.

"Beyond reach, shit," he said. "What does that mean? It's not beyond reach. The ship's down there. I photographed her propeller. What is 'beyond reach' about that?"

"Well, I don't like it either."

"Can they do that, boy? Just change the title?"

"They did it. But, no, they can't do it. If you make a fuss about it, they'll have to back down."

"Think I should?"

"It's up to you, Jack. I don't like the title. But if you argue with them, it will slow the book's publication. They'll argue back."

"Slow up our getting books?"

"Right."

"They've got me where it hurts, boy."

That night Joe and I ate with the Grimms. Jackie Grimm had through the months served as a sort of buffer between me and Jack, who really wasn't qualified to judge the book's literary merits. To his credit, he relied on Jackie, much better read, who commiserated with him about how long it was taking while maintaining that a good job was being done.

Jackie enjoyed playing "Ghost," a spelling game where the object is to give letters keeping a word going but not spelling a complete word. The person completing a word loses. I considered myself really good at this unimportant diversion, and recently had been amazed that Jackie had begun to beat me. She had an A-1 vocabulary, but in the thirty-odd years I'd been playing the game I'd memorized virtually every combination possible. Jackie would occasionally call on the telephone and we would play a round or two of "Ghost." This night, with the *Titanic* book finished, she decided to make me feel better. She admitted she had been playing with an open dictionary.

The point is, Jackie Grimm was competitive, and probably a big reason Jack had been so successful. She professed to be a better gambler than her husband, and I believed it could be true. Jackie also provided college scholarships, sometimes overruling Jack when he had doubts about a youngster's merit. She exercised a reasoning influence on her often impulsive husband. And being a competitor, she never let him forget he would have *won* the world championship of poker had it not been for a rare mistake, a mistake she would never have made.

This night the dinner was turkey, and Jack and Jackie were having a heated argument I could tell was of long standing. Neither liked the dressing the other made, so each fixed a separate one, and now they were badgering Joe and me to say which was best. This was no light matter with the Grimms. The debate had apparently raged for years.

"They're both good," Joe said. It was the only thing to say, since he'd been backed into a corner, but the answer satisfied neither Grimm. In fact, both became upset with Joe. Instead of regarding his statement as a compliment — each made a good dressing — they were upset that he praised the other's obviously inferior concoction.

Jack later took me aside in the living room. "Tell me the truth, boy," he said. "I can take it. Who makes the better dressing, me or Jackie?"

"You won't tell Jackie what I say?"

"On my word, boy."

"You make the best dressing, Jack."

Jackie saw us out to the pickup truck when we left. "Had to get you alone," she said. "Tell me, for my own sanity, isn't Jack's dressing just dreadful? And isn't mine — I don't like to brag — very good?"

"You won't tell Jack?"

"I promise."

"His is terrible. The pits. Yours is super."

Jim Gosdin came to visit in Abilene in May. As I found out later, he called ahead to say he was coming. I was out, so he called Grimm and asked him to forward the message. "Be happy to, boy," Grimm assured. But the millionaire forgot, and when Gosdin showed up at my door no one was home.

It was a Saturday morning, and Grimm was in one of the rooms at the Petroleum Club, playing poker. He was also eating breakfast when Gosdin found him. The breakfast was on a table behind Grimm, so it wouldn't get in the way of his card playing. Grimm only spoke to Gosdin when another bite of food was called for.

Gosdin inquired as to whether or not I got the message about his visit.

"Guess I forgot to tell him," Grimm said, around a fork full of ham.

Gosdin asked about my present whereabouts. "No idea," Jack said.

Gosdin remarked on Grimm's large stack of poker chips.

"Looks are deceiving, boy. I'm the second best player in the world, but only seventeenth in Abilene. These guys are pounding on me like a nail."

"Was he really losing?" I asked, when Gosdin returned to the apartment and found me. Joe and I had been at Albertson's.

"Of course not. You've played with him."

"I'm in a different league from the boys at the Petroleum Club."

"Grimm's in a different league from the world. He just wanted to get rid of me. Figured I'd leave and let him concentrate if he said he was behind."

Gosdin stayed the night. He had been visiting his parents in Lubbock, and stopped on his way back to Dallas. He kept telling me I should ride back with him, spend a night or two.

"I've got bad memories from the last time," I said.

"Not everybody's like Art," he said. "Let me prove it to you."

"I don't know. I'm really not excited about Dallas."

"You may like it so much you'll decide to stay."

"No chance of that."

"Well, I promise you, no one like Art. And you've got nothing better to do."

"I've got a novel."

"On which you're not working very hard. Abilene's not the place for you to be. You talked about spending a year. It's almost up, isn't it?"

"In August."

"Abilene was okay for your *Titanic* book. Grimm there with all the information. But you need a bigger place, where you have more in common with the people.

"That's Dallas?"

"You bonehead, not everybody in Dallas was at L.G. Mosley's party. The rest of the stuff was by accident. Look at it that you were lucky. You got all of the bad out of the way in one visit."

So I came to Dallas for a second time. And I did meet many people I liked, friends of Gosdin's, with outlooks and interests closer to my own.

On my second night Gosdin said he was inviting his friends Brenda and Gerald over for lasagne. "Brenda's nice," he said. "You'll get along fine with her. Gerald's something else. Gerald doesn't like anybody."

"Why are you having him for dinner?"

"He's a good guy."

Gerald arrived with a can of beer in his hand and wearing a tee shirt with the message, "KILL 'EM ALL, Let God Sort 'Em Out," emblazoned on the front. He immediately started making fun of Gosdin, an easy target in his Pierre Cardin apron. I had figured Pierre, for a price, would put his name on just about anything, but an apron was going too far.

"That's nothing," Gerald said. "Gosdin's got his dishcloths, too."

"Designer dishcloths?"

"Show him, Gosdin."

It was true. And it was true I had a good time those two days in Dallas. Even Gerald was all right. He was just a grump.

The next day, I went to visit the deal-maker, Satterfield, at his ranch outside of Dallas. I wouldn't say he was worried, certainly not that he was beginning to sweat, but he did want to know about my progress on the novel. He had found out that movie rights were much more valuable if the book was completed.

"How's the work going?" he asked.

"Slow," I said.

This isn't what he wanted to hear.

"Well," I said, "I'm trying hard. It's a tough book." This was God's truth.

I had come to see Satterfield, but instantly was more interested in his office manager, Judy. She was a journalism graduate of the University of Georgia, had been a newspaperwoman, TV host, and a teacher. I asked her if she'd go out for dinner, and she was about to say no, when Satterfield, bless his heart, piped up. "Why don't you go with him?" he said.

We ate at a good steakhouse and talked the night away. At my request she had driven her car; Grimm's pickup, fond as I was of it, didn't seem appropriate. But we talked so late the parking lot was closed when we went to get the car, and the attendant who'd been given the keys was missing. This piece of good luck meant we had to make the very long ride to Satterfield's ranch in a cab to get the pickup, which meant in turn that the next morning I got to see her again to take her to her car.

I persuaded her to visit two days hence, "spend an afternoon and meet Joe and Jack Grimm. You'll like Joe a lot, and you haven't lived until you've met Jack." This ploy worked, though of course I had no intention of having Grimm help us form a threesome, and since it was the Memorial Day weekend, she agreed to drive over to Abilene. Judy enjoyed herself and we saw each other often through that hot Texas summer.

On a late afternoon in June I heard a familiar loud knock at the door. The walls rattled. It was either Jack, an angry bill collector, or the police. I wasn't far enough behind with any bills for it to be a collector, and there wasn't the kind of night life in Abilene that was likely to get me in trouble.

"Come on in, Jack."

"I've got a project you'll be interested in," he said, sliding past me into the living room. He was as ever in a hurry, and I had doubts that I'd really be interested. The last project he'd suggested had been an exposé of the mayor of a small town outside Abilene. This worthy was probably corrupt, as Jack alleged, since he seemed to be in charge of counting votes on election day, and managed to provide important services to the town, services normally handled by a third party, services for which he was handsomely paid. From what I gathered, he was almost a modern-day Judge Roy Bean.

I had told Jack there wasn't really a market for the story. It wasn't as if the man were Mayor Daley, head of a big city and arranging for the votes of dead people to be counted towards his reelection. The town the mayor in question headed was *tiny;* it wasn't even on any maps I ever saw. But Jack was righteously outraged, and wanted me to do something. I had never seen such zeal for rooting out corruption in him before. I wondered, perish this thought, if Jack hadn't gotten a speeding ticket while going through the hamlet, an indignity that might indeed have kindled his yearning for clean government.

"What project are you talking about?" I asked.

"You know about the paraplegics, right?"

Yes, I did. Grimm was sponsoring six paraplegics who intended to go up the highest mountain in Texas — Guadalupe Peak — in their wheelchairs. The event's purpose was twofold: provide an example for other handicapped persons, and raise money for charity. The scheduled climb, a most worthwhile project, had received considerable attention in the local newspaper.

"Right," I said. "I think it's good you're sponsoring it."

"If you want to see it, you can come with me," Grimm said.

I shrugged my shoulders. "Why not?"

"This should be getting more attention than it has," Jack said.

"I agree."

"It would be good for *Sports Illustrated,* boy, the magazine carries this sort of story."

"I agree. Adventure and the outdoors. One of the long pieces they run at the end of the magazine. They've done stories on grizzly bears and prairie dogs. They shouldn't have anything against people in the outdoors. Especially the handicapped."

"Why don't you do the story and sell it to them. It's promotion the event deserves."

"That is a good idea, Jack. I'll do it."

"I figured you would, boy. All the equipment you'll need for the climb is ready."

"Wait a minute. I'm making the climb? The mountain climb?"

"Of course. You can't do the story properly if you're not with them."

He had a point. But I couldn't see myself climbing any mountain. Guadalupe was 8,751 feet high.

"Maybe you should get somebody else," I said.

"What's the matter with you, boy? I thought you were a fearless journalist. Writing that book on Rockefeller."

"I didn't have to be in good shape to write the book on Rockefeller. Look at me, Jack. I'm a candidate for a heart attack. I read that I'm just at the right age."

"You didn't have any trouble on the *Titanic* search."

"I didn't do any heavy work. Took a lot of notes, and lost to you at blackjack. My duty on ship, if you recall, was the same as yours: the winch-watch. If something went wrong, all we had to do was switch off a motor and yell."

"I know you can make it. Show some desire, boy. Some drive."

"Maybe I could do the story from on the ground. Listen to their radio reports. Talk to them when it's over."

"It's better if you're along."

"I think you're right. Get someone else. Let Joe write it. He's helping carry their supplies up the mountain."

"He's just a boy, boy."

"But he's my son. A writer's son. Got it in the genes and all that stuff."

"I'm asking *you*. You're here. You're a writer. It's perfect."

"Jack, I just wouldn't make it. From what I hear, that's a rugged mountain. I used to climb *hills* as a kid. Scale short cliffs. Almost killed myself doing that. And I wasn't out of shape then."

"The paraplegics are doing it. And in wheelchairs. If they can make it, you can."

"Don't give me that. I've seen those guys. They've got arms like Hercules. I admire them, don't get me wrong, but those paraplegics are specimens. And I hear *they* have worries about making it. They use words like 'treacherous' and 'dangerous' to describe the climb."

"This is your chance to do something good for your fellow man, boy. You're always talking about doing good."

He was making me feel bad. But I really didn't believe I could climb that mountain. One of the paraplegics had mountain-climbing experience, but except for him everyone would be new to the sport. They wanted it that way. They wanted to do it on their own.

"Jack, look at it from another angle. I'd just slow them up. Be in their way. They've got enough to contend with without having to worry about me."

"I think you could make it."

"Are *you* going up the mountain?"

"No. I'll be there at the bottom, coordinating."

"Well, I'm willing to be right along with you."

"You disappoint me, boy."

Joe later told me he had never seen such courage as those handicapped people exhibited. Their hands and even their rear ends had all the skin rubbed off, but they refused help of any sort where scaling their mountain was concerned.

As it turned out, the story received plenty of national and international attention without my help, and, best of all, three of the climbers made it all the way to the top.

I spent most of July thinking about the weekends when I would drive Jack's pickup the 150 miles to see Judy. A memorable occurence took place, late, very late, one particular night.

As usual, I was in bed and asleep by midnight. At 1:30 A.M., I was jarred awake by Grimm pounding on the door. Sleep-drugged, brain not functioning, I was confronted by a wide-awake millionaire in a hurry. "Throw some clothes on, boy," he said. "You'll want to see this."

"What?"

"I may be bringin' in a well."

"Let me fix some coffee."

"No time for that, boy. Come on. I'll show you what Texas is all about."

He was going a hundred miles an hour as soon as we were out of town on the highway and kept it at that speed.

"Don't you ever get a ticket for speeding?" I asked, slightly awake now as we jetted through the star-splashed Texas night. The stars are big and bright in Texas.

"Not too often," he said. "I can outrun most patrol cars. One time I had this cop chasing me. Was going a hundred and twenty, just fast enough so he could keep me in view. Pretended I didn't know he was behind me. Went twenty miles before I finally let him pull me over. He was in his sixties and said he'd been right close to having a heart attack trying to keep up in that little old Plymouth they gave him."

"Did he give you a ticket?"

"Nah."

Grimm, the speedometer stuck at 100, passed the time by telling jokes. "Know the difference between your wife and your job?"

"No."

"After five years your job still sucks."

And this one: "Know why a black person won't marry a Mexican?"

"I don't know."

"Afraid their kids would be too lazy to steal."

"And just," I said, "when I was beginning to think you might not be racist."

"Only told it, boy, to get you upset."

Actually, Grimm was very nearly a Renaissance Man compared to most rich Texans I'd met where race relations were concerned. To hear most of them talk, welfare recipients, known collectively as "niggers," never mind that whites got welfare also, lived a life of carefree ease. Medical bills, which hard-working folk had to pay, were willingly taken care of by a leftist federal government. Legal services, food, housing, all were taken care of for welfare recipients but not working people. If I'd believed what I heard, I would have rushed to get on welfare rolls. At Mosley's party I'd heard a banker say "every" black drove a Cadillac. When I offered to bet him we could take a ride and would see that the vast majority of people tooling around in Cadillacs were white, his expression was wonderment over how I'd gotten an invitation to this party.

The Ku Klux Klan in Texas was at this time making noises about patrolling the border to keep Mexicans out. The Klan in Texas seemed very small, but they weren't without secret sympathizers. Grimm judged "the Klan should just stay out of it. I guess the Mexicans are willing to do work most Americans won't." This was hardly the most enlightened reason for muzzling the Klan, but was downright radical coming from an oil baron. Many rich people I met who tried to use the word "black" simply couldn't. It stuck in their mouths, like Fonzie on "Happy Days" trying but unable to say "I'm sorry." They'd go "bl . . . bl . . . bla . . ." but couldn't get any farther. What the hell, their expressions would read, "nigger!" But it was a word even in Texas that could get you in trouble. One rancher used it on a black field hand and was nearly beaten to death by his formerly docile "boy."

Grimm and I were three hours on the road. Nothing in that barren landscape under the big sky had changed when he announced. "Here we are, boy."

"Where?" Nothing, *nothing,* was in sight.

"Here." Screeching his tires he wheeled left into a field and we were swallowed up. Simply disappeared, if anyone had been watching. The grass, or whatever it was, was over the roof of the car, and visibility was zero. To overcome this handicap Grimm stepped on the accelerator and went faster. The Cadillac banged over ruts, took off over hidden hills, collided with rocks I thought would tear its bottom out.

"Why don't you slow down?" I asked.

"Get stuck if we do."

I could imagine us running smack into a big boulder and dying in this Godforsaken field. We hit another rut and my head banged the roof of the car. We skidded and slowed, as though in mud. We seemed to go over the side of a hill and the Cadillac threatened to turn over. The grass slapping the windshield began to resemble millions of slender snakes trying to grab us and being mowed down.

We emerged into a clearing dimly lit as a small town might be at 4:30 A.M. Grimm had crashed from the high grass into what might indeed have been a very small town, but no one stopped to take notice. That he owned this little outpost on the edge of the world didn't impress anyone either. People who had been working kept working.

The ground was muddy and I sank in to my ankles. Dominating everything, the pickup trucks, the trailers, a makeshift shack, was the mighty derrick, rising stark and elemental into a clean dark Texas sky. I thought of great dinosaurs — none had ever been a tenth this tall — as I stood awed by the derrick. The noise was terrific, as it might have been when a tyrannosaurus roared, but here the din was caused by steel pounding steel.

Grimm strode through the mud with the confidence of a man who had visited places like this for thirty years. I followed, uncertainly, the nervousness of a white-collar worker in a blue-collar's domain carrying an added weight of guilt. The men who worked these wells provided a product the entire world needed. Writing books was important, but not so important as this. I wondered if people in jobs I considered totally useless, such as writing ads for toothpaste, ever felt morose when comparing their work to that of people who farmed, or built homes, schools, and hospitals. It was probably an ad man, I thought, who came up with the word "consumer" to describe everyone but a rich industrialist. The ad man was the real consumer, in the sense that word implies using rather than producing. The roughnecks sweating on that derrick were the real producers.

Grimm first rapped on the door of a small trailer. I was right behind him, and we were admitted by a man in a Stanley Kowalski undershirt who greeted Grimm as "old turd." He was six feet four inches tall, and his nose must have been broken a hundred times. So also his knuckles, which had no individual shape. He was maybe fifty years old, and although a rough life looked like it had been behind him, he seemed ready for more of the same.

"This is Ed," Grimm introduced. "Ed is my tool pusher."

A tool pusher, I learned, was a sort of super foreman. One of the main qualities sought in a tool pusher was his ability to stomp any roughneck. Ed and Grimm seemed to have been together for a long time, and they settled comfortably in the cramped trailer over coffee recalling "war stories."

"Know how the boss — here that's Jack — used to have to fire a tool pusher?" Ed asked me.

"No," I said.

"Had to fight him. It was an unwritten law. The boss had to get down on all fours with the tool pusher and prove he was the better man."

"I never did that," Grimm said.

"Like hell," Ed said. "He was a wild, tough young buzzard, don't let him tell you anything different."

"It's not so much fun to fight any more," Grimm said.

"Called getting old," said the tool pusher.

The two of them talked about drinking, fighting, and oil. The tool pusher, surely because he was without Grimm's economic clout, was a record-setter where getting traffic tickets was concerned. He seemed always to be in a hurry, with cops just around the next bend. Just as you had to fight a tool pusher to fire him, evidently the same was necessary to effect an arrest.

Oil was indeed king in Texas, as was readily discerned listening to Grimm talk with the tool pusher, Ed. The "world's richest acre" had stood on a portion of a downtown block in Kilgore, Texas, containing the planet's most intensive concentration of oil wells. A well was sunk through the terrazzo floor of the Kilgore National Bank Building.

In Crane, Texas, oil wells outnumbered people. The score: more than 6,000 oil wells, 3,366 people.

There was even an oil well in the middle of a maximum security prison near Palestine, Texas.

Grimm, apparently in no hurry, remarked that the only person he knew tougher than his tool pusher was his tool pusher's wife. Her husband had once been arrested outside a tavern, *before* he got in his car, and this injustice — the cop should have waited for him to be caught DWI — so outraged her that she attacked the officer, who had to radio for four other policemen to bring the situation under control.

I imagined that conversations such as I was hearing in the trailer would someday soon be as extinct as passenger pigeons. Wildcatters like Grimm were rapidly being replaced by giants like Exxon and Gulf. Under the best of circumstances — say the 1920s oil boom in Texas — an independent had to possess tremendous amounts of luck and courage. With oil harder to find, and larger amounts of investor money needed to begin, the wildcatters of old were disappearing. Grimm himself had come close to failing. His first 24 wells, drilled shortly after graduating college, came up dry. On what might have been his last chance before going to work for one of the majors, he hit the jackpot.

Jack had said he might be bringing in a well this early morning, and I had hoped to see a dramatic geyser bursting towards the sky, but that wasn't the way it was going to be. Laughing and joking, Grimm exited the trailer, me right on his heels, and headed for the derrick itself. We scrambled up on the platform and I gave silent thanks that Joe had been a roustabout, not a roughneck. The job looked dangerous, and was. A person who was not careful could lose an arm or a leg, or life. You could be the most careful person in the world, and still be killed, if any one of a hundred parts of this ugly, deadly machinery decided to break down and go berserk. Just one of those chains, drawn tight as piano wire, could snap and lash out, slicing a man in two.

Grimm had trod gingerly aboard the search ship *Gyre,* but here he was in his element. The men on the rig sensed it, that here was a person not to worry about. *I* sensed they could tell I didn't belong there. Well, I agreed. I stood in one place, where it seemed nothing was happening, so I didn't blunder into causing some disaster.

Fingers were missing from several of the workers' hands. All the men on the rig were young. Grimm had told me about arms being crushed or sheared off. He said the roughnecks made good money and deserved every cent of it. I told him I thought it was like fighting Joe Frazier: whatever you made it wasn't enough. Since I didn't see missing limbs, but *could* see how they were a likely result of this sort of work, I guessed people were forced to pursue another profession when they lost an arm or leg. Of course they were. You could have six legs and eight arms and still not have enough to perform all the needed tasks.

Satisfied, Grimm climbed down from the derrick and slogged through mud to a more modern trailer than the one occupied by the tool pusher. "How's it going, men?" he asked the three seated inside, the use of the word "men" (he called the tool pusher "boy") being a giveaway that this was the serious part of the trip.

The three men in the shack — all of them young, maybe five years out of college — were hunched over computers in a room jammed tight with technical equipment. Their dress was the same as the roughnecks, but cleaner. Still, I guessed that plenty of times they had scrambled aboard that rig.

I listened, but didn't understand a word of what was said. It was the talk of geologists. I watched Grimm's face, looking for him to betray emotion, but his face was as unreadable as it was at the card table. And these were higher stakes. I understood $320,000 was sunk into this operation, and the outcome could be anything from another Spindletop to a dry hole. I glimpsed what was meant when wildcatters were referred to as gamblers.

Grimm had his face in a geology map and I heard "damned deep," which I supposed meant the oil, or whatever, wasn't sitting right near the surface. The men he talked with were matter-of-fact. They were paid to do a job, did it well, but had no stake in the outcome. They couldn't deposit oil where it didn't exist; there was no reason to become morose if it wasn't found. Besides, Grimm was a geologist, good enough to be offered a university position teaching the subject, and had probably chosen the spot himself.

"Are you richer?" I asked, when we headed back to the Cadillac.

"Looks like plenty of natural gas. Not much oil."

"That good?"

"Oil'd be better."

"You gonna make money?"

"Maybe some. Not so much as if it'd been oil."

We reached the car, and I changed the subject. "You're not going to go through that field again, are you?"

"Only way out, boy."

"Why didn't you hack out a road?"

"The farmer wouldn't like it. I got mineral rights, not farming rights. Old boy'd take a shotgun after me if I messed with his crop."

"He doesn't mind your knocking it down with your car?"

"How else am I gonna get there?"

The return trip through the field was even more harrowing than the first, but Grimm's Cadillac was as sturdy as the pickup he'd loaned me. No matter how big the rock he hit, or how deep the rut, the car kept going. At times all four wheels were off the ground, but we never flew high enough to see the night sky above the tall grass. We came out of the jungle unexpectedly and with a rush, and Jack had to wrestle the Cadillac's wheel to right the car on the road and keep it from hurtling into a field on the other side. In comparison, the 100 mph return to Abilene seemed inviting.

Grimm asked my opinion of Texas and I told him the best part was the attitude of people who assumed you were up to something good, not pulling a fast one. Being taken at face value until you were proved otherwise was different from New York City, where violent crime was so epidemic people often were afraid to stop and give directions to an inquiring stranger. Grimm was a native Oklahoman, son of lower middle-class parents from Waggoner County, but had made himself into the most Texan of Texans. I knew he didn't want to hear anything negative from me — he considered himself my host — so I didn't mention that the ubiquitous religious fundamentalism was not my cup of tea. The zealots — and their numbers were legion — made me nervous, and I could envision their even becoming dangerous. Often there were books, like *Huckleberry Finn,* someone thought should be taken off the shelves, and every imaginable war (I think there were about thirty going on at this time) found apologists who were delighted with it, quoting Biblical prophecies to prove God's will was being fulfilled. The appearance of an "anti-Christ" was a thought consuming the minds of many fundamentalists, and it wasn't a long step from there, I thought, to saying someone *was* the anti-Christ, and from there to a rerun of the Salem witch hunts, with each person having a different idea who the anti-Christ is.

But I didn't say anything about this to Grimm, nor did I mention that there didn't seem to be any feverish intellectual activity going on in Abilene. If you didn't come to Abilene already exposed to the arts, you weren't likely to be enticed to them there. But when Grimm persisted that there must be something I would prefer was improved, I mentioned the weather.

"It's not always this hot, boy."

"I know, but it's sure hot now. And it's worse when the wind blows. The only place I've ever seen where the wind makes things hotter. It's hot in California, too, but at least it gets cool at night."

"Well, there are a lot worse places than Abilene for weather."

Of course, this was true. And many of them were in Texas. The previous summer, 1980, Dallas had 42 consecutive days when the temperature reached or exceeded 100 degrees. The state's high temperature that sizzling summer was 119 degrees in Weatherford.

An average of 109 tornadoes touch down in Texas every year; in 1967 there were 232. The hurricane that hit Galveston in 1900, killing an estimated 7,000 people, was the worst natural disaster in U.S. history. The largest hurricane of record, Hurricane Carla, hit the Texas coast in 1961.

There are blue northers, sandstorms (I saw a few of these), icestorms, snowstorms, droughts, and floods (I saw one of these also — it made Grimm nervous when it threatened to wash away the Petroleum Club).

But the seemingly endless heat was most depressing. Most people spent as little time in the heat as possible. Most cars out of necessity had air-conditioning. I'd heard that some people, down on their luck, drove around with their windows rolled up even when they didn't have air-conditioning, rather than admit they couldn't afford it.

One hour and a hundred miles after we'd burst out of that field Grimm wheeled into the parking lot of a small diner set in the middle of nowhere. A dozen pickup trucks, windows dusty and bug-spattered, each equipped with the obligatory gun rack, were there ahead of us. "Best Mexican food in Texas," Jack said, and hopped out of the Cadillac.

The food was good. Many of the roughnecks and roustabouts in the diner recognized Grimm, and those who didn't had heard of him and came over to shake hands. He was a celebrity in these parts. I had driven once with Drury and him to Eastland, Texas, where he had to bail an employee charged with DWI out of jail, and the entire inmate population asked for autographs. Drury, of course, was a drawing card, but Grimm's autograph was just as eagerly sought. He and The Virginian plunged into cells to shake hands and sign scraps of paper.

Grimm and one of the roughnecks in the diner talked about a bar in Pampa, Texas. "Rough place," Grimm agreed.

"Rough? It's more than that. A shooting there every weekend."

I could see Jack playing Can-You-Top-This. "When you go there," he said, "they search you for weapons. If you don't have one, they give you a gun."

We were served ice cubes in our tea that were the shape of the state of Texas. Without question this was the most popular design in the state. There was stationery in this form, swimming pools, cookie cutters, the ever-popular belt buckle, and even bath soap and eyeglasses. You can fry a steak in a pan shaped like Texas.

The crowd in the diner was exceptionally well mannered. I saw very few examples, ever, of the loud-talking stereotypical Texan. If anything, most Texans I met seemed to speak softer than the average Easterner. Grimm, aboard that oil derrick platform, had actually seemed uncomfortable when forced to shout to be heard above the drone of the engines.

"What are you going to do, boy, when you get home?" Grimm asked when we were just a few miles from Abilene. It was 7 A.M. and beginning to get light.

"Go to bed," I replied.

"It's morning. Time to work."

"You going to work?" I figured he had a card game planned somewhere. There seemed to be one going on at any hour you chose.

"Gotta round up my buffalo. They broke loose again. They're rampaging through a neighbor's field, or so he says."

"Why are you so interested in buffalo? They were near extinction at one time, weren't they?"

"Don't know about that. I do know my buffalo will be extinct if I don't get to them before that farmer does."

"Well, good luck."

"Want to go with me? Good experience for you, rounding up buffalo."

"No thanks."

"That's probably right thinking, boy. You want to get back to work on your new book."

I did? I hadn't slept in 24 hours, and had already told him I was going to bed. But I didn't repeat myself to avoid hearing his make-something-of-yourself speech.

August came. My self-proclaimed last month in Abilene. I wasn't really sorry I was leaving. I'd miss Grimm, I liked him, almost everything he did struck me as funny, but these were not reasons to stay. There had been the chance he would go back again to look for *Titanic* this summer, and had I gone with him that might have delayed my departure, but he couldn't find a suitable search ship so the hunt had been postponed for a year.

There wasn't really anything to pack. I guess the packing was done in my mind as the day to go approached, and consisted mainly of overcoming inertia, the natural tendency to stay put. I've heard there is no good place to work and live; it's all in your head. No matter where you go, you always take yourself along, and right there is the problem. Nonetheless, I persuaded myself "somewhere else" would be better than Abilene for me, that the experiences and people one needs to be able to write were missing here. I knew I was not a candidate for being born again, for example, and that eliminated a large part of what Abilene offered.

It hadn't been bad at all, not nearly as bad as some of my friends had predicted. I'd found I'd much rather count on a neighbor in Abilene to help, than one in New York. And I'd had some fun.

Yes, there had been good times in the year, and a book completed, which is not to be sniffed at, and especially the chance of learning about another part of our country and its people. And that, as a wise man said, had only taken time, which if we do not spend we cannot save.

I visited Jack in his office the day before I left. I had come to return his pickup, his super-duper typewriter, and to thank him and say good-bye.

"Well, this is it," I said.

"We made a Texan out of you," he said. "Just like I told you we would."

"I'm not a Texan."

"Goin' to live in Dallas, aren't you?"

"Yes, but . . ."

"Another one of your kids is here, right?" My daughter Terri had come to Abilene to take advantage of one of Jack's scholarships.

"Yes. But . . ."

"You're a Texan, boy. You're roped."

"I'm just moving to Dallas to be near Judy."

"That good Southern girl will keep you here, boy."

"Maybe she will," I conceded.

"Well, if you get married, you might consider doing it on top of my mountain."

That would have been an idea. But the date we finally set, in December, made it impossible. In December we would have been blown right off that mountain.

Jack got up from behind his desk. "Come on, boy, let's go for a ride."

We got in Grimm's Cadillac and drove out to his mountain at Buffalo Gap, where he intended to have his giant sculpture, almost seven football fields long, hacked into stone. The car came to a stop.

Jack said, "Well boy, you going to come back and visit?"

"I will," I said. "Some Sunday morning you'll look up, you and the boys, and I'll be there at Albertson's with my plate of scrambled eggs."

"I know you've found a good girl. I hope you find the *place* you want to live, too."

"A Jason's Quest," I said.

"How's that?"

"Something hard. But it can be worthwhile. Maybe I've already found it."

"Maybe you have, boy."

We got out of the Cadillac and he looked up at the mountain. "I guess you write books," he said, "for the same reason I look for *Titanic,* or commission the memorial that's going up there. I'm told it will last millions of years."

"You want to be remembered. Leave something behind."

"Damn right, boy! Show I did something while I was here."

Who could argue with that?